NAVIGATOR
IN THE
SOUTH SEAS

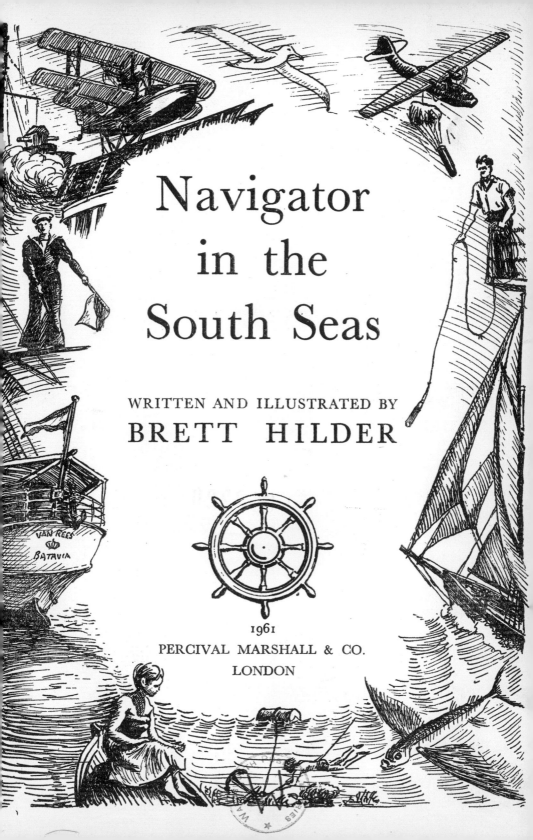

Navigator in the South Seas

WRITTEN AND ILLUSTRATED BY

BRETT HILDER

1961

PERCIVAL MARSHALL & CO.

LONDON

1961 © Brett Hilder

Printed in Great Britain by Electrical Press Ltd., Cordwallis Works, Maidenhead, Berks, for the publishers, Percival Marshall and Co. Ltd., 19-20 Noel Street, London, W.1.

CONTENTS

Part One. The Years of Preparation 1928-1938

Part Two. The Years of Action and Reaction 1938-1946

Part Three. Adventures of Peacetime 1946-1960

TO MY SHIPMATES
whose long-suffering loyalty is my
most treasured reward

PART ONE

The Years of
Preparation
1928-1938

Chapter One

Going to sea : the East Indies

THE DECK SLOWLY LIFTED UNDER MY FEET, A GENTLE 'SCEND and dip to the ground swell coming in through the Heads, and then I knew that I was, at last, really going to sea. Half an hour previously the main engines had come to life, sending a pulse through the ship as her fine hull gathered way through the water.

She had been lying at the wharf for a week, inert and dishevelled, her holds open to the sky and being stuffed with a cargo of food by the stevedores. A graceful ship being prostituted by cargo operations and indignities to her mechanical innards. Then her holds had been closed, her hatches covered and battened down, her decks and gear all shipshape and Bristol fashion, to resume her role as a lovely lady of the ocean. Her name was *Marella*, and she was my first ship.

Only five days before, I had called at the office of the Burns Philp Line, not very hopefully, for I had been trying to get to sea for nearly a year. My one-and-only rich uncle had given me an introduction to the managing director, who promptly called for the Marine Superintendent. This bearded old sea-dog appeared, heard my request, and gruffly announced "You can join the *Marella* as cadet . . . she's sailing on Tuesday ! "

Those next five days were filled with the excitements of getting my uniforms and packing my gear for my new way of life.

Once aboard the ship I found that I was the junior in a half-deck of four cadets, the others having been to sea for periods varying from two weeks to two years. The *Marella* had been built in Germany in 1914 and reputedly fitted out as a yacht to take the Kaiser around the world after he had won the war. Her appointments were lavish indeed; her dining saloon, smoke-room and music-room were lined with marble. On the boat-deck was a gymnasium, fitted with electric vibrators and other equipment to shake up sluggish livers and reduce excess fat. Over the gym was a swimming bath, 20 feet long, and the most coveted goal of the four cadets.

The ship had lain in Hamburg all the war and her maiden voyage was to England under the flag of the League of Nations, as part of war reparations. Her original name was *Hilda Woerman*, and this was changed to *Wahehe* by Shaw, Savill & Albion who used her on the run to Australia for some time.

In 1922 she was given to Burns Philp to compensate for the loss of the steamer *Matunga*, which had been captured and sunk off New Guinea in 1917 by the German raider *Wolf*. As the *Marella* was worth a lot more, the new owners had to pay the difference, amounting to about £75,000. She was an expensive ship to run and had been known to consume 100 tons of coal in one day. Her boilers were therefore put on a restricted diet by bricking in the furnaces. She had a long narrow hull like a warship and twin screws, which gave her a speed of 12 knots. Her gross displacement was 7,475 tons.

Most of the *Marella's* life was spent on the run from Australian ports to Java and Singapore, where her crew were signed on. They consisted of Malay sailors, Bengali Indians in the engine-room, and Chinese cooks and stewards from Hainan. This mixed crew and the white officers all spoke Malay as a common tongue, like the population of Singapore itself.

The Captain was a rigid and rugged old sailing-ship man, with an Extra Master's certificate and was a retired Lieutenant of the Royal Naval Reserve dating back to about 1911. He was very keen on semaphore signalling and after his early morning swim in the pool used to call up the bridge and plague the officer-of-the-watch with signalled orders and questions. This generally caught the Fourth Officer, who kept watch with the Chief Officer. Another trial of the Fourth's was to give the cadets an hour's schooling each day at sea. In port we were always too involved with cargo work to have time for studies.

MARELLA

After reading the adventures described later in this book you may be surprised to hear that the worst part of going to sea is the deadly monotony. The clock never moves more slowly than in the long dark watches of the night. The first ten or fifteen years are the worst, for after that you may be finished with watches, or be a Chief Officer at least. His watch is the best, from 4 to 8 both a.m. and p.m., so that his watch is broken by sunrise and sunset.

Cargo work is nearly as deadly as watch-keeping. Certainly you do have more company during the long hours down the holds, white stevedores in Australian ports and coolies in the Indies.

Cargo hours are much longer than watches, which are four-hourly, for you are sometimes down a hold for 24 hours with only breaks for meals. This stops you spending too much time and money ashore. In my time, cadets were paid only 15 shillings a week (about two dollars) for the four long years of apprenticeship. This barely paid our simplest expenses, for we had to have our white uniforms washed and ironed, even if we did the rest of our washing ourselves. We wore uniforms at stand-by, entering and leaving port, at gangway watch and at boat drills and other public occasions. When doing seamen's work on deck and cargo work we wore dungarees.

The monotony of my first ten years at sea was increased by the amount of study I chose to do. This was encouraged by the need of getting a job and keeping it, for the first chilling blasts of the depression were reaching Australia. I was also ambitious to do well at sea, having been born a snob without any real reason and I badly wanted to get to the top of the ladder.

The *Marella* had called at Melbourne before I joined her in Sydney and she was bound up the eastern coast of Australia, calling at Brisbane, Townsville, Thursday Island and Darwin, each of these places seeming worse than the last. Two days after leaving Brisbane we entered the tropics, in which so much of my life has been spent, or perhaps mis-spent!

At Townsville we were inside the Great Barrier Reef, which extends some 900 miles before it reaches the coast of New Guinea. The passage inside the reef gets narrower as we go north and takes three days and nights of intricate navigation before the ship clears Cape York Peninsula and heads away into the west.

Our captains have been allowed to pilot their own ships through this route since 1927, instead of employing Torres Strait pilots who charge high fees. Thursday Island is one of the many islands in Torres Strait, the scene of many early visits by navigators to

Australian waters. Torres was the first to pass through this reef-infested passage between Australia and New Guinea in 1606. Tasman sailed close to the western entrance in the same year. Then Cook passed through in 1770, after discovering and naming New South Wales, and Bligh sailed through in his small launch after the famous mutiny of the *Bounty*.

Thursday Island and Darwin are bases for the fleets of pearling luggers which range over the shallow tropical seas to gather mother-of-pearl, the gold-lipped oysters. These are worth about £1 a piece, or £1,000 a ton. Before World War II the luggers were very numerous, but the industry has only partly recovered since 1945. The divers are of all colours and castes, black, white and Japanese. The pearls they occasionally find are only rare excitements, as they occur so seldom unless cultivated.

Torres Strait is only 40 feet deep, so there must have been a connecting strip of dry land once between New Guinea and Australia. This was probably some thousands of years ago, but it is known that the sea level at the equator has been rising slowly during the last 50,000 years, ever since the last peak of the ice ages. This would account for the similarity of flora and fauna across the Strait, while to the north and west are the later and fiercer species of Asiatic animals in the Indies.

Darwin is a desolate place. It is the chief port of North Australia, which is real Blackfeller country. The coastline is fringed with mudflats and mangrove swamps, the haunt of savage crocodiles, while the higher land is stony and barren and thinly populated with large lizards called goannas. In pre-war years the main export of Darwin was empty beer barrels, some salted buffalo hides, crocodile skins, and a few small bags of mineral ores. The real value of this land has proved to be in various mineral deposits, including uranium from a place with the delightful name of Rum Jungle. At present the cattle trade still holds first place and beef is exported from several ports around the north-west coast of Australia. The salted hides are from wild cattle which are shot, skinned and left to rot in the sun. It is a wasteful land, indeed, and small wonder that Dampier was so disgusted with the miserable conditions of the natives he saw along the coast in 1688.

After leaving Darwin for dead we sailed over 1,000 miles to Java, along the lovely chain of the Lesser Sunda Islands. First we passed Timor, of which the eastern half still belongs to Portugal, a fragment of their former empire. Then past Sumba or Sandalwood Island, to Sumbawa and its great volcano. On the northern coast of this island is an area of abnormal magnetic variation, which affects ship's compasses to over 10 degrees.

If we are lucky we may see the little island of Komodo, famous for its living dragons, which are huge monitor lizards up to eight feet in length.

All these islands are inhabited by natives of Malay type, but of pagan or animist beliefs. They revere all forms of nature and of animal life, especially their hill ponies.

The next island is Lombok, where the natives are Buddhists, a result of the early conquerers from Ceylon and India. The huge but delicate temple of Borobodoer in Central Java is a relic of the same Buddhist period in Java, and is modelled after a recumbent woman's breast. The next wave of conquest was Hindu and their living tradition is now confined to the lovely island of Bali, justly famous for the graceful beauty of its dancing girls and for the Hindu festivals which are not to be seen in the other islands of the East Indies. A number of European artists live amongst the inspiring beauty of Bali, where the natives make exquisite wood-carvings, often of the temple dancers. Such works of art cannot be made by the natives in the more populated islands of Java, Sumatra and Borneo, for a very strange reason.

The Indonesians of the larger islands are all Moslems, apart from a few early Christians, and date from the Arab conquests in the fifteenth century. The laws of Islam include the Ten Commandments of the Jewish and Christian churches, forbidding the making of any graven image, or any likeness of anything in heaven above, in the earth below, or in the waters of the deep. Moslems can there-

The temple of Buddha at Borobodoer in Central Java, and two carved heads from Bali

A Balinese dancer and a Timor horseman

fore make neither sculptured nor painted portraits, which handicaps
their artistic work.   They have to stick to caricature and abstract
design, like the very modern schools of contemporary art.

It has been said with great truth that most Malays worship
Allah; in Bali they worship the Hindu gods; in Lombok they
revere the Lord Buddha; further East they worship animals and
nature, while in Australia the greatest religious emotion seems to
be devoted to . . . racehorses !

Our first port in Java was Sourabaya, spelt in different ways, and,
after the tired and barren ports of tropical Australia, I was amazed
at the fertility of the land, the size of the port, the number of ships,
and the patient and endless activities of the millions of natives.
Fleets of fishing prows, square miles of paddy fields, uncountable
villages, and cultivation extending right up the sides of the volcanoes.   I had never realised that there were nearly 50 million
natives on Java alone, an average of 1,000 to every square mile.

Java is a prolific country, very well organised by the series of
successive conquerors, though today it is reverting to disorder
under the little dictators of Central Java.   In pre-war days the
country was happy and prosperous, where even the coolies working
on the ships could have a four-course meal for about sixpence.
They had soup, fish, goat meat, spices, fruit, ginger-bread and a
glass of iced syrup.   Certainly the plates provided were only fresh
green leaves and the table silver consisted of the fingers of the right
hand.   The left hand was reserved for washing the bottom after
defecating in the nearest river or off the edge of the wharf.   There
was no toilet paper in the country and even the European homes
only provided a bottle of fresh water in the lavatories.

The surprising thing about Javanese culture is that the masses
are just peasant farmers, yet they have a rich tapestry of tradition
in their etiquette, their languages, their colourful clothes of rich
designs and their studied deportment.   They make delicate and
artistic silverware, in which symbolism blends with natural motifs.
They are an active and intelligent people, if rather hot-headed, and
it may be for this reason that their best period of progress and
prosperity was under the cool-headed Dutch.

The ports of Samarang and Batavia were specially interesting to
me because they were known to Joseph Conrad and mentioned in
his books.   Old Batavia is like a Dutch town with canals, but
disguised with an Eastern flavour like a theatre backdrop.

After Batavia, now called Djakarta, our next port was Singapore.
This is a teeming city of a million people, mostly Chinese.   There

are also a lot of Indians, and indigenous Malays. The port owes its importance to the entrepôt trade, rather than to local trade or industry. All the foreigners in Singapore speak bazaar-Malay, which has been simplified from the more complicated Malay used by the cultured natives and in the courts of the Sultans.

Bazaar-Malay seems to be the easiest language in the world, being spoken successfully by Javanese, Indians and even Chinese. It has now been adopted as the official language of Indonesia, as the tongues of Java and the other islands were too varied for any attempt at standardisation.

Malay is both elastic and simple to use. The verbs have hardly any changes for tense, mood or number, while the nouns only change when they are doubled to form the plural.

Thus " orang " means a person, and " orang-orang " means people. Orang-utan means a jungle-man, for the Malays have always regarded the simian species as man's close relatives, rather forestalling the Darwinian theory of evolution. Malay may be written in Arabic characters, from right to left, or in Roman letters from left to right. The British and Dutch spellings of Malay words vary a lot, the adverb " slowly " being spelled " plan " by the Dutch and " perlahan " by the British. In Java I was surprised to see a traffic notice reading " PLAN^2 " or plan squared, a short method of forming the plural of Malay words instead of writing " plan-plan," which means " very slowly," or " dead slow." I found the Arabic writing very easy, rather like shorthand, but it is easier to write than to read back, as most of the vowels are left out. I didn't try to learn to read or write Chinese, though I learnt quite a lot of words from the Chinese coolies in Singapore during the long hours of cargo work in the holds. They mostly spoke Mandarin, or Northern Chinese, whereas our stewards spoke Cantonese, which is very different.

The next language I studied was Dutch, as I had fallen in love with a girl from Holland who was living in Java with her parents. That was at the end of my first year at sea, when I was only 17; I had to wait four years to marry her, but that is getting ahead of

JAVANESE FISHING PROWS

the story. Other complications with passengers included adventures with eccentrics and dipsomaniacs, who at least enlivened our days in the half-deck of the *Marella*. Our most famous passenger was the lovely dancer Anna Pavlova, who travelled with her husband and company to Australia after a tour of the Indies.

We were leaving Sourabaya one trip, going out stern first from the wharf, when the ship got too much way on her, and churned the port propeller into a concrete wharf. This broke one blade off, bent the other three, and also bent the tail shaft slightly. The ship had been fitted with streamlined bronze screws only a month before, at the cost of £800 each, so that it was a costly accident.

We steamed on one screw to Batavia and on to Singapore, where we went into dry-dock after unloading the cargo. Here the damaged screw was removed, and the tail shaft drawn out. In the foundry the shaft was straightened under the blows of a steam hammer, and then it was replaced in the ship and fitted with a spare propeller for the homeward journey.

After one day at sea the stuffing came out of the stern gland and the screw had to be stopped to prevent the flooding of the shaft tunnel. When we anchored at Samarang, local Japanese divers were engaged to replace the stuffing with oily cotton waste under-water, but they gave up the job because of the strong tide and perhaps because of the sharks. So the Captain called for volunteers and a party of us spent several hours trying to do the difficult job under 14 feet of water. The attempt was not successful and we had to proceed to Sourabaya on one engine. The job was done there by divers in suits and helmets, and we went on our way with two propellers pushing us homewards.

When I had completed my first year in the *Marella* I was transferred to the motor ship *Malabar*, also on the Singapore run. She had never carried cadets before, and I was joined by my cousin, Willis Hilder from Brisbane, on his first trip to sea.

In the *Malabar* we were very lucky in having a helpful Chief Officer, who gave us all the interesting jobs in seamanship he could think of and plenty of time to study. During the next two years I

THURSDAY ISLAND PEARLING LUGGERS, TORRES STRAIT

completed my studies for Second Mate (foreign-going), and was therefore one year ahead of the syllabus. I could take and work out all the standard sextant sights of sun, moon and planets, but had to wait another year to complete my apprenticeship and sit for the examination. Then I found that I could sit for the Coast-Trade Second Mate's certificate, as that only called for three years at sea.

In the meantime I had joined the Naval Reserve as Midshipman, and amongst other things was able to brush up my signalling by morse and semaphore. When I left the *Malabar* for my holidays I sat for the Second Mate's exam and also passed Voluntary Signals. Having no money to spare, I didn't go to a navigation school to be coached, which made the examiner very dubious. He had never had a candidate before who hadn't been to a navigation school for a few weeks at least. I passed quite easily, but it was only a practice run, as I had no intention of entering the coastal trade.

My first naval training was 28 days in H.M.A.S. *Australia*, a Washington Treaty cruiser of 10,000 tons displacement. She carried the flag of Rear-Admiral E. R. G. R. Evans, who was known as Evans of the *Broke* after the first war, and later became Lord Mountevans. He was a distinguished seaman, and a most likeable Admiral. One of his exploits was in a typhoon in the China Sea, when he dived overboard from a cruiser of which he was captain, to help a ship in distress !

I discovered that midshipmen of the permanent Navy had to keep a large personal journal, like those of Dampier and Cook, written up daily and inspected weekly. This contained a brief summary of what happened in the squadron, to train our powers of observation and description. We had to include at least one full-page sketch a week, either of artistic style or of technical interest. The whole idea appealed to me so much that I adopted it for my own use in the Merchant Service as well as for my periods of service in the Navy. I drew a new journal from the Paymaster's store and started to write it up immediately. Into it went plans of every port on the Singapore run, with descriptions of each country, and plans and details of every ship I served in. I kept this up until war broke out in 1939 and must have learned a lot which otherwise would have been overlooked.

The cruiser *Australia* carried 710 persons, of whom 70 were officers of some sort or another. It was an endless job trying to identify them, learn their names and ranks and find out their jobs. Half the crew were away on winter leave at the time and this gave me breathing space to catch up on the strange naval customs and way of life. There were a lot of traditions and naval practices to learn and I took copious notes of gunnery and torpedo work, which were all new to me. There were plans of the various types of naval vessels to copy out for my journal, mostly from the well-known book, *Jane's Fighting Ships*.

Naval seamanship is very different from that of merchant ships, being apparently based on using the maximum number of men instead of the minimum. This is to give the crew full employment. Being aboard for the purpose of learning all I could in 28 days, I concentrated on subjects we didn't have in our own ships.

Much of my time was spent in charge of a motor-boat running between ship and shore and I learnt a lot about handling boats under power and under sail. The social side of naval life was also an education to me in itself; it ran so efficiently that I acquired a great respect for the way it was organised. I was also very impressed with the methods used to maintain discipline; how people could be ticked off without showing any personal animosity or inviting impudent replies. The Golden Rule seemed to be based on giving direct orders and advice, instead of using provocative questions such as " Can't you make a bigger mess of that ? "

After my first three years at sea in large ships I didn't realise how remarkably free from accidents those years had been. I knew that our ships running to New Guinea occasionally ran on coral reefs, or damaged a propeller, but those things could not happen to a fine and respectable ship like *Malabar*. My brief holiday was over soon enough, and I left home for the wharf to rejoin *Malabar*, which was due to berth at 8 a.m. The newsboards were carrying the headline " Liner Ashore " but I didn't buy a paper and found out when I got to town that the liner was my own ship !

She was on the rocks at Long Bay, six miles south of Sydney, so we went out to see what was happening. The lovely ship was not

CHINESE JUNKS AT SINGAPORE

only fast on the rocks, but already abandoned as a total loss, as she was damaged beyond any chance of salvage.

Her permanent Captain was on leave at the time, like myself, and had been relieved by Captain Leslie, a retired Sydney pilot who was aged 71. He had not served in our ships except to pilot them in and out of Sydney and relieve masters on the Melbourne leg of the trip. He didn't speak Malay, which had an important bearing on the loss of the ship. We always made a point of giving the helm orders in Malay to the quartermasters and kept a strict eye on them when a pilot was giving orders in English.

It may sound unbelievable, but the helm orders in English, up to the year 1933, were always given in an opposite sense. That is, one said " Starboard the wheel " to turn the ship to port, and vice versa. This was plain pig-headed conservatism from the days when ships were steered by a tiller, which is pushed in the opposite direction to the intended turn.

The *Malabar* had been steaming up the coast that morning and ran into a bank of fog, caused as usual by the smoke from the Bunnerong Power Station. The Captain immediately ordered " Port five degrees " to take the ship further off the coast in the fog. Unfortunately the Malay quartermaster not only turned the wheel to port instead of to starboard, but kept on five degrees of helm in the naval fashion. In the Merchant Service the normal practice is to just alter course by the amount ordered.

The Captain was alone on the bridge at the time, having sent the Chief Officer and my cadet-cousin down to get washed and dressed for the arrival at Sydney. He was too intent peering into the fog to see that the quartermaster in the wheelhouse put the wheel over the right way. Nor could he see in the fog that the ship was turning to port instead of to starboard. By the time the ship struck the rocks she had turned 35 degrees off her original course. The ship was doing about 13 knots and she hit the rocks too hard ever to get off again. The time was 7 a.m., and the date was 2 April, 1931. The tide was full, and, as it fell, the ship settled down aft and her bottom was pierced by more and more rocks.

After running the engines full speed astern for a while, without success, a steam trawler tried to tow the ship off, but the situation had become hopeless. The passengers, mails and most of the crew were sent away in the boats and some racehorses carried on deck were swum ashore. That was all that could be done. Later in the day my cousin and I set out with some slightly sober fishermen in their open launch to try to get our gear from our cabin. When the motor failed we hoisted the sail, but the wind and sea were rising fast and, after bumping into the rocks at the foot of the cliffs, we had to bow to the force of circumstances and the strength of the rum and get back to safety while we could. The wind increased to a gale, developing into a cyclone that night, which smashed the ship to pieces by the next morning.

The loss of the *Malabar* shook me to the bottom-boards and I resolved never, ever, to take any risks in navigation, or to neglect any safety precautions. The Company issued strict instructions to captains on the theme that " safety in navigation must be your first consideration." Very good intentions and very sound instructions; it's a pity that we cannot stick to them religiously. Captain Leslie lost his certificate as a result of the wreck and we were filled with sorrow for the fine old gentleman.

During my first three years at sea I had served in four ships. I doubt if any of them are still afloat now. The cruiser *Australia* survived heavy damage during the Japanese war, and was later scrapped. Her sister-cruiser *Canberra* was sunk in a night action against the Japanese in the Solomons in 1942. The *Marella* was sold to the Greeks after the war and was renamed *General Marcos*, *Liguria* and *Corsica* in turn. She has probably been scrapped by now.

The wreck of the *Malabar*, which gave her name to a new suburb of Sydney near Long Bay, finished my first three years off with a dramatic but sobering note for the future.

THE WRECK OF THE MALABAR 1931

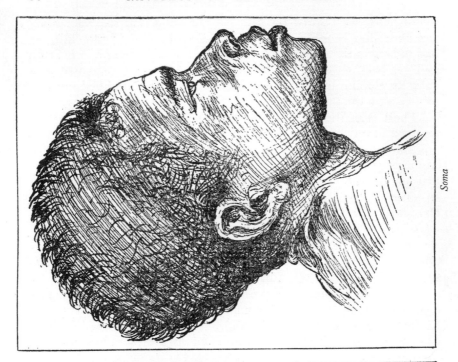

Soma

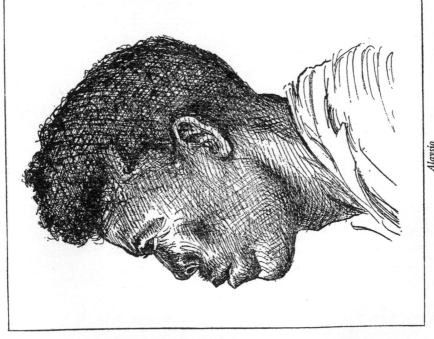

Alaysio

Chapter Two

Off to New Guinea

ON THE VERY DAY THAT THE *Malabar* WAS WRECKED A NEW ship for the company was leaving England en route for Sydney. This ship was the m.v. *Macdhui*, of 4,561 tons gross, very similar to *Malabar*, but with a more modern funnel and a supercharged engine, giving her a speed of 15 knots. The new ship was designed for the New Guinea run, an entirely different trade to that of Java and Singapore. Having one year of my cadetship still to do, I was very keen to get to know the island trade, although our New Guinea ships had not previously carried cadets.

I applied to join her on her maiden voyage. This was refused, so I did 28 days' naval training and was allowed to join her on her second voyage. I found that there was a lot to learn about the new trade, as I had hoped, for it was far better for me to learn it as a cadet than later on as an officer. The ship had an Australian crew, working under union rules, while the ports in the islands were as primitive as the natives. It gave me the opportunity to learn Pidgin English, which is the medium of converse between natives of different districts as well as between whites and natives. There was also the added difficulty of navigating in badly charted waters, some areas and ports being quite unsurveyed. That is still the case to-day, and the heavy rain storms of the area make navigation largely a matter of local knowledge.

New Guinea is one of the largest islands in the world, with mountains up to 17,000 feet, and dense jungles holding about two million stone-age Melanesians. This race is distinguished by very fuzzy hair, brown to black skin colour, and stocky stature. They vary greatly from tribe to tribe and extend over the heavily wooded islands from New Guinea to New Caledonia and Fiji. The name Melanesia means " black islands," as they appear so dark with jungle growth when compared with the coral islands of Polynesia.

Melanesians have a sullen expression as a rule, but I think that they have basically a much stronger and more reliable character than their neighbours, the Malays to the west, the Micronesians to the north, the Polynesians to the east, and the Australians to the south.

New Guinea is divided into three parts: Dutch New Guinea to the west, Papua (or British New Guinea) to the south, and old German New Guinea to the north. The last was captured by Australian forces in 1914, mandated to Australia by the League of Nations in 1920, over-run by the Japanese in 1942, recaptured by American and Australian forces in 1945, and is now a Trust Territory of the United Nations administered by Australia in close amalgamation with Papua. So much of the country is hidden in high mountain country, or buried in jungles, that the last of these fastnesses are only now being contacted by Government patrols, which are welcomed by bows and arrows, spears and stone axes.

The ships of my company started trading around the savage coasts of New Guinea about 1880, collecting shell, copra and other products of the islands. This trade has increased all through the years with the increasing white settlement, but was dwarfed in 1927 by the discovery of large quantities of gold in the highlands. The gold output eventually reached a value of three million pounds annually, just ten times the value of all other products.

Two new ports were developed to serve the goldfields, which were up in high valleys surrounded by mountains 6,000 feet high. The fields were only 35 miles from the coast, but took native bearers weeks on foot to get there. Finally, all the cargo was taken in by aircraft, from the two ports of Salamaua and Lae, each of which was furnished with an airstrip. The largest planes were three-engined Junkers, carrying up to seven tons, and this air service was the largest air-freighting service in the world before the war. A lot of the gold was alluvial and was sifted from the valley flats by large dredges, similar to those bucket-dredges used to dredge muddy harbours and rivers. All the construction materials for these dredges were flown in with the rest of the needed cargo and the thousands of natives from other districts recruited for the goldfields industry.

The runway at Lae is very good, leading out to sea over a high bank, which is subject to erosion from the open sea. The whole shore is so steep-to that we had great trouble anchoring there; we had to veer out 45 fathoms of cable (270 feet) and steam slowly towards the shore until the anchor touched the bottom; at that moment we paid out to 90 fathoms and were then able to swing safely without scraping the beach. On one occasion, the breeze came off the land and the ship drifted slowly off, taking the anchor with her out to sea, hanging uselessly down at a depth of 540 feet. It took all the king's horses and all our steam winches to get it up again.

The ocean swell which surged into the open anchorage at Lae made the work of unloading heavy cargo very hazardous. We carried surf boats for use in other ports, but at Lae we used the large steel lighters available and heaped them up with mountains of mixed cargo, foodstuffs, building materials, machinery and often a motor vehicle to top off with. The light railway line from the airstrip ended in a platform over the sea, like the beginning of a jetty and there was a travelling crane which could lift the cargo off the lighters and into small trucks on the line. The steep bank eroded several times and the jetty disappeared down into the deep sea, on one occasion taking the crane with it to the unknown depths.

Over at Salamaua, only 19 miles away, there was a sheltered bay for an anchorage, but the airstrip was low-lying and frequently flooded in heavy rain. There were no lighters in this port, so we used the surf boats. We used to lash two of them together, side by side, and build a deck on them of wooden hatches, to serve as a raft. Each boat was fitted with a sweep oar for steering, and a painter for towing, manned by natives. All the cargo was thrown on to the

Guinea Airways plane loading 3½ ton lift at Lae, 1932

beach, often half in the water and, as we worked day and night, and often in rain, the effect on the more fragile cargo was disastrous.

While in New Guinea waters, we carried about 100 natives aboard to do the cargo work and man the boats and launches and, as I had a lot to do with them in a slave-driving capacity, I learnt a lot about them. We tried to introduce some humour into the business to make the work more agreeable for all of us and I got to like my black-skinned toilers. Amongst themselves they were very gregarious and sociable, taking pleasure in each other's company, which is a very good trait in the human species. Where there is too much insularity and reserve there is always an opening for anti-social attitudes. Natives from different tribes have entirely different social arrangements, superstitions and taboos, but these were all accepted without question. Each small district had its distinct language, which forced the natives to converse in Pidgin, in which they take great interest and pleasure. Recruits from the interior seem to pick up the language in about a week, partly because it is constructed like their own tongues. Indeed Pidgin is really a Melanesian language, being built up by the natives with words picked up from the first visiting ships, though spiced with some native words in different territories. Its simple form of grammar is very similar to Malay, but then all the native tongues of the Pacific are related to Malay in vocabularies and to a lesser extent in grammar.

Many people outside Melanesia regard Pidgin with great distaste, especially political and educational groups like the United Nations. They say that it is degrading and calculated to keep the natives a depressed people. Just a bastardised form of hacked-up English. They are quite wrong in both theory and practice. For what language is a pure one ? They may coin a theory of the purity of languages, like Hitler's theory of the pure Aryan race. For what is English itself, but a pidgin form of Anglo-Saxon, developed by the English by commerce with their Norman conquerors; and what are the romantic languages but pidgin forms of Latin ?

The word Pidgin came from business and it is a language of trading, as was Malay around the coasts of the East Indies. Now Malay has become the official language of Indonesia, in spite of being a degraded lingua-franca of bazaars and seaports and unlike the polished languages of the native states.

So many of the words in Pidgin have different meanings, or additional meanings, to those in the King's English, that it is a difficult language for the English to learn. It can best be learnt from the natives. Foreigners find it easier to master, when they don't know much correct English and it is quite a common experience to have to converse in Pidgin with German and French missionaries, in the same way as Indians and Chinese in Singapore are forced to use Malay as a matter of course.

In Pidgin the verb " to find " also means " to seek," so when you tell a boy to " You go find-im something " he is likely to return after a long interval and report " Master, me find-im, me find-im, but me no find-im something."

Many are the stories of misunderstandings of Pidgin in the various islands, often caused by the rather elastic meanings of simple words. In Malay the word for milk is su-su, which is plural, as a woman's breasts, and probably derives from the various forms of the Chinese word suey, which include the meanings of soup, water, milk, to suck, to drink, to smoke or suck a cigarette, and is to be seen in the compounds chop-suey, and sam-suey, or " fire-water," otherwise whisky. In Pidgin su-su includes milk, female breasts, and even the lugs or ears left as handgrips when a bag of copra or wheat is sewn at the top. There is the perennial story of the lady of the house playing hostess at a tea party, calling for the boy to bring a cover for the milk jug, " calico belong su-su," and he returned with a pair of brassieres !

Now the word kai-kai means food, or to eat. One young man returned from New Guinea for leave in Australia got himself a flat, invited a girl to dinner, and prepared a seductive meal, complete with soft music and romantic candle-light. When the girl arrived he plied her with a few sherries before popping the question, " What about some kai-kai ? " To which the girl replied, " Let's have something to eat first."

The spelling of Pidgin is a problem. Either the words should be spelled as in English, or they should be in phonetics. The different missions have made several attempts and there is no doubt that the phonetics are easier for natives to learn. On the other hand it will make it more difficult for them ever to master the complications of correct English spelling.

One of the amusing things about the missions in New Guinea is that they have been obliged to register as companies in order to carry on commercially and train their adherents in technical work, such as timber-cutting and engineering. The result is that we now have the " Mission of the Holy Ghost Limited," and the " Catholic Mission of the Sacred Heart of Jesus Christ, Limited."

The missions are of all denominations, but the various forms of theological dogma do not trouble the natives, but they do worry some of the missionaries and the trained native teachers. The missions are doing good work, but then so does nearly every white man and woman in the islands, traders, planters, officials, all carrying the white man's burden in a sweltering and fever-ridden climate. They all do medical work and all strive to train an endless flow of bush kanakas into the ways of the more civilised world, as well as giving them regular food and the idea of regular work. Most natives think that work is for their women, the men's energy being saved for fighting, hunting, politics and talking, and the initial stages of procreation. In the more demoralised parts of the Pacific there is agreement that " Work is the curse of the drinking classes."

The *Macdhui* used to call at about a dozen ports in New Guinea, including the off-lying islands of New Britain, New Ireland and Bougainville. Some of these ports were townships and possessed a wharf, others were plantations where the ship anchored to land stores and load the copra. This is the dry and cured flesh which lines the inside of the coconut and when crushed it produces coconut-oil, used for soap and margarine.

The name copra used to be spelled cobra, while the coconut palm used to be cocoanut, apparently under the illusion that it was the source of cocoa, while this in turn is more properly known as cacao, and is the fruit of a small bushy tree.

Coconuts commence life as small buds like acorns, taking 12 months to mature into ripe nuts, when they drop to the ground and start to sprout both roots and leaves, so that the nut develops into the ball-and-socket joint between the grown palm and its roots. In fertile ground a palm may be bearing as many as 200 nuts at once, in different stages of maturity. The nuts contain a fluid which is very refreshing, and quite sterile, so that it is much better than water to drink, especially if a little gin is added " to kill the germs." Coconut palms or trees start bearing at about seven years, grow about a foot a year, and have been known to live for nearly 100 years, and to reach a height of 90 feet.

Most copra is produced from European-owned plantations, but a lot is made by natives from their village groves, and traded for their needs and fancies, including motor trucks to take the copra to market. It is worth about £60 a ton, but it takes about 6,000 coconuts to make a ton of copra.

The other products of New Guinea are timber, cocoa, coffee, rubber, desiccated coconut, coconut oil and pearl shell. Now that the highlands are being opened up by airways and roads there can be a great increase in agriculture and cattle-raising. Much of the higher country consists of grassy plains, but the grass is six feet high and as tough as sword-grass. Such areas are hardly populated by natives at present.

Air navigation in mountainous New Guinea presents grave risks of crashing into mountainsides in cloud and the pilots have had to use unusual methods of local knowledge. Flying always starts early in the morning, when the valleys are often clear of cloud, and the heavily laden aircraft can wend their way up to the goldfields by eye. They steer no set courses, calculate no winds, but get to know the heights of every mountain pass and the cloud base which tells them whether the other end of the valley will be clear or not. The oldest strip is at Wau, where the absence of level ground forced the runway to run uphill. They land the aircraft up the slope, and take-off downhill, when they are often only lightly laden. Nowadays the network of airways over New Guinea is a big system, but many small aircraft have to be used for the home-made strips in remote places.

Some of the missionaries have their own planes and the Catholic Bishop at Wewak flies his own Cessna, to cover his huge territory including the vast Sepik River area. The natives in this area are prolific artists. Everything they make is designed with imagination and artistry and decorated with bold designs of traditional form. Even a small block of wood to serve as a head-rest will be in the form of a crocodile doubled over, for the teeming crocs of their river are an ever present danger as well as a supply of meat. Their long low canoes each turn into a crocodile at the bow, while their masks, shields, spears and houses are all works of decorative art. Yet a few miles up in the mountains there are more primitive tribes whose carved shields and spears have no sign of pattern or decoration of any sort.

Most native art is far more inflexibly ruled by tradition than that of ancient Egypt or of any more modern academy, and contemporary artists who object to academic traditions, claiming freedom to paint like the carefree natives, are a long way off the beam. I believe that native art is so stylistic, symbolic, and unrealistic that their motifs can be traced back through the centuries to the earliest civilisations of which we have examples.

Melanesians in their native state did not live lives of carefree ease and plenty. They suffered under heavy social debts and obligations, chronic shortages of food, constant war with their neighbours and with nature in the raw, lack of meat, lack of salt, lack of variety in their food, the despotic rule of their chiefs and elders, and the ravages of malaria, yaws and other debilitating diseases. Many men went through life without much chance of buying a wife to grow vegetables and feed them, while an old chief might have many young wives to tend his pigs and gardens. The young bachelors mostly lived in a separate house, under grave suspicion of sodomy, for death was the usual penalty for being caught with a married woman. These are the villages from which the boys were recruited to work on distant plantations, and they benefited enormously by the regular work and food, medical attention and freedom from village fears and troubles. All this is education and elementary civilisation.

The discipline of a plantation must seem like a Sunday school picnic to the savage kanakas who come out to work for Europeans for a year or two before returning home to be denuded of their boxes of trade goods by their relatives. The Germans had the reputation of being harsh masters when they colonised the coasts of New Guinea. They flogged and hung the natives when rough justice demanded it, while they died off in hundreds with malaria. The Australian troops who took over in 1914 carried on a military discipline and this has proved to be a very sound foundation for the civil administration to build upon. Natives do respect physical strength and also strength of character and are as sensitive as children to injustice.

They despise a master or mistress who is always threatening them but never strikes them. When you have to strike a native, the harder you hit him the more he'll respect you. Once aboard a ship I had trouble with a native winchman, who had to be called smartly to order several times. A little later I was looking down the hold and happened to turn just in time to see the winchman about to slay me with a steel marline-spike. I had a cane walking-stick in my hand and laid into him so fast and effectively that there were strips of skin flying through the air before the cane had broken to pieces. He shot ashore very much chastised and I was surprised to get a present of fruit from him on the next trip. He often told strange natives just how hard I could hit and that I wasn't just trying to bluff them.

As you navigate a ship around the badly charted coasts at night or in heavy rain, you often turn a corner and find a point of land trying to wrap itself around your bow. " Hard-a-starboard," and steam around the point, only to see a row of trees appear in the rain, asking to be rammed. So it is " Hard-a-starboard " again and hope for the best. When a naval navigator asked me how far it was around Cape Orford, I replied " About four hard-a-starboards ! "

As a cadet in my last year I used to keep watch with the Chief Officer, which was most valuable experience. I finally made a sketch of Cape Orford with its many headlands, and only eight years later I made a survey of the coast while captain of s.s. *Maiwara*. This sketch-survey was only in 1955 incorporated into the Admiralty charts of the area. The years certainly pass quickly and we have so much to learn, often not knowing at what future date the knowledge may be vital.

While in the *Macdhui* we called once at Manus in the Admiralty Islands and at Wewak near the Dutch border of New Guinea, and I saw nothing of these ports until I called 20 years later as captain. In more civilised ports with good charts and pilot services these things don't matter. But some of our stops in the islands are hard to identify and many don't even get a mention on the charts. All this time I was studying hard for my Second Mate's exam and the year passed quickly enough. Finally my four years' cadetship was complete and we got back to Sydney to pay off one Thursday night. By the following Thursday I had sat for the exam and passed, and was ready to start off my career as a ship's officer, as soon as I could get a job.

MACDHUI IN NEW GUINEA

Chapter Three

The South Seas Islands

HAVING PASSED FOR SECOND MATE, MY FIRST THOUGHT WAS to get a ship, but that had suddenly become a most difficult matter. For Australia had been struck by the great financial depression which was putting one country after another out of business. Every shipping company had ships laid up, excess officers, and many men, even with master's certificates, signing on as A.B.s as there were no jobs available ashore. According to the books, I must have had about seven weeks' holiday and no doubt the sunny days passed quickly and happily enough, though I had no money. There was plenty of swimming and surfing, which costs nothing, and when I had been ashore a month there was the great and dramatic moment when the Sydney Harbour Bridge was opened. But not by the Labour Premier, as intended, but by a reactionary ex-cavalry officer on a horse, who charged up and cut the silk ribbon with his sword !

At this time the State of New South Wales was verging on civil war. The Government Savings Bank had failed and closed, and this state was the first to default on its interest payments on British Loans, all owing to the depression. The Premier was dismissed by the Governor and things settled down again. Only a week later, my 21st birthday occurred when I was hiking in the Blue Mountains. There was still no job, so I went into the Navy for 28 days' training in my new braid as acting Sub-Lieutenant.

After that I went back to see our Marine Superintendent, the fiery but kindly old Captain Green, who proceeded to regale me with his family history. Two of his uncles were sea-dogs; one, Uncle Jim, was captain of the fine ship *Dunbar* which was wrecked off Sydney Heads some time in the 1880's. His other uncle had " been taken by the press gang in '96." When I asked whether the press gang had been operating as late as 1896, he roared out " Seventeen ninety-six my boy, *seventeen* ninety-six." After he grew up a bit the said uncle later served at Trafalgar.

Cappy Green was naturally the President of the Ancient Mariners League in Sydney, though he wasn't the oldest member. He was only about 90 when he died about 1943, but he had been at sea in 1870, and so was much older than my own grandfather. Thinking about Cappy Green makes me feel a very young man, despite my greying beard, my 28 years at sea and my young officers who were not born when I went to my first job as Third Mate. For the company had purged its ships of some dead-beats, purged just one too many, and I was able to jump into the vacancy.

Not that I was happy in the job, for it was an old and cranky coalburner, with a cranky set of master and officers. I was full of my superior learning and naval training, a cocksure young snob, and the only officer in the whole company without a Master's ticket.

I had thought my job as a ship's officer would be a sinecure; carefree watches in the balmy tropics, after the heavy toil and study as a cadet. We sailed from Sydney in mid-winter, headed into a cyclone and had to heave to the first night as the fore deck was awash and the cargo of petrol and oils was all adrift and had to be secured again. I lost my dinner over the side, the only occasion

s.s. Morinda *landing cargo at Norfolk Island*

C

this has ever happened to me, but the ship's jerky rolling was too much after my weeks ashore. The crew were mostly the worse for wear and not interested in the lashing of the deck cargo. The ship's motion was due to her being much too stable, or stiff, as some genius had put a load of old anchor cables in her fore hold to improve her stability, but had only succeeded in making her a lot worse. Her speed was variable and dependent entirely on the humour of the stokers. Her steering was poor, because she had an old type of sailing-ship rudder, designed in the old days to turn easily by hand, without much interference with the direction of the ship.

Nowadays ships have large square rudders, for they are turned by engines in any case, so that ships make very good tracks across the ocean, apparently not affected by the variable and powerful currents which used to get the blame.

My three seniors, the Captain, First and Second Mates, were all Scottish, though of different varieties. They had all risen from the forecastle, their studies had been just sufficient to pass the exams and they all shared the same dislike of me. I'm sure they didn't appreciate my sterling value, nor did they try to help me in any way. The Captain was a man of over 50 but had just got his first command; he was rather unsure and evasive, but was probably quite good-hearted really.

The Chief Officer was an old Highland giant with a very mixed history. He had been master of a schooner 30 years before, had vanished under a cloud, only to appear in the company again after a dubious absence of 25 years. He had risen to command, but his ship had just been laid up and he was demoted again. He was a very capable sailorman and I gained a great respect for his seamanship, especially in hurricanes and bad weather. He really had a heart of gold, but effectively hid it under a very gruff manner, especially to me. The Second Officer was also a giant Scot, from Oban, who had been recently demoted from Chief Officer to Third when he refused to serve in the inter-island trade in the Solomons. He was now up to Second and spent his time scheming to get me the sack, to make room for an old A.B. friend of his in Auckland who was out of a job.

When our first cyclone had passed, we were 150 miles off course and a few days late making our first port, which was Lord Howe Island. This improbable island is a volcanic effort, like most of the odd lumps of rock in the Pacific, but time and its geological eras have mellowed Lord Howe into a perfect place for a holiday. It is barely five miles long, nearly a mile wide, but would take months to explore thoroughly. At the southern end of this little island are two square mountains both over 2,500 feet high, like a giant Notre Dame de Paris. Fifteen miles away, a Gothic spire points out of the sea to a height of 1,800 feet, even more improbable than Lord Howe itself.

The island has two sides, but no harbours. Ships must anchor wherever they can find some shelter to lie at anchor. Each side has a landing place; one on a sandy beach protected only by rocks and shallows, the other in a large lagoon encircled by a coral reef, the most southerly in the world, for its latitude is 30½ degrees south, and therefore well out of the tropics. Apart from the sheer mountains and volcanic cliffs, the island is sandy and undulating, lightly wooded with sub-tropical trees and wholly delightful to the easy freedom of bare feet. To the visiting shipmaster, however, the price of safety is eternal vigilance. For to be anchored on the rocky edge of a stray islet in the wide open battlefield of the Pacific is a dangerous predicament. Every morning the ship is moved in as close as is safe to the reef off the landing place, if the sea is not too rough for the surf boats to be loaded alongside and towed into the landing. Every night the boats and launch are hoisted and the ship moved out to a safer anchorage for the night, but the engines are kept at the ready and full sea watches are kept all night in case of a change in the weather, or a sudden squall. The ship would be much safer stopped in the middle of the ocean.

The island was discovered in 1788 by an expedition from Sydney on its way to Norfolk Island, for both these islands lie on the same straight line from Sydney. The island was not settled until about 1830, as a supply station for whaling vessels. They had been using the island since 1788 for fresh supplies of birds, eggs, turtles and some wild green vegetables. Nowadays the population consists of about 100 permanent inhabitants and about 100 visitors, who provide a sufficient income for the island.

The history of the island is replete with wrecks and near misses, and I've had a few near misses myself. About seven years ago, our company decided that it was no longer profitable to call there, owing to the delays with bad weather and the rising costs of running ships. Since then several small ships have tried to serve the island, but one foundered with all hands on the way, another was wrecked on the reef, and a third was nearly blown ashore and has never called at the island since. At the present time there is a flying-boat service from Sydney, twice a week, carrying passengers and supplies. The island grows most of its own vegetables, fish are plentiful, but

they have to import such staple foods as flour and sugar, which get
mighty expensive by air freight. The flying-boats land in the lagoon,
in about 10 feet of water, but this is only safe at high tide, and the
timetable has to be made out to fit the times of the tides.

Our usual stay at Lord Howe was two days, but in bad weather
it might be a whole week before we got no our way, sometimes
taking some of the cargo on with us. Our next leg was 600 miles
over the trackless ocean to Norfolk Island, another volcanic outcrop
halfway between New Caledonia and New Zealand. It was discovered by Cook in 1774, and named by him after the noble family
of Howard, who were Dukes of Norfolk. The island grows a fine
big type of pine tree which was not known anywhere else, though
it has been since transplanted to many other parts of the south
west Pacific.

Cook also noticed a wild flax growing there and thought that
the island could furnish the raw materials for masts and sails for
the Royal Navy. Norfolk is a fairly circular island, about seven
miles in maximum diameter and the shape of the island does not
provide as much shelter as Lord Howe. The weather is able to
wrap right around the island, leaving no lee side in cyclonic weather,
so we have to be alert at all times and be ready to up anchor at
short notice and dodge around the cliffs looking for the most sheltered spot to anchor. There are two landing places, on opposite
sides of the island and several other anchorages where cargo cannot
be landed.

The island is fairly high, surrounded by sheer cliffs about
250 feet high, except at the two landing places where valleys open
out to the coast. The rest of the island is undulating, rising to a
hilltop named Mount Pitt, 1,000 feet high. The beauty of the bright
green grass and the heavy masses of pine trees makes the whole
island a park worthy of any feudal monarchy.

This paradise of the temperate Pacific was once a hell on earth,
the scene of the worst penal settlement in the cruel old times of
1800. Floggings, murders, hangings, drownings and shipwrecks
punctuated the almost constant state of suppressed rebellion and
mutiny. The convict age left Norfolk Island with many fine stone
buildings, roads, bridges and a good jetty also of stone. Not volcanic
stone, but the coral limestone which has grown on the southern
shore since the island arose from the sea-bed. The last members of
the convict settlement left the island in 1856 to make way for the
present unusual community.

These are the Pitcairners, mostly descendants of the mutineers of the *Bounty*, who settled on Pitcairn Island after the mutiny, with their Tahitian wives and with the help of a few additional colonists managed to overpopulate Pitcairn by 1840. In 1856, the whole Pitcairn community was moved, at their request, and at Government expense, to Norfolk Island, where they were given large grants of land. Surprisingly little of interest has happened on Norfolk in these 100 years, compared with the excitements of the previous 85 years.

Some of the homesick Pitcairners, out of the total of 194, went back to Pitcairn, where their descendants still survive. Farming has always been the main occupation on Norfolk, with several periods of whaling activity. Until about 1920 the whales were chased, harpooned and towed back to the island by small boats under oars and sail. In about 1950 another method was in use, with a high speed motor chaser about 40 feet long, with a harpoon gun on the bow. At present a large whaling station is under construction, costing a quarter of a million pounds, and it will employ a small fleet of Norwegian whale-chasing vessels during the season of three months. At the end of the season, or when the quota of whales has been filled, these vessels will lay up in some safe Australian port. There is no safe port for them at Norfolk Island, in fact hardly more than temporary anchorage. In the past, the whale blubber was boiled down in large coppers and the rest of the whale wasted. The oil was exported in drums, but in future it may be run out to ships in a pipe-line, with the end secured to a buoy anchored offshore.

Before reaching Norfolk Island we must study the wind and the seas, and the different sets of ocean swells which may be running in different directions. From this we will have a good idea which side of the island, if any, will be calm enough for boatwork. We then get a radio from the island telling us which side to make for and on our arrival there we should see a flag flying with the latest news of the working conditions. If neither side of the island is workable the ship can dodge around the cliffs looking for the least uncomfortable anchorage to lie in.

Eventually we can start work, and put our launch and surfboats in the water to ferry the cargo ashore. A launch and some larger boats come off from the island, manned by a crew of what looks like pirates and mutineers. The swarthy islanders in the boating company and those who work as stevedores on the ship have stepped straight out of the pages of " The Mutiny of the *Bounty*," but there is no Clark Gable among them. On my first

innocent visit to Norfolk I was astounded to see one of the young
boatmen wearing a naval rating's cap bearing the legend in gold
letters, H.M.S. *Bounty*. For the islanders are worried by no qualms
of conscience on their ancestors' behalf. Rather they regard them
as the historic characters in a saga of the sea. Our cargo for the
island consisted mainly of groceries and necessities, including a
fair quantity of alcoholic beverages, although the islanders have
several home-brews of their own.

The exports from the island used to be bananas and oranges,
the bananas going to Australia and the oranges to New Zealand.
Both those trades have now ceased, and there are practically no
exports nowadays. It's one of those conundrums of economics to
which the answer is . . . " invisible exports." Apparently there is
enough money coming into the island through tourists, through
elderly people settling there to retire with money and all those
people who get pay from the Government for some reason or other.
There are no State social benefits on Norfolk, because there are no
taxes. The only votes the locals have are to elect the members of
the Advisory Council, who assist the Administrator, appointed by
the Australian Government.

The total population of the island is only 900, of whom 100
would be visitors at any time, from New Zealand and Australia.
The only value of the island, except as an historic souvenir, is its
role in wartime as un unsinkable aircraft carrier. In 1943, a strip
was built on the island and this has been extended and maintained
for civil use; it has brought a lot of Government money to the
island. New Zealand is only 400 miles away to the south, New
Caledonia about the same to the north and Australia 800 miles to
the west. These are very small steps.

The standard of education on the island is not high, though it
has increased very greatly in the last generation. I believe that the
only subject these children of nature show much interest in, sex
education, is not in the school curriculum, but is the most popular
of the extra-mural subjects.

The island has a perfect climate, tempered by the vast Pacific,
so that frosts are unknown. Fruit, of all kinds except apples, grow in
profusion; passion fruit grow wild up the hillsides, among masses
of wild and juicy guavas, the oranges are the most succulent I have
ever eaten and most of the inhabitants are able to live from their
orchards and vegetable gardens. The island is a splendid base for
fishing and the rocky coastline also provides edible shell-fish and
innumerable sea-birds, some of which, like the tern, produce very

good eggs. These have colourful yolks, of sunset hues, and the white of the egg never turns opaque and white, but remains transparent when cooked.

Norfolk was uninhabited when discovered, though it lies on the route to New Zealand, and must have been an occasional stopping place for early Pacific native voyagers, the Polynesians and earlier races.

But the ship is now loaded with oranges for the market in New Zealand and we must sail without further dalliance. The road to New Zealand is generally a very rough one; this is especially so in winter when an endless series of Antarctic cyclones sweep along the Australian southern coastline and always include New Zealand in their wild path. It's only a few days' steaming from Norfolk Island to Auckland, but we had only been going 24 hours when the weather became too bad to carry on. So we bore up head into wind and seas and swell, eased the speed down and so became " hove-to." In this suspended state of locomotion the ship has to be kept moving through the water fast enough to give her steerage way, so that the ship's head can be kept into the seas. Her speed when hove-to was between one and two knots, which doesn't take a ship very far in the wrong direction.

After a couple of days of this we were able to resume our correct course and revert to our normal bracket of speed, which was between five and eleven knots. The time of year was mid-winter, June, July and August, so I got a rather cold and unfriendly impression of the rocky coasts of New Zealand.

On alternate trips to Norfolk Island from Sydney we omitted Auckland and went up northwards to the isles of the New Hebrides where I received my introduction to the more lawless of the South Sea islands. We called at about ten ports there, mostly on separate islands, and full of interesting items of native custom and early history, but rather devoid of much modern commercial activity. This was during the depression of course.

After three months in the old *Morinda* I was suddenly transferred to the inter-island trade in the New Hebrides, in a still older vessel, which ran around the islands without calling in Australia or any other civilised ports. I soon found myself almost back with Cook as far as navigation was concerned and in the days of piracy on the Spanish Main as far as trade was concerned. I was to learn more in the next 18 months than I had learned in my previous 21 years, despite all my previous studies, and my reputation as " a bloody young know-all."

Chapter Four

New Hebrides Condominium

ON ARRIVAL AT VILA, CAPITAL OF THE NEW HEBRIDES, THE *Morinda* came to anchor and the old s.s. *Makambo* came gingerly alongside and made fast, with large coir rope fenders between the two ships. While the *Morinda* was discharging her cargo for Vila into boats and lighters to be towed ashore, a supply of bunker coal was being transferred to the *Makambo* from the *Morinda's* bunkers.

While the *Morinda* called at about ten of the main ports in the New Hebrides, the *Makambo* called at about a hundred spots, very few of which contained more than six Europeans. Some of them were only trading posts in charge of a native and often were very hard to identify as we sailed along the reef-fringed shore. Some of these ports were good harbours, though not a single one possessed a wharf at which we could berth the vast hull of our great ship, over 1,000 tons gross.

Sometimes the reefs were so steep-to that it was too deep to anchor alongside them and in these places the ship had to stop and drift while the boatwork progressed, using the engines from time to time to keep near the landing place.

I transferred to the *Makambo* as Second Mate, as they didn't carry a Third and this had the drastic effect of putting me on six hour watches with the Mate. I was on the 12 to 6, both a.m. and p.m. After being on the bridge from midnight till dawn, when the ship normally arrived at the first port for the day, instead of going off duty for six hours I had to work instead.

The first light of dawn was a very busy time for me, after keeping my lonely vigil on the bridge with only a native at the helm who couldn't speak English. My principal job was to get the ship to the entrance of the port by first light, calling the Captain, the Mate, the supercargoes and the boats' crews of natives. As they came reluctantly on duty I went aft to the poop, cleared away the two surf boats there in their davits, and stood by to lower them into the water as soon as the Mate on the bow dropped the anchor on a signal from the Captain. I then set off in the boats towards the passage through the reefs, or landing place on the beach, under tow by the ship's launch. The work of landing cargo and loading copra was often very difficult in a heavy surf, with the boys carrying out the copra in large bags on their shoulders and the boats rearing and grinding on the jagged coral. Most of my time seemed to be spent refloating boats which had been thrown up ashore, despite their stern anchors, and the rest of the time in pushing them off the rocks and trying to keep them safely afloat as they were loaded.

Sometimes the surf was too rough and the danger of having the boats smashed forced us to put off the loading until another day. Our timetable was very elastic, the Captain having the liberty to call at the ports required just how and when it suited him. He always made sure we were at a comfortable anchorage by Saturday afternoon, so that he could spend Sunday ashore shooting pigeon or duck, fishing on the reefs, or dynamiting fish in suitable waters.

Between all the boatwork and week-end excursions I had plenty of exercise, though I ran very short of sleep owing to the watches, and some weeks only averaged four hours' sleep a night.

One of the Captain's favourite week-end spots was off the Jordan River, in the Bay of St. Phillip and St. James. This was the site of the imaginary city of New Jerusalem, founded by Quiros, Portuguese leader of a Spanish expedition in 1606. This visionary thought he had discovered Australia, and named the island " Tierra Australia del Espiritu Santo." The island is now known simply as " Santo," and the bay with the big name is called " Big Bay " by the locals. Near the Jordan River was a coconut plantation where we picked up some copra, but the river itself yielded us both fresh fish and boatloads of fresh water. The fish teemed in the rapidly flowing water and even sharks could be seen well up in the shallows of fresh water. It was common to have fish bumping into your legs as you forded the stream in three feet of water; a plug of gelignite produced some hundreds of stunned fish which had to be rapidly gathered before they recovered from their concussion and before too many sharks arrived on the scene.

The stick of gelignite has to be plugged with a detonator, with a fuse only about two inches long. The thrower stands ready with a lighted cigarette in his mouth and, when a sufficient number of fish have collected nearby, he lights the fuse and then throws it

without delay. It should explode just as it falls in the water and any
delays in throwing have usually the effect of costing the man both
his right arm and his right eye. There are a lot of resultant Lord
Nelsons in the New Hebrides, both native and European. One
forgetful Chinaman lit his fuse with a box of matches, threw the
box into the water, put the gelignite in his pocket, and blew himself
unexpectedly into kingdom come.

The good ship *Makambo* and her motley crew were an incredible
experience. The Captain was " the biggest bastard that ever sailed
the South Seas," and was often told so, but less politely. Apart from
him there were six European officers, comprising two Mates, the
Supercargo and his two assistants, who were also wireless operators,
and the Chief Engineer. The rest of the engine-room and boiler-
room staff were Chinese from Hong Kong, as were the cooks and
stewards. The deck crew were natives from Aneityum, and the boats'
crews were from Tanna and other islands in the New Hebrides.
There were also odd assortments of native and white passengers to
add to the variety and spice of life.

The Captain, Chief Engineer and myself lived abstemious and
reasonably virtuous lives, trying to save our money. The other
four officers lived a rollicking life under the motto " Cigarettes,
whisky and wild, wild women." With them, however, the first love
was the grog, mainly beer and gin; next favourites were the less
reluctant female native passengers, to whom rape was rather the
normal salutation from a strange man in the native way of life. In
the ship the grog led also to brawls with the native crew, which was
regarded as a sport, though I think the natives gave back as good as
they received. These occasions were announced as " an open
season on coons." A much milder form was the marking of the
lighter skinned natives with their names in great letters on their
chest or back in scarlet marking ink. Their names are strange
corruptions of English ones as a rule, including Biblical ones, and
any misspellings were liable to be indecent by choice.

I was generally working too hard and studying for my First
Mate's examination to be involved in the dissolute pastimes of my
shipmates, who were very kind and considerate to me. They
couldn't resist having some fun at my expense and I was rather
easily embarrassed. Having a healthy young man's usual frustrations,
I blushed very readily, and the French gave me the nickname of
" Pinkie," the slang expression for " vin rouge ordinaire," or good
red claret. At every new port the local folk were greatly amused
by the news: " What do you think we've got for a Second Mate ?

A *virgin* ! " The French freedom of speech in the unmentionable topic of sex used to shock me by its unexpectedness in front of wives and teenage daughters and I soon knew all their bad words, which only added to my discomfiture. My theoretical knowledge of sex advanced in great strides, which was perhaps very necessary, as I intended to marry as soon as I had saved £100, my intended bride being my Dutch girl living in Java, whom I hadn't seen for two years.

Every trip, we got back to Vila about a week before the *Morinda* arrived again from Sydney and in that week we gave the ship a gentle overhaul, both hull, engines and boilers. We therefore took her around to Havannah Harbour, 20 miles along the coast where we could obtain fresh water and lie in safety from sudden squalls or seasonal hurricanes. We anchored the ship there and I went ashore to arrange the watering. This harbour should have been the site for the capital of the Group, but now it is quite deserted except for a cattle ranch whose owner pays occasional visits. It is run by natives, with a half-caste in charge, while some of the more skilled labour was Tonkinese, from Indo-China.

The water came from an inland spring, flowed around the cattle ranch, on to the beach and over the half-tide reef into the sea. My job consisted of clearing out the decaying debris from the narrow watercourse. Most of the debris was dead and rotting pieces of cattle and birds, as well as general refuse, but the water would eventually run clear and clean enough. In the meantime the ship's

WATERING SHIP IN BOATS

boilers would be cooling down before being scaled and other necessary work put in hand.

The stream had to be dammed up and diverted into a wooden trough, made in sections which fitted into one another and these, supported on sticks, led the water over the reef to the waiting surf-boat. The boat had to be cleansed of its rotting fragments of copra and other cargo and sunk to dislodge the rats and cockroaches which lived in the double bottom and lining. When each boat was filled with fresh water it was towed off to the ship and pumped out with a flexible hose into our water tanks.

The worst taste the water ever had was after a murdered Tonkinese woman had been found in the stream and, although none of us ever drank the water, except in emergencies to quell an alcoholic fire, we did have showers and the water tasted very rich and colourful.

The watering was a slow process, taking about two days, by which time the beach and the bush ashore had become unbearable with the heat and the cattle-flies. While the ship was riding empty we took the opportunity, to scrape and paint her around the waterline, the area known as " between wind and water," where she suffered the most wear and tear. Scraping off the paint and rust carefully often exposed a hole in the hull, an inch or two wide, and I was surprised that she didn't spring a leak and sink while I was serving in her. About a year later she did this very thing, after being made fast alongside the *Morinda* in Vila Harbour, and had to be hurriedly beached before she sank completely. The engineers used to patch up the small holes effectively, but she was nearly 30 years old and had had a rough life, so she couldn't keep going for ever.

Another of my duties was that of Medical Officer. Every British ship carries an excellent booklet called *The Shipmaster's Medical Guide*, and the *Makambo* was also provided with a large collection of medicines, drugs and rusty instruments from her former days in the passenger trade when she carried a doctor. None of the crew succumbed under my experiments in witchcraft and the Chinese patients were consoled with opium drugs.

We called one day at the large island of Erromanga, famous for the martyrdom of several Presbyterian missionaries and the treacherous nature of its natives. We were boarded by a young man from Sydney who reported that his mate, Tom Buffett of Norfolk Island, was lying sick of blackwater fever. So we formed a party, landed through the surf on the beach, walked two miles along the Williams River (stained with Martyr's Blood) up nearly 500 feet to the homestead where poor Buffett was at his last gasp. He had been down with malaria for three weeks, which had led to more serious symptoms. We carried him all the way back to the ship, by which time he was in considerable pain. He bore up with great fortitude, objected to being put into a suit of new pyjamas because " they made him look like a queen," and he was a rough cattleman. While I was searching through my book for his bad symptoms, he kept drawing his knees up to his chin to ease the pain. I had just decided that he had peritonitis when he gave his last kick, and the Mate laid him out for burial. We went straight to Tanna, arriving at dawn, to get the missionary doctor to look at the corpse, before sewing up the body in canvas. We then repaired ashore and buried Tom on a grassy knoll overlooking the palms of Lenakel.

The island of Tanna was discovered by Cook in 1774. He landed on the island, risking his life in contact with the treacherous, constantly warring tribes of cannibals. He got from them the names of the neighbouring islands, but when he asked them the name of their island, pointing to the ground, they replied " Tana," which is also the Malay word for earth.

Tanna is famous for its volcano, which is easily accessible to visitors, being only 600 feet high, but it has the disconcerting habit of erupting about every five minutes. Most of its energy is spent by pumping up great volumes of ash and steam and there is no record of anyone being struck by the flying rocks and ejaculations of red hot lava. This activity has never been known to stop during the memory of the natives, nor has there been any great eruption, though the island is subject to violent shakes.

Cook found and charted a fine little harbour, named it after his ship, Port Resolution, but in 1860 the coastline suddenly lifted up about 60 feet, which put the port out of reach for any ships larger than launches. The red glow of the volcano can sometimes be seen for 20 miles at night and, when the ship is anchored for the night barely a mile away, the fireworks' display is magnificent.

The next island of call is Aneityum, the first of all the New Hebrides to be settled and converted to Christianity. Here lived a fine race of 10,000 savages, who numbered 3,000 by the time they were all converted, and nowadays there are only 120 of them left. The ravages of the blackbirding trade gave place to grog and firearms and the spread of European diseases like measles and scarlet fever to which they had no immunity. The natives are also crudely proficient in procuring abortions and in 1933 there was not one child on the island, the youngest person being a man named

Dopi (intended for Toby?) aged about 20 and serving in the *Makambo* as a sailor. Things have improved a little since then.

Aneityum contains much earlier relics than the other islands, and on a large boulder of rock is a prehistoric inscription which remains undeciphered, like those on Easter and other islands in the Pacific. There are some cannons rusting away without any history attached and I collected a small one bearing a British crown to put in my collection at home. I also took the brass bell of the s.s. *Trucanini*, a ship built for my company in 1877. She was wrecked by a hurricane in 1893 and her rusty bow still stands among the trees at the head of the beach as an ever-present warning to seafarers sheltering in the bay.

In the native village one sees cannon balls collected from the reef, where some old ship must have perished; there are crumbling stone walls of the whaling station of 1840 and some tripods and cauldrons from later whalers. An ancient figurehead is the only trace of a French blackbirder of unknown name and date, along with some boats' davits and brass lanterns of later wrecks. There is a good description of the loss of the Presbyterian mission's *Dayspring* in a hurricane in 1873, and again of the wreck of the Anglican mission's *Southern Cross* on Aneityum during my time in the Group in 1932.

My own baptism by hurricane came soon afterwards, in the early part of January 1933. It was at the beginning of the season, which is usually limited to the potentially dangerous months of January, February and March. This is during the hot and airless days of the north-west monsoon, monotonously calm except for occasional squalls of rain and wind. During the south-east season in the winter months the climate is more bearable. We left Tanna because the weather had become too rough to work and made for Aneityum for shelter. We anchored there at 5 a.m., on January 7, when the falling barometer read 29.77 inches. The wind started to veer from north-east to north, and for the next two days it increased steadily in violence as the glass fell right down to 29.38. The ship had been securely battened down, all canvas and awnings removed, all boats well lashed, and we were riding to our two anchors and most of our cable. The wind continued to blow from north, over the top of the mountain, with squalls from either side and torrential rain.

It was painfully obvious that the centre would pass almost over the island; if it passed slightly to the east of us we would get the renewed force of wind from south, which would leave us in safety, but if it passed to the westward the wind would blow us ashore near the *Trucanini*, as the harbour was open to the westward. As the centre got close the wind force nearly dragged our anchors, so we had to go slow ahead on the engines to take the weight off them and to enable us to steer to some extent and so prevent the bow from yawing in squalls.

An hour later the calm of the centre arrived and the wise old Captain sprang into action. We hove up the anchors as fast as we could and shot out the passage between the reefs just as the screaming blast came from the west, after which we turned and ran for shelter around to the lee side of the island. On our wallowing way we just sighted the remaining half of the wrecked *Southern Cross* in the gathering dusk. So ended lesson one of the law of tropical storms.

Two months later my bride arrived in Vila from Java all unknown to my family in Australia, who disapproved of foreigners and especially Roman Catholics. I was still 21, sound in mind and body, a rather nominal Anglican, and still a virgin. As it was in the middle of Lent, we needed special dispensation from the dear old Catholic Bishop Doucere to marry immediately and at the High Altar of the Cathedral. The service was in French, translated into English for my benefit and into Dutch for my wife's, though I made my responses in French and my bride answered in English. The service was at about 6 p.m. and, as we had already celebrated our civil ceremony at the British Office at 10 a.m., none of those present was entirely sober.

Three weeks later my ship was reported missing, as we had been caught in another hurricane off Malekula island. The radio aerial had blown down around our necks, the face of the clock on the bridge had blown off, and as we lay in shelter for five days we saw many small vessels part their cables and pile up on the reefs ashore. The glass got down to 29.30 and the centre of the storm passed so exactly overhead that we saw the eye of the storm, a small patch of blue sky which marks the centre of the vortex.

Another three weeks later we were anchored in Havannah Harbour when I particularly wanted to be in Vila, to attend a friend's wedding and to see my wife. So I took two days off and hiked about 30 miles overland, through bush and jungle ravished and made almost impassable by the hurricane. It was quite an education, as I got bushed many times, while the return journey next day after the champagne and celebrations was utterly exhausting. It was a very happy experience in retrospect.

I should have explained earlier that the New Hebrides has an experimental form of government, called a Condominium, the first

of its kind in the world. It started as a no-man's-land, full of lawless
spirits, until in 1907 France and Britain agreed to govern it jointly.
The experiment has been a success, though not a very flourishing
one, and peace has been maintained for nearly 50 years between the
French and British settlers, of whom the latter are mostly Australians.
The natives don't count for much, being only 45,000 in number and
without any nationality. The New Hebrides are not a colony, nor
any kind of sovereign state, but they are one of the few places left
on earth where the inhabitants are not over-governed or even taxed.

After 15 months in the Group a man was sent to replace me,
so I worked my passage to Sydney in the *Morinda* with my wife,
landed in Sydney on a Saturday morning, and sat for my First
Mate's examination the following week—I passed quite easily.
Then came two years as Third Mate in ships running to New
Guinea, the New Hebrides and the Solomons, while I was busy
studying towards my Extra Master's certificate, on which I had
set my heart and my hopes. But they were to be long years before
I achieved this ambition.

Frigate bird

Chapter Five

The Royal Australian Navy

BY 1936 I HAD DECIDED TO GO INTO THE NAVY FOR nine months' training as a Lieutenant of the sea-going Reserve, which is the Australian equivalent of the R.N.R. This period was to start with three months of specialist courses ashore, followed by six months afloat. My intention was to achieve the maximum qualifications as an officer of the Naval Reserve and at the same time to see more of my wife and home than was possible in the Merchant Service. I also hoped that the naval training would help my studies for Extra Master, and give me more time to study. I still had ten months to serve before I had the qualifying time to sit for my Master's ticket, after which I could sit for Extra. The naval pay was much less that I had been earning, being about £300 a year compared with £500, but we only had one child to keep, and considered that the objectives in view were worth it.

Life in the Navy was much more civilised than in our ships trading to the islands; it was, therefore, a great change and a great education. My wife and small son went with me to Flinders Naval Depot where the specialist courses were held, situated on the shores of Westernport harbour in Victoria.

Having been there before, in winter, I made sure that my three months there were the Australian mid-summer months of January, February and March. The days were very hot and the nights cold, after my eight years in the tropics. We got a week-end cottage by the beach at Somers and I had a swim every afternoon that I wasn't detained by duties at the Depot. After two miles fast walk cross-country I would reach home in a sweat, change into swimming trunks and run into the sea for a swim. The waves were not high enough for a good surf and the water was so cold that I could never stay in for more than five minutes, or I would have been frozen stiff.

43

In the meantime I had to swot up all sorts of books on gun-drills for my gunnery course, which occupied my first month. After that I went to the Torpedo School, which also included electrical subjects and the gyro compass. This was a golden opportunity, so I concentrated on the mystery of the gyro and its behaviour, which was most engrossing, as well as being very necessary for my Extra Master's studies. After learning just enough torpedo work to satisfy the Lieutenant in charge, I was sent to the Signal School for my final course. Here I had a lot to learn, and had to practise daily on Morse signal light to achieve the required speed. The semaphore was no trouble, either frontwards or backwards, as used in destroyers in line ahead, but my big trouble was to master the whole gamut of code-books and cyphers. These were due to be completely changed the next month, but I was unable to do the new books as they hadn't all been received at the depot. So all my labours on the old books were a waste of effort, except that I got a First Class pass, while only Seconds in gunnery and torpedo.

The passes won me a reward of four months' seniority as Lieutenant, and I was really a completely unskilled gunner or torpedoman when I was appointed to destroyers for two months. My very first destroyer was the old V and W Class vessel of the first war, H.M.A.S. *Voyager*. She seemed more like a submarine to me, with her cramped spaces, steel decks, trapdoors and vertical ladders. I fell foul of the Captain in the first hour, for being in the heads (lavatory) when he wanted to be there, and the ship was due to sail in a few minutes. It was far from being a happy ship. The Captain rode rough-shod over the ship, the First Lieutenant was in trouble for drinking too much, the Second Lieutenant was Captain's secretary amongst other duties and was so broken in spirit that he left the service shortly afterwards. The Navigator was a Sub-Lieutenant, a very good lad, but I wasn't allowed to keep a watch by myself. The best fun we had was exercising old stocks of torpedoes which dated from the first war.

These tin-fish were very uncertain in behaviour, so we fired most of them in the sheltered waters of Jervis Bay. The bottom here was rocky, good for fishing, but bad for any torpedoes which might go too deep. After firing two of them we had to turn and race full speed to the end of the bay to collect them again if they came to the surface and signalled for help with the correct procedure. One of them went right to the bottom when we fired it and had to be retrieved by divers. It had failed to start running when it was shot out of the tube.

Another rogue torpedo started running but dived down to the rocks, bashed the side of its head in, then surfaced and ran at full speed in erratic circles, apparently determined to ram us on the waterline out of spite. We managed to elude it, largely by luck, but we weren't able to recapture it because it sank when it had run out of breath. A week later the flotilla of three destroyers was ordered to fire all their torpedoes in the open sea, using the Admiral as target. He was flying his flag in the cruiser *Canberra* at the time and all the torpedoes had to be fired to pass well astern of her.

The three destroyers each fired six fish, not fitted with warheads of explosive, of course, but with practice or blowing heads. These blow the water out of the head when they have stopped running, so that they float vertically, popping up and down, burning a carbide smoke float to attract attention.

At this period of peacetime the Navy was cut very low by the Parliamentary estimates, so that all expenditure on gunfire, fuel-oil and other necessities was severely limited. The cost price of a torpedo was on the books as £5,000 and there was great and lasting consternation whenever one was lost.

On this occasion, as soon as the destroyers had fired their fish they all rushed to retrieve them and cutters were sent away to collect the fish one at a time. As each one was hoisted inboard a signal was made, so that the flotilla was a mass of bunting showing the number of fish in sight, the number aboard, and which destroyers they belonged to.

The flagship hoisted a signal saying that she had actually been struck by a torpedo near the stern and as we combed the sea collecting and sorting out the fish it began to dawn on us that it must have been one of our rogue torpedoes, which had apparently committed suicide in the effort. For we finished up one short and the Admiral led us in line abreast up and down the area until it started to get dark. The flag then made a memorable signal—"HONOUR IS SATISFIED: SQUADRON WILL RETURN TO BASE."

Another day the flotilla practised " evolutions," and this game has always impressed me as the most interesting and worthwhile of all naval occasions. The day before is filled with secret preparations by all the ships. The decks become traps for the unwary, being littered with ropes, lines, wires, tackles and shackles, and the boats are stripped of all gear which might impede their handling. When the fun starts at 9 a.m. the Admiral, or in our case the Captain (D), issues a stream of unexpected orders and each ship must signal the moment the evolution is complete. There is fierce competition between the ships and the most outrageous tricks are tried out. Many of the evolutions are only half completed before the next orders break out from the bridge of the flotilla leader.

To give some idea of the extent of the exercise, it is not uncommon to have to strike down a topmast and the topmasts are, therefore, half unshipped and held by a ropeyarn at the ready.

As the men rush from job to job around the decks, letting go a second anchor, lowering boats, launching a Carley float, firing a gun, and so on, there is always the danger of tripping over a line and performing some evolution unexpectedly. Everything is likely to be the subject of the next order, except that the main engines are not used. We had to send all our boats away to pull around the flotilla, changing crews each time they came alongside. We rigged stages overside to expedite the crew changing and also had a boat rope rigged from the bow to give each boat a flying start while they couldn't be seen by the other ships.

Then we had to rig the hand capstan and heave up the second anchor with it. Immediately afterwards, a collision mat had to be fitted under the hull in a certain position; fortunately the necessary ropes were already in position. All this only occupied $1\frac{1}{2}$ hours, but it seemed like a lifetime. One of the usual criticisms of the Navy by the Merchant Service is that they take 50 men to do a job of seamanship which in merchant ships would be done by one man and a deck boy. This is largely correct, because the large naval crews needed in fighting ships have to be kept employed and exercised. But on these days of " evolutions " it is a pride and joy to see the speed, efficiency and ingenuity of the Navy.

My last ten days in the " Boats," or destroyers, were spent decommissioning *Voyager* and commissioning *Waterhen*, another old vessel of the same class. We had carried out a full power trial along the coast and had worked up to 28.9 knots, at which power the whole midship part of the narrow-gutted craft was too hot for the engine-room crew to remain below for long. I now went to the flagship and soon felt much more at home. In fact, to my surprise, instead of being a useless piece of ullage, my services were in great demand. All sorts of jobs came my way, in the various phases of the ship's life. I became the assistant to the squadron navigator, who was a Commander and a specialist navigator. I learnt a lot of interesting theories from him, especially on the handling of large ships with multiple propellers and in shallow waters. Bringing a whole squadron into an anchorage at once so that all their anchors could be dropped simultaneously was quite a novel procedure to me. There was also a lot to learn about the use of the echo-sounder, rangefinders, searchlights and other aids to navigation.

Another of my jobs was in the gunnery sphere and I eventually had command of " X " turret of 8 in. guns, as well as the after magazine. Later the Captain granted me the naval watchkeeping certificate, which allowed me to keep a watch at sea.

There was also the duty of parades, divisions, parts of ship, and many other routine matters which filled in the daily round, while leaving some scope for recreation, boat-sailing and racing, sport, including swimming, and high social occasions in Sydney and Brisbane. As usual, I found the younger naval officers so devoted to the naval service that they had no time for me or the Merchant Service. Four-stripe Captains and Admirals were much more broadminded, having seen some war service, so that the Staff Captain and the Rear Admiral were my best friends in the ship. This was to lead to some delicate situations later on, when we made a voyage to New Guinea.

Perhaps I should mention here a little about naval idiom. While in the Merchant Service one serves on a ship, and lives aboard her, in the Navy one serves in a ship, which I have explained as due to the following facts. The hull of a merchant ship is full of cargo, so the crew live on deck or in the deck houses or super-structure, while the complement of a warship live in the hull itself. Another idiom, which I regard as rather senseless, is that a warship is not given the article " the " before her name. Thus one may mention the *Queen Mary* but not the *Vanguard*. One way out is to refer to the battleship *Royal Sovereign*, or H.M.S. *Victory*. Nowadays when so many warships have names of places, cities or countries, such as *Australia, Birmingham, Canada* or *Washington*, it is very ambiguous to say: " I'm appointed to *Washington*," and it is, therefore, neither good English nor effective speech. And unfortunately this affectation has spread through the B.B.C. to similar mention of merchant ships.

While I was serving in the cruiser *Canberra* I shared a cabin with an Air Force pilot, who was carried with a few men to fly and maintain a spotting aircraft carried for fleet work. This machine was a Walrus amphibian, a flying boat with retractable wheels, widely known as a Pusser's Duck. It was a great advance on the flying machines designed by Leonardo da Vinci, but it did not appear to have much in common with the era of modern aeronautics. It did fly, not fast nor very far, and it could carry four men or seven cases of beer at a pinch.

For some years past one such aircraft had been carried on board *Canberra*, which carried a very tall crane to lift the aircraft from her nest near the after funnel into the water and back again after a flight. In this way the Walrus took off from the sea and alighted on the surface again. The pilot had to taxi the craft carefully alongside the ship and hook on to the crane to be brought inboard. They had tried doing this at sea, with the ship still moving through the water, but the aircraft was lost in the process.

When I joined the ship, she was just being fitted with a catapult to shoot the plane into the air, though it had to be landed on the sea and picked up by the crane as before. Before firing off the plane for the first time, we had to test the catapult with a large piece of timber the same shape as the bottom of the flying boat, and the same weight, which we shot off several times in harbour. It went flying through the air and then skidded over the water very effectively. Then we tried the plane out with only the pilot in it a few times, just to make sure, before we were allowed to fly with him. There was a lot of competition for the thrill of being catapulted off, but I was one of the first as I was his cabin-mate. The catapult is 60 feet above sea-level, and can be extended to a length of 60 feet too, and turned around to point as nearly as possible into the wind being felt by the ship. A charge of cordite is inserted in a cylinder, about the same as an eight-inch gun, the plane's engine is revved up to its full power, and when pilot and passengers are wedged against pads to take the shock the gunnery officer fires you off into utter unconsciousness. All aboard the plane just black right out.

If all goes well, the plane flies off, rather hesitantly as it leaves the end of the rails, but very seldom falls into the sea. Consciousness returns after a few seconds and away you stagger at a speed of 60 miles an hour, with a top limit of 85 knots. This was my very first experience of flying and it makes a normal take-off from the ground a very tame affair. The plane has wings which fold back like a bird, though not as gracefully, and the wonder is that the wings don't fold back on take-off.

It took us about a month before the Admiral would trust his kindly soul to the shock of the catapult and when he finally did, the dear old man flew his Rear-Admiral's flag from one of the struts between the two wings.

We next did a cruise to show the flag to the natives of New Guinea, for a German cruiser had recently called there, one of the six-inch gun cruisers. We had to go one better and show them a larger ship, with eight-inch guns. The Admiral and the Captain

asked my opinion quite a lot about New Guinea and the Admiral
even wanted to leave the ship at Port Moresby to visit the goldfields
in the mountains in our Pusser's Duck, but finally decided against
it, much to the pilot's relief. We were practising picking up the
aircraft at sea and, thanks to the inborn seamanship of the pilot,
were finally successful in achieving this with the ship steaming at
10 knots.

Our squadron navigator was scared of bad charts and the reefs
we would meet around New Guinea and wanted to keep so far off
the coast that we got lost trying to find our way from Port Moresby
to Samarai. Early next morning the Captain sent for me on the
bridge, having got rid of the navigator somehow, and told me they
had just sighted a certain-shaped island in the rain, and where
were we? This was one of the hundreds of small islets of the area,
but I guessed that it was Dumoulin, in the outer fringe, and that
we were only about 20 miles out of position. The ship had been
slowed right down but, assuming that my guess was right, we went
in through the rain and got to Samarai only a couple of hours late.

From this port we had to go north through the dangerous
China Straits, which our ships did both day and night, in any
weather. The navigator wanted to take us right out around the
Louisiades instead of through the Straits by daylight. While still
at Samarai we had some heavy rain squalls and, when they cleared,
we saw that the *Macdhui* had entered unseen and had berthed at
the wharf. Not only that, but she was due to sail at midnight and
did so, much to the amazement of the incredulous navigator and
other officers. When the flagship went through the Straits next day
we had lookouts up the masts, the echo-sounder going and the
Walrus doing an anti-reef patrol ahead of the ship. We got safely
to Rabaul after several adventures, and created quite a stir. All
the native chiefs for 100 miles around came to see the big guns and
some of them were delighted to find me on board, obviously acting
as local guide.

Our next delightful port of call was Noumea, capital of French
New Caledonia. Here we had a wonderful time and even had an
expedition into the mountains to hunt deer, which was most
successful. We then had an official banquet of venison steaks and
were very sorry to leave Noumea after a few days of high revelry.

When we were returning towards Australia we had action
stations at sea for a couple of days, including full power trials in
which we exceeded 30 knots. I found myself in an embarrassing
position, as the navigator wanted me on the bridge and the gunnery

officer said I should be in " X " turret during action. The Admiral intervened and I stayed in the turret until I was made officially dead during the action, so I repaired to the ward-room for a drink and rest, that being the Casualty station.

Having paid off from the Navy, I had only three weeks to get ready for one of the quarterly exams for Extra Master. Three more seasoned veterans sat at the same time, one having his eleventh attempt, another his fifth, the other his third, and I was the only maiden candidate. Only one man had passed the examination in Australia since 1931, when the regulations made it one of the most difficult examinations in any profession. I was successful a couple of years later, in 1938, and from that year to 1956 no one has passed it in Australia.

In England, where there are plenty of navigation schools for coaching men for this certificate, only a bare ten per cent. are successful and I suppose only five per cent. of men with their Master's Certificates ever attempt the Extra Master's exams.

I failed with the other three men on my first attempt, not to anyone's surprise. A month later I went for Master and passed, for an old loophole in the rules had permitted me to sit for Extra as soon as I was qualified to sit for Master. Another month later I passed for compass adjustment and, a month later, again made my second attempt for Extra Master. I failed again but I heard later that it was only a matter of about one per cent !

My funds had long since run right out; I had to get back to hard work and good pay on the New Guinea run and try to study in my spare time for yet another attempt at Extra.

Chapter Six

The eruption at Rabaul

AFTER NINE YEARS' SEA SERVICE, AND WITH A MASTER'S
Certificate, I rejoined Burns Philp as Second Mate of the s.s.
Montoro on the New Guinea run. This was my favourite ship,
partly for the sentimental reason that she had been launched in
the same year as myself, 1911. She was a popular ship, loved as
much for her failings as for her homely virtues.

On my second trip in her we were lying at the wharf in Rabaul,
discharging cargo in the humid heat and surrounded by the circle
of dead, dormant and steaming volcanoes. At mid-day we were
sitting out on deck having our lunch, when a violent 'quake shook
the ship and rattled the plates around the table. Rabaul is noted
for its shakes, locally known by the native name *guria*. This last
shake was one of a series which had been getting worse daily, but
as there hadn't been an eruption for nearly 60 years, there was no
undue alarm. The sea-level fell several feet and rose again like a
flood tide or bore and it was reported that some reefs near the
entrance had risen a few feet and were now nearly awash. We left
Rabaul that afternoon for our next port, Kavieng, and had just
left that port the following day when we got our first news of the
eruption. This included an S.O.S. for us to return to Rabaul to
help evacuate the town.

By midnight, when I came on watch, it was bright moonlight,
in fact everything seemed to be whiter than usual. I soon found
that this was due to a fine white dust carried by the wind, the south
east trade, over 150 miles from the eruption at Rabaul.

The heavier dust, ashes, pumice and rocks were falling on the
area around Rabaul from a brand new volcano. This had arisen
on the site of a low muddy island near the harbour entrance and
called Vulcan Island by the Germans because of the hot springs

there. Between this island and the shore was a sheltered little
strait, and a local firm had built a slipway nearby to take ships
up to 500 tons. One of these ships, s.s. *Durour*, was up on the slip
for overhaul and, this being completed, the crew were standing-by
to get her back into the water. The violent shakes were ringing the
ship's bells continuously and had shaken all the props and ladders
away from the ship's side. The crew could hardly be blamed for
going over the side down ropes and they made their way up to the
main road to head for Rabaul. They had just left the ship in time,
for Vulcan Island gave a couple of convulsive heaves, then blew
straight up into the sky like the cork from a bottle of champagne.

The column of smoke, steam, hot ash and black mud went to a
height of about six miles, like a more modern atomic explosion.
Red-hot rocks, up to the size of motor cars and small cottages, fell
at intervals out of the column. The *Durour* received many direct
hits as well as being half buried in pumice. The new volcano built
itself up to 600 feet in the first 24 hours, as well as joining Vulcan
Island on to the mainland. The little strait is no more and the
Durour is in the same spot to this day.

During the first terrible night the main road nearby was buried
under 40 feet of pumice, so that the few European houses were

The town and harbour of Rabaul with the six volcanoes

completely covered and hundreds of natives were buried in their villages. Next morning did not dawn in the town of Rabaul, for the dense pall of ash kept the area in darkness and provided a steady shower of pumice and stones.

The Government decided to evacuate the population to Nordup, the nearest part of the sea coast, three miles over the ridge to the east of the town. The great trek was under way all day, streams of choking people and crawling cars with headlights on making their way with visibility down to three feet. In the harbour the small ships had been washed ashore and back again by tidal waves. The only large ship in port, the American freighter *Golden Bear*, was caught with her holds open, receiving a few hundred tons of pumice into them instead of a cargo of copra.

She made her way out of the harbour, but was heavily bombarded by a jet of steam and pumice from Vulcan Island, which painted her Navy grey on the starboard side. By this time the *Montoro* was getting near the scene and we spent the morning preparing for the embarkation of evacuees. We turned out all the lifeboats and stripped them of all gear except the steering oar. Our two gangways were turned out, rope ladders rigged over the side, and all the cargo nets we could muster to use as scrambling nets, as became common practice in amphibious landings of World War II.

The Montoro *at the evacuation from Nordup Beach*

As we approached Nordup the boats were lowered to the water, ready for rapid dropping with our surf boats and two launches. There is no charted anchorage at Nordup, so we lowered down the anchor on 35 fathoms of cable, which brought us up close to the beach. All of a sudden a loud explosion came from the direction of Vulcan, but much closer, and we saw a jet black mass arise from where Matupi volcano had been steaming away fitfully for years. Now it went into full production and greatly encouraged the mass exit from the town, firstly because it was much closer than Vulcan and, secondly, because its blast furnaces contained some sulphur to add to the discomforts of suffocation.

All our boats and launches were immediately manned and went to the rescue of the thousands who thronged the foreshore, the ash showers falling a few yards behind them. The evacuation was carried out with urgent efficiency. Most of the population were too overawed by the gigantic scale of the eruption, and by their relief at being still alive, to make any fuss or noise. There were several schooners near the shore loading up with the first arrivals, and the *Golden Bear* had taken off a few hundred whites before making out to sea. We used ten boats in all, towed two at a time by our launches, which were thus able to run continuously between ship and shore. Each boat filled up in the shallow water with over 100 persons each, while other pairs of boats emptied their loads up the ladders and nets into the ship. After six hours' continuous running there was nobody left ashore but a few police, both native and European, who remained to look after the deserted township.

The lifeboats, certified to carry 54 persons, were found to be loaded with 110 in most cases, a mixed bag of natives, Chinese and Europeans of all ages and conditions.

The ship's decks were packed with a crowd of about 6,000, including about 250 Europeans. Most of them had a bundle of clothes with them, and one old Chinaman carried a bucket of what appeared to be potatoes. It was very heavy, for the potatoes were only a veneer over a mass of silver coins.

After dusk, we hoisted all the boats and moved off to sea, stopping for the night off the harbour entrance where we were safely to windward of the two erupting volcanoes. Most of us stayed up to watch the satanic celebrations; the two volcanoes, on each side of the entrance, were throwing up a solid jet of red-hot dust and stones to a great height and the two columns appeared to meet somewhere over the town of Rabaul. The lightning was fantastic, some flashes bursting like bombs, others running horizontally around the ascending columns, while forked lightning zig-zagged down to the surface of the sea.

I don't think anyone slept that night. The noise of eruption and thunder, and the thump of falling rocks was continuous, while our mass of human cargo had plenty to look at while they stood packed on all the decks. We had a number of native police to keep lanes of access clear to the bridge, but the passengers were no trouble at all. During the night the Government sent a signal to the Prime Minister at Canberra, and our local manager sent one to our Head Office in Sydney, with lists of urgently needed stores. I still treasure the original drafts of these messages among my souvenirs of the occasion. My own part in the evacuation had been running one of the launches. The other was run by the Chief Officer, while the Captain and the Third Mate got the people aboard and packed them on each deck.

The next morning dawned at last and we steamed in towards the coast at Kokopo, a small outpost of Rabaul, to which it had been connected by 20 miles of good coastal road. It was a Government post, and there was a depot of Burns Philp, but the largest establishment was the Catholic Mission of the Sacred Heart. This mission, under Bishop Vesters, a Dutchman, really performed a miracle that day. They took in the whole mass of evacuees and repeated the story of the little loaves and fishes. All the pregnant women were installed in the school, as many had started premature labour-pains. Camps were established in the neighbourhood for the thousands of natives until they settled down elsewhere.

It took five or six hours to ferry all our passengers ashore, after which we commenced to dig into our cargo, intended for other New Guinea ports, to provide essential supplies for the camps. On deck we had some 20 head of cows for a projected dairy farm at Lae, all in calf, and they all commenced to produce still-born offspring, much to the dismay of the carpenter, who had charge of them.

People who had looked into Rabaul from distant vantage points reported that the harbour had filled in between the volcanoes, and if this were true the port of Rabaul had ceased to exist. On the second day at Kokopo we took a launch to survey the entrance of the harbour. The Captain, Chief Engineer and I took a sounding line to check the depths and a thermometer to test the water, setting out for the seven-mile run to see what we would find.

Rabaul has not a long history as a port, for in spite of its excellent harbour it did not become the capital of German New Guinea

until 1913. It has a much longer history of volcanic activity,
stretching back beyond human memory into the geological ages.
According to the geologists who examined the area after the
eruption, the harbour of Rabaul marks the site of an ancient
volcano which stood about 10,000 feet high. At some unknown date
the lava cooled off and plugged up the crater. Later eruptions
broke out through the sides, forming a ring of smaller cones which
still exist as a circle around the harbour. When these choked up
in their turn the father of them all had to save up his frustrations
until he had the energy for a mighty explosion; this completely
demolished the main mountain, throwing blocks of old lava as
big as houses up to 35 miles away, where they can still be seen.
The bomb crater which was left was open to the sea, which rushed
in to form the present harbour.

The earliest record of an eruption is in notes from Dampier,
under the date 10 March 1699: "The next morning we saw a
Burning Mountain in the country; it was high, round and peaked
at top [as most volcanos are] and sent forth a great quantity of
Smoak." The next visitor was Carteret in 1767, but there was
apparently no eruption at that time. The earliest native story of
an eruption was about the date 1840, while the next one, in 1878,
was seen by a white resident on a nearby island, so bringing the
volcanic history of Rabaul into modern times.

The entrance of the harbour is a canyon 100 fathoms deep,
so I was not surprised to find no bottom with the lead-line, as it
was only 20 fathoms long. As we neared the two volcanoes the
harbour looked all clear. This was really a mirage, a reflection
of the sky due to heat. We soon saw a long line of sand barring our
way, and as we got closer to it the mirage beyond shrank away.
Then we saw that it was not sand but a bank of pumice, floating
on the surface like pack ice. Some of it was under water, but about
a foot of it was above the sea, the edge of the mass being kept
compact by the fresh trade wind. Thinking that we could force
the launch through it to the open water beyond, we steered into it
at full speed. We didn't get far, for the engine ran hot, and would
have seized up if we hadn't stopped.

At this moment I dipped the bucket overside to get a sample of
water, but found that it collected no water at all, only dry pumice.
The water-pump for cooling the engine had choked with pumice
and had to be dismantled and cleared before we could get back
into open water. From our vantage point between the two volcanoes
we had a marvellous view of the eruptions. The noise of the

explosions and of great rocks dropping down to earth was most impressive. The strangest thing we saw was a white mass coming over the edge of Vulcan's crater and tearing down the side in a parabolic curve like a Roman chariot in a cloud of dust. It met the sea in a cloud of hissing steam. Whether it was a spurt of lava overflowing, or something else, I will never know, but there is still a deep groove down the mountainside today, with a small bay at the water's edge.

We were about to leave the harbour and its pumice when we spied a small schooner coming out from Rabaul. She seemed to be getting through the pumice well enough, not under sail but driven by a diesel motor. When she passed us we saw that she had a 44-gallon drum of water on deck which was being used to cool the engine. A hose led down to the water-pump of the motor, and the exhaust water was pouring back into the drum, where it may have cooled off slightly in the air. Aboard the vessel were two old characters of the town, who had been arrested for being found drunk in the club. They had broken into it and decided to spend their last few hours of membership sampling the stocks of grog before the town was buried like Pompeii. They may have finished up as two figures in a museum, immortalising the New Guinea Club as members who had stood by the club to the last bottle, faithful even unto death. Instead of achieving immortality they were charged with looting, as were many wandering natives who were after plunder from the deserted homes. The few police and Government officers who stayed on in the town were provided with meals at the Hotel Rabaul by Kathleen Bignell, the only

Vulcan and Matupi erupting over Rabaul Harbour, 1937

woman left, who stayed right through the eruption and was later awarded the M.B.E.

Only two Europeans lost their lives, one being the wireless operator of the *Golden Bear*, and the other a local photographer who went off to climb Matupi to get a good picture of the new volcano across the bay. He must have just about reached Matupi when it blew up in his face, and he was never seen again.

Approximately 1,000,000 tons of ash fell on the town area from the two volcanoes, raising the level about four feet around all the houses. Only a few houses were damaged, but every tree in the district was leafless and battered by stones. The fine dust in the town was both unbelievable and unbearable for many months afterwards. After a couple of weeks the two craters calmed right down and the town was re-occupied again. During the eruption the roads were torn apart by cloudbursts and floods, as the drainage system had all been blocked. Huge drains had to be dug beside the roads to drain the town during the heavy rains and a lot of the loose pumice was washed down into the harbour, silting up some of the shallow areas. Most of the European women were sent to Australia to recover from shock and to wait for the town to be made livable again.

Finally, the townsfolk found one morning that the leafless frangipani trees had suddenly burst into flower, a joyful sign of life and former beauty returning to Rabaul. Every year since, with the exception of the years of the Japanese war, the New Guinea Club has celebrated the event by the Frangipani Ball held on the anniversary of the eruption, the 29th of May.

On our first visit to Rabaul after the eruption, we were able to enter the harbour and passed through a solid field of pumice. It really looked like dry land. There were pieces of dead trees lying on it, old cases and empty drums, like an abandoned army camp in the Sahara desert.

We stopped off the wharf, ran our lines ashore, and found that all the heaving in the world wouldn't get the ship right alongside. We did get to within 15 feet of the wharf, by just compressing the floating pumice into a denser mass between the ship and the wharf. During the cargo proceedings, the odd cases which fell out of the slings landed safely on the surface of the pumice, to be retrieved by natives walking safely on the dry surface as though there was no water underneath.

The scene at night by moonlight was like the Arabian Nights. The pumice around the ship was about five feet deep, and the harbour remained like this for about six months until the nor'west monsoon started to blow the surface out to the open sea. Some of it sank to the bottom of the harbour, making it a little shallower, but that was of no importance in this deep port.

Before the eruption, Rabaul was the healthiest place in New Guinea, the whole of Crater Peninsula being cleared of mosquitoes and, therefore, free of malaria and dengue fever. After the eruption every house and building formed a lake underneath when it rained, for the higher level of the ground left a hollow under each house. These lakes were ideal for breeding mosquitoes and so there is still a danger of malaria and dengue fever, as I have found to my own cost.

The Government decided to move the town, or at least the seat of Government, away from Rabaul. After about five years the administration had settled at Lae, but the town refused to move to a place like Lae, which hadn't any harbour at all.

The Japanese occupied Rabaul early in the war, used it as a naval base to hold as many as 100 ships at a time, but were the cause of the town being bombed completely out of existence during the three years of allied retaliation. So the Government decided to re-create the town in a safer place while the chance remained and various sites were proposed and rejected in turn during the five years after the war. By this time the town of Rabaul had been rebuilt by private effort and it was too late.

To guard against future eruptions a vulcanologist has been stationed in an observatory on the ridge overlooking the town. Here they can feel the best effects of the shakes and visit all the volcanoes and other hot spots daily to keep check of the blood-pressure and pulse of the whole emotional area. Public notices indicate the special escape routes out of the town to evacuation camps at Nordup and Nonga and most residents keep a small suitcases of necessities in case they have to leave home in a hurry. The odd chance that the next eruption may be worse does not worry the people of Rabaul. They are much too busy with commercial development and the more domestic problems of living in the tropics.

PART TWO

The Years of
Action and Reaction
1938-1946

Chapter Seven

My first command

THE YEAR 1938 STARTED AN EVENTFUL PERIOD IN MY LIFE, leading up to the Second World War. Most of 1938 was occupied for me with the final passing for Extra Master, my first promotion to Chief Officer in the company, and then my first command.

This was not in the company, but came as an offer from the Red Funnel Trawlers, who wanted a deep-sea master to take one of their large trawlers for a trial run to New Zealand and back. I knew nothing at all about trawling, but jumped at the chance of becoming Master at the early age of 27 years. I had only been ten years at sea, and a few months previously had been only Second Mate.

Half the crew of the trawler turned out to be old enough to be my father and, of the crew of 13, the youngest was myself. They still referred to me as "the old man." The ship herself had quite a history, for she had been building as a trawler for the Iceland trade when the first war broke out in 1914. The Admiralty took her over on the stocks, as H.M.S. *Gunner*, ostensibly as a sweeper, but really for service as a Q-boat or mystery ship. She was fitted with a 12-pounder and a 6-pounder gun, a hidden radio, and was disguised as a Norwegian cargo vessel. Although she had some brushes with enemy submarines she was never credited with a kill.

She was based at Granton throughout the war, becoming the mother-ship of the trawlers and Q-boats there. After the war she became a merchant ship, with a superstructure built over the engine-room, and went off to Tahiti to trade in the South Seas as the s.s. *Temihani* for the French. I could still see signs of her previous employment in her deck construction, for she had to be specially strengthened for the gun mountings as a mystery ship.

In 1926, the Government in New South Wales was trying to

encourage the trawling industry and the *Temihani* was bought from the French, stripped of her superstructure, and became a typical trawler again. Her name was changed to an Australian aboriginal one for a fish, in this case *Millimumul*. This is particularly long when spelled in morse code, so we used to shorten it down to plain " Milli " for reporting purposes at night.

Now the fishing fleet does not form part of the Merchant Service, though it is a sister service and probably is even older in origin. Very few trawler men or other fishermen ever serve in merchant ships and they remain a race apart, with their own traditions, superstitions, and primitive but effective methods of navigation. I found the ship to be a wonderful sea-boat, capable of nine knots, so that the voyage to New Zealand across the Tasman Sea took us

Diagram of steam trawler

five days. This deep sea navigation was quite beyond the trawler-men and they regarded my sextant work on the sun and stars with great admiration.

I realised that I was a foreigner among them, but found them wonderfully helpful and ready to teach me all I wanted to learn about the mystery of trawling. We were supplied with a new trawl net, two old spares, 45 tons of crushed ice for the fish holds, and 70 tons of coal to get us to our first port in New Zealand, which was the coaling port of Westport. We arrived off this port after dark one night, right on our track and E.T.A., much to the surprise of the crew after five days in the trackless ocean with no land in sight.

Westport is a river port on the west coast of the South Island of New Zealand, and the bar at the entrance has a habit of silting up with sand in westerly gales, which are quite common in these latitudes. The lighthouse-keeper called us up by morse, to which we replied " Milli," and then he asked us our draught. We told him 14 feet, to which he replied " O.K." I headed for the bar with the leading lights in line and prepared to plunge into the unknown river in the dark. I had studied the details of the port in the sailing directions and was a fearless and reckless young shipmaster of five days' seniority. Before we reached the bar the keeper flashed the morse letter " U," which means *You are standing into danger,* so we turned and got clear again. He then told us that there wouldn't be enough water on the bar till later that night and, as the harbour-master had to bring a small French ship out then, he would be able to pilot us in. This was really much more sensible, as it was a dangerous bar, and by midnight we were safely berthed at a wharf.

We had to put our clocks on two hours, as New Zealand had just gone on to summer time, the date being September 27. When dawn broke I saw the snow-clad mountains up river and felt the icy draught down the valley; it didn't feel like summer to me, fresh from the tropics. That week was the fateful week of Munich, 1938, when Czechoslovakia went off the map and Chamberlain saved England from war for 12 months.

Bridge of a trawler

In Westport we had to fill our bunkers with coal before we started trawling around the coasts, for once we started that we would have to keep outside the three-mile limit and not enter territorial waters except under stress of weather, as we were a foreign ship in New Zealand.

Owing to heavy rainstorms there had been a landslide up the valley railway to the coal mines and the only coal available at the port was very small stuff, which gave our firemen and stokers a lot of trouble. We had to take what we could get and also some fresh meat and stores to last us for three weeks. Unfortunately, the cook wasn't used to victualling the ship for more than two weeks and he didn't order enough. When we were ready to sail, the river bar was too shallow and we were bar-bound for 24 hours.

When the harbourmaster allowed us to sail he asked me to give a blast on the whistle if we touched on the bar on the way out, so he would get a good idea of the depth available. Before we left port, most of the crew had spent some time in the taverns and had tried to get some local information about the trawling grounds around New Zealand, but fishermen are very cagey about giving away their knowledge of these things, which are trade secrets even between different trawlers of the same company.

We sailed northwards and then through Cook Strait, to try the eastern coast near the Kaikora rocks. Here we found suitable depths, but after trawling for several hours on our night of arrival we caught nothing but rocks and snags and tree trunks. So we made up north for Hawkes Bay and had better luck there.

Before I joined the ship I had no idea of the work involved in trawling, and certainly no conception that the trawl net was rather like a great Christmas stocking and larger than the ship herself. Nor did I realise that this net had to drag along the actual sea-bottom, where most fish are to be found, while the mouth of the net was held open by two great wooden doors which acted like vanes and rubbed along the bottom on their edges.

Knowing how rugged the sea bottom can be, and what sunken obstructions can foul the net, it's no wonder that the nets are often damaged and, sometimes, when wrapped around a rock or wreck, have to be cut away and written off altogether. The trawl is towed by two heavy wires led from a winch on the fore deck and out over the quarter. These wires are each 250 fathoms long and the trawling is done in depths between 20 fathoms and 140, which gives a limiting depth of 840 feet. Steaming at half speed, the

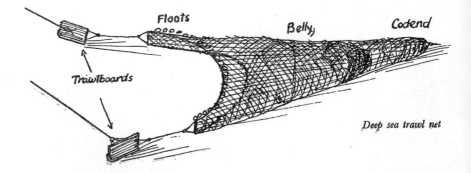

Floats   Belly   Codend

Trawlboards

Deep sea trawl net

ship only makes about three knots when towing the trawl and to make her steer properly we always rigged a stormsail on the mizzen-mast.

After towing for three or four hours, the net is assumed to contain about three tons of fish and the 'ship is stopped to haul the net. This requires all hands on deck, every man in the ship.

Then the wires are hove in and the net hoisted in by hand except for the cod-end, which contains the catch; this is hoisted by the tilson and emptied out on the foredeck. The net is then streamed again, before the crew set to work on the catch. Half of this consists of sharks, sting rays and mullock from the bottom.

The sharks and larger fish have all been spending their time waiting in the net by gorging on the smaller fish, not stopping when their stomachs and gullets are full, but having their mouths full too, with the fish tails hanging out. Half the fish are suffocated in the cod-end and when it is brought to the surface the deep sea fish expire very quickly. When the excess fish have been taken from the larger fishes' mouths, the sharks and rays are killed and dumped overboard. Then the smaller fish are put into baskets and stowed in the ice of the hold, while the larger ones are first gutted and cleaned before stowing below.

As each handful of entrails was thrown over the side they were caught by a hungry horde of albatrosses, molly-hawks and many types of seagulls, which arrived in squadrons every time the ship stopped to haul the net. In fact the working of the winch was their dinner bell, both day and night, for the trawling did not stop until the hold was full. We spent nine days and nights trawling continuously, except for ten hours when we had to shelter from a gale.

The trawlermen are really tough, for it was still mid-winter weather, generally with icy seas breaking over the decks and not anyone's idea of Saturday afternoon yachting. When all the catch was stowed away below, the bridge and engine-room watches resumed and the rest of the hands turned in for a couple of hours' rest. I don't think any of them owned pyjamas, and they turned in all standing, complete in oilskins, sou'westers and sea-boots, just pulling a blanket over the top.

There was a lavatory in the fo'c'sle, but I was the only man to use it, for these deep sea sailormen just used to squat on the lee bulwark with one hand on the rigging, and never mind the state of the weather. Most of the men were trained around the North Sea and all the way to Iceland. The Mate's name was Jim Kenney, aged about 63, and he had served as skipper at times. He was born a gipsy in England, ran away from his tribe and never saw them again. He went to sea in trawlers from Hull and wore a small gold anchor in his ear for a charm. He was a lovable man and reminded me of the Italian fisherman in Kipling's book " Captains Courageous," about the Grand Banks' fishermen.

The Second Mate was a massive but amiable giant who loved garlic so much that he took a sugar-bag full to sea each trip. Every time he came on watch his pockets bulged with it and he just chewed it raw like sticks of celery. The tiny wheelhouse was glassed in, with just room for the large steering wheel and helmsman, besides the officer of the watch. The gaseous atmosphere, after a few hours of the middle watch, was quite devoid of normal air, but apparently the garlic-gas was quite healthy.

The only unpopular man in the crew was an old Dutchman. He had a sour disposition and a stinking great pipe and was reputed to have married a woman with money and property in Sydney. He was very grimy, for the rest of the crew did wash their hands and faces regularly. And I'll never forget the great Second Mate having a bath on the fore deck with a bucket of water amidst the fury of a wintry gale.

A week after Westport we were fresh out of meat, but we had plenty of fish to choose from. Now an occasional meal of fish, especially freshly caught, can be very welcome, but when it's on at every meal it gets very insipid. We tried all kinds of fish, cooked in every possible way, including pieces of liver and the wingtips of the sting rays. Then the Mate sawed up some timber to sawdust and made a smoke-box from a kerosene case, to produce some smoked fish to vary the menu. We ran out of vegetables except for potatoes and then ran out of tobacco !

The Mate was the only man with any left and, every time he rolled a cigarette secretly in the night for a quiet smoke, he soon found a few friends gathering around him pleading for a few puffs. I was a non-smoker myself, but the crew asked permission to clean my cabin out, removing the bunk and all, in the hope of finding a few forgotten bumpers or fag-ends. I was really ashamed of the abject degradation of these men, who were as pitiful as opium-addicts deprived of their drug.

When the fish hold was full we clewed up all the gear and set out for home. We first had to get through Cook Strait; if I had realised what the weather could get like there we would have sailed home north-about past Auckland. From Cape Kidnappers we beat down to Cape Palliser, fought our way past " Windy Wellington," and struggled against a great westerly storm through the Strait. I had never seen such huge waves and the only safe spot on deck was right aft where the lifeboat was stowed under the mizzenmast boom. My cabin was under the wheelhouse and the only one on deck; it had no door, and its portholes had never been opened. This appeared strange to me when I joined the ship, for the only access was down through a trap door in the wheelhouse. But when I saw the waves which wrapped themselves around the cabin in rough weather, I realised that it was all for the best.

We emerged from Cook Strait at last into a cyclone which was blowing a gale from the sou'west, with mountainous seas. We had to steer about north-west, so the gale was abeam to port and we set stormsails on both masts to keep her steady and help her along.

We managed to do six knots and I was amazed at the ease with which she slipped through the heavy seas and swell. We soon found another ship in the storm, the passenger liner *Wanganella*, of 10,000 tons, but she was hove-to in the gale, while we slipped past her, very proud of our ship's seaworthiness.

As the storm continued day after day, we had nothing to do but rest when off duty and catch up on our lost sleep. We all messed together in the after cabin, in homely style like one happy family, and I found the crew a very interesting study. They would have made the trip worthwhile even without the absorbing interest of the trawling and handling of the ship.

The run home was 1,407 miles, which took over a week, and was not without incident, thanks to the cyclone. On the second day the small hatch to the fish hold, being continually swept by seas, started to come adrift from its covers. These canvas sheets were battened down with wedges and lashings and it was a difficult job to get them secured again, while the ship's head was paid off and we ran before the wind. Otherwise we could have filled up and foundered.

The following day found the wind backing to the south, so coming more on our port quarter, but the swell became more confused, as is common in the Tasman Sea; where the swell crests crossed there arose a pyramidal breaker. These are worse with every fifth wave in a storm and so are few and far between. One of them arose and hurled itself at our funnel, just missing it but sweeping the engine-room casing with all the nets, spare anchor and steel stanchions, which snapped like carrots to our amazement. We cleared up the mess and restowed all the gear, being thankful that the nets hadn't gone overboard and into the propeller.

On the following night we thought we were running out of the storm, but it had one last crack at us. This occurred at about 2 a.m., a popular time for storms to make mischief. We all awoke at a loud crash, like a collision, and as I rolled out of the bunk and started up the vertical wooden ladder to the wheelhouse I was met by a solid mass of water coming down. I got out of its way, then climbed up to find the giant Second Mate gasping for breath, not from his garlic but from having taken the full force of the wave after it had smashed through the windows of the port side of the wheelhouse. The water soon went, mostly into my cabin, which had to be baled out, and the Second Mate survived the unusually fresh air for the rest of his watch. There was no other damage and we set to at daylight to board up the missing windows with kerosene cases. The wave must have been just the crest of a pyramid, to strike us so high and not strike the rest of the ship. That was the end of the storm.

Since leaving Westport I had omitted to shave, thinking that as a skipper I should look the part, instead of being a beardless youth, as I was so young for the job. As we neared Sydney we ran out of most items of food, though we didn't go hungry and, when we made Sydney Heads at midnight, after 25 days away, we only had some tins of treacle left and two tins of pepper! We paid off next day with a few prize fish to take home and a good packet of pay, including our bonus on the fish, which in my case was 2d. per basket for our 977 baskets.

The "Milli" came to a sticky end in 1941, when she caught an enemy mine in her net. This wasn't seen until the net was being hauled aboard and it exploded against the side of the ship, blowing her to pieces. The Captain and half the crew were lost; the surviving five men found the capsized lifeboat, righted it, and spent 24 hours off the coast before they were picked up. Only one of them had been with me on the trip and he was John Lowe, who had become Second Mate of the ship. He was one of the few Australians in the ship and I hope he was able to survive the rest of the war, either in trawlers or minesweepers.

So ends the story of my first command and of my only voyage in a gallant and seaworthy trawler of 287 tons.

Chapter Eight

Disguising a ship

MY NEXT COMMAND CAME LESS THAN SIX MONTHS LATER, IN New Guinea waters for my old company, Burns Philp. I had been asking for command of an inter-island vessel for some time and was suddenly offered the s.s. *Maiwara*, which was based on Rabaul. As I would have to live there, my family had to pack up, let the house and make a new home in Rabaul. We travelled to New Guinea as passengers in the m.v. *Macdhui*, got a house from the company at a low rental, and gathered up some furnishings as our own furniture was let with our house in Sydney.

The *Maiwara* was of 600 odd tons, a coal-burning steamer, built in 1924 in the Free State of Danzig. After two years in the Baltic pit-prop trade she was sold to Burns Philp in Scotland. She was built as a raised quarter-deck vessel and had some superstructure added before setting out for her new base in New Guinea.

When I joined her she did not call at the mainland of New Guinea at all, but devoted her runs to the large islands of New Britain, New Ireland and Bougainville. These formed part of German New Guinea, or the Bismarck archipelago, and their coasts were dotted with large coconut plantations. We worked on a six-weekly schedule, to fit in with our Sydney ships and the *Maiwara's* time was divided into three short trips of two weeks each. Most of our ports of call were uncharted, although there was a Captain's Notebook containing sketches of most of the ports. This enabled them to be identified and the ship to be safely anchored, but the sketches were a strange mixture of plan and elevation.

Unfortunately, a lot of the coastlines were uncharted, which made the ports hard to find, and some of them weren't in the Notebook. On my first visit to New Ireland we had to call at one of the Company's plantations, named Punmalum, to drop stores and

collect the copra. This part of the coast was shown on the chart as
a straight dotted line and the preceding captain had put a pencil
cross on the coast with the name Punmalum. This gave me no
information at all about the port, but when we were at the right
spot we found a headland, a small bay, and a small river flowing
into the bay. There was the manager's house, a copra shed and the
surrounding plantation to show that it was a port of call, but I
have always maintained that these places needed a large sign to
show the name, like railway stations.

Having no instructions about the anchorage, we proceeded in
with a man sounding the depths with a lead-line. We soon found
ten fathoms and, when it shoaled to six, I dropped the anchor in
the mouth of the river. The water was muddy, so we could see
no reefs, except the breaking ones in the distance. Ten minutes
later, as we swung to the wind, our stern grounded on some coral,
much to my dismay. Our launch had been put in the water, so we
gave it a sternline to tow the stern clear of the shoal, while the
anchor was hurriedly weighed and the ship moved out to deeper
water. No damage was done and I later made a careful sketch
survey of the place, along with about a dozen other uncharted ports
and pieces of coastline.

One part of the coast of New Ireland turned out to be six
or seven miles out of position, the chart apparently having been
put together from odd pieces of coastline marked down by the
earliest navigators, starting probably with Dampier in 1699.

Parts of the New Ireland coast were well charted, but in this
stretch of 90 miles the whole coastline needed charting. This
took me several trips, charting and checking and getting the
distances averaged out by means of the ship's speed. I didn't make
a new chart, but plotted the correct coastline on to the Admiralty
chart, as my survey joined up at each end with good naval surveys.
During the war all my efforts at hydrography, together with those
of other shipmasters, were printed and distributed by the Allied
Geographical Section. But it has taken ten years since the war for
my corrected coastline to be officially incorporated in the Admiralty
charts.

Some of our ports were hazardous in the extreme. Buka Passage
is one of these, a passage about five miles long and narrowing down
to a width of 100 yards or less between the great island of Bougainville and its small sister called Buka. A tidal stream of five or six
knots runs at unpredictable times and it is only safe to travel against
the current, for steaming with it takes a ship too fast to turn the

Lat 4° 30 S

Long
154° 13 E

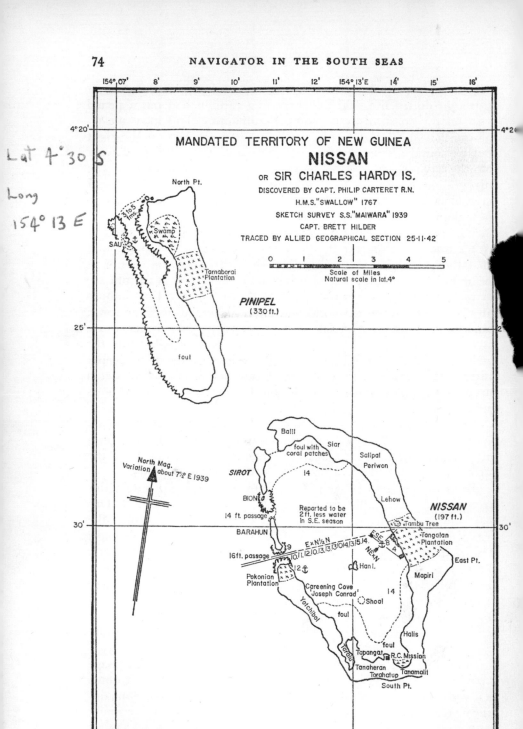

MANDATED TERRITORY OF NEW GUINEA
NISSAN
OR SIR CHARLES HARDY IS.

DISCOVERED BY CAPT. PHILIP CARTERET R.N.
H.M.S."SWALLOW" 1767
SKETCH SURVEY S.S."MAIWARA" 1939
CAPT. BRETT HILDER
TRACED BY ALLIED GEOGRAPHICAL SECTION 25·11·42

0   1   2   3   4   5
Scale of Miles
Natural scale in lat.4°

North Pt.

3 to 5 fms.

Swamp

SAU

Tarnaborai Plantation

PINIPEL
(330 ft.)

25'

foul

North Mag.
Variation about 7½ E 1939

Balil

foul with coral patches

Siar

Salipal
Periwon

SIROT

14

BIONO

Lehow

NISSAN
(197 ft.)

14 ft. passage

Reported to be
2 ft. less water
in S.E. season

Tambu Tree

BARAHUN

30'

Tangalan
Plantation

16 ft. passage

E x N½ N
9   10.11.12.10.13.13.10.4.13.5.14.

Han I.

East Pt.

Pokonian
Plantation

12

Mapiri

Careening Cove
Joseph Conrad

Shoal

14

Yatchibal

foul

Halis

foul

Tapangat

R.C. Mission

Tanaheran

Torahatup   Tanamalit

South Pt.

corners. We had three stops in the Passage, one for the Government Station, one at Chinatown, and one at a plantation. There wasn't room to turn safely, though I did succeed in doing it twice, once in daylight and once by force of circumstances, at 8 o'clock at night when the tide turned.

Our most breath-taking navigation was the port of Nissan, an atoll also called Green Island and Sir Charles Hardy Island. This atoll is a rough circle of coral about seven miles in diameter, having a lagoon in the centre and several narrow passages leading into it. The main passage was about a mile long and a few yards wide, with an official depth of 16 feet. The passage is difficult to locate, as it is really a gutter running through a submerged bank of coral.

We used to stop the ship outside, get up a good head of steam, and note the position of the passage by the tide rip which marked the gutter. The ship then lined up roughly on a tree about six miles away, on the other side of the atoll, and then dived at the passage while I sent an urgent prayer to the God of Navigators. As the ship entered the long, straight but shallow groove, the bottom rushed up to meet us, appearing to be no more than six feet deep, instead of 16 feet exactly. As the ship forged her way against the tide, I was scared to try to alter course at all, for fear of bumping the stern on the sides, so I generally got through the long mile with only faint-hearted alterations of course. Once inside the atoll it was easy steaming to the plantation anchorage.

Believe it or not, the audacious Alan Villiers took the ship *Joseph Conrad* into Nissan under sail. He was looking for an atoll in which he could safely careen the ship and, having chosen Nissan, he stopped off at the entrance and sent a boat ahead to find the passage and check the depth available.

The boat showed an affirmative flag, so Villiers made straight for the passage under full sail, to have enough speed for stemming the tide. He himself took a perch aloft to con the ship through the passage, but the sight of the shallow reef from his vantage point was simply paralysing; he uttered not one word of command until the ship was safely through. After careening the ship on a sheltered beach she was towed out through the passage by boats under oars, with all hands much wiser for the experience. I made a survey of this atoll, and was very proud to see it published with the note: Discovered by Captain Philip Carteret, R.N., H.M.S. *Swallow* 1767; sketch survey by s.s. *Maiwara*, Captain Brett Hilder, 1939.

Sometimes my five-year-old son came on a trip with me, sometimes my wife and small daughter as well, and this year of my life

was really full of interest. It was also a prosperous year for us and
the only year of my life so far when I had any money to spare. But
the sands of time were running out very quickly.

In Rabaul we bought an old car and toured the interesting
district of Crater Peninsula, visiting the several volcanoes and
having lots of adventures. The old ship was in bad need of an
overhaul, which was overdue, so I got around each trip as fast
as possible, to get more time in Rabaul for repairs. On one of these
occasions a cruise ship arrived for a visit, the triple-screw ship
Katoomba, of 9,000 tons. I got the job of piloting her to a wharf,
which was quite a thrill for me, and the Captain was most indignant
when I charged him the regulation fee of £9.

The next item on the programme was the very serious disturbance which has since become known as World War II. This was
a great inconvenience to a lot of us, and added to our responsibilities
at sea. One difficulty about New Guinea was that it was a League
of Nations Mandate, and therefore was not able to be fortified for
defence. The harbour of Rabaul lay wide open with its shipping
wharves to any passing raider. Then there was the story of the
Burns Philp ship *Matunga* to remember. She was caught on the way
to Rabaul in 1917 by the German raider *Wolf*, her cargo and bunkers taken, her crew and passengers made prisoners and the ship
scuttled. The *Wolf* had steamed up close disguised as a merchant
ship and the hold-up was sudden and inescapable.

As a Naval Reserve officer, I determined to avoid a similar
fate, but as we only did nine knots and had no radio, we would have
only one means of escape. That was to disguise the ship as a neutral,
which might deter a raider from attack, or of giving away her
identity by stopping us for search and checking. The Admiralty
had issued us with full instructions, including the use of disguise and
camouflage, but it seemed to me that to be of any use a disguise
would have to be complete and permanent. It would be useless to
show a neutral flag if the names and markings on the ship and
funnel did not tally with the neutral flag. So I decided to disguise
the *Maiwara* as a neutral Dutchman from Batavia, assisted by our
having a native crew aboard and my knowledge of Dutch if a
raider stopped us.

A lot of people thought that the first few months of the war
were too early to worry about raiders, but I knew that some German
ships had escaped from Australian ports just before the declaration
of war and would be making up through New Guinea waters to
Japan to fit out as raiders. My small and slow ship couldn't stand

up against even a potential raider, for they would be able to capture
or ram her if we tried to put up a fight or attempted to escape.

We were in Rabaul when the balloon went up and during the
next few days I made all preparations for the defence of the ship.
The Admiralty had officially taken over control of all British merchant shipping and therefore their orders and instructions overrode
any other regulations or the orders of the owners. A merchant
ship becomes a national asset, rather than a chattel of her owners,
and the Master's first duty was the safety of the ship; the safety of
the crew and cargo, and any other considerations, must be secondary.

I went to see the company's manager at Rabaul, who agreed
with my ideas and issued me with the dozen rifles he had in store,
plus two boxes of ammunition, and the necessary drums of paint to
disguise the ship. The rifles were to repel a boarding party if we were
stopped by a raider and I was determined to try to ram an enemy
rather than give in without a fight, if our disguise did not prove

sufficient. We started by painting
the funnel cream, to fit in with our
assumed identity as a vessel of the
K.P.M. Line. The new funnel
made a new woman of the old
ship, like a woman in a new hat.
We made a Dutch ensign and a
K.P.M. house-flag, which wasn't
easy.

Next we had to paint the ship
white instead of black and this
took several weeks as we travelled
around the islands on our normal
run. At one stage the ship was
white one side and black on the
other. To save time between ports
we had the crew over the side on
stages at sea, painting away. The
white paint made the ship look
very much larger and we then
painted in the name *Van Rees* and
port of registry, Batavia. We also
had to change the name on the
lifeboats, to avoid detection by
close scrutiny and at last we were
completely disguised.

*Painting the funnel was the first step in
disguising the ship*

By this time several objections to the disguise were voiced including some terse signals from Navy Board in Melbourne, but to these I replied that I was acting under Admiralty orders, that I was doing what I thought necessary for the safety of the ship and that the Australian Navy Office could go to blazes. This proved quite successful, for they were in a weak position and when they appealed to my company to intervene I was able to tell our board of directors where they could get off, too.

In a long letter to them by airmail I pointed out the legal position and signed it " Your most loyal but disobedient servant." I believe that they were privately amused at my fight with Navy Office. We later called at a Government post on New Ireland where the District Officer had been putting the defences in order. On sighting us steaming in, he ordered panic stations to repel a German raider and we were surprised to see men running with rifles to take up positions near the boat jetty. We dropped anchor and sent the

Dutch ensign and false name on stern

launch in with the purser, as was normal practice. At this moment I remembered to give two blasts on the whistle, to advise the neighbourhood of our arrival. Now the *Maiwara's* whistle was unmistakable, being of two notes and of great volume. The whistle turned the panic ashore into hoots of mirth and saved the launch from rifle-fire.

What the next move from the Navy Office would have been I cannot say, for at this stage I was called up for service in the Navy by another department. The company sent up the former captain of the *Maiwara* to relieve me. His name was McManus, and he had orders from the company to change the disguise to the ship's correct flags and name.

I sold up the furniture and car and sailed with my family in the *Macdhui* for Sydney under full war conditions of black-out and I thought the chapter had closed when we

The s.s. Maiwara *on her lawful occasions*

Disguised as s.s. Van Rees

got to Sydney. When I got to Melbourne to report to Navy Office I was in plain clothes and, as I felt sure they didn't know I had been called up, I went in to find out just whom I had been fighting, so I could give him a piece of my mind. The man turned out to be a four-stripe captain, the Deputy Chief of Naval Staff, and an old enemy from my time in H.M.A.S. *Canberra*. When I tackled him, secure in my plain clothes disguise, I was very surprised to find him in a friendly and conciliatory mood. He said we couldn't afford to annoy the neutral Dutch by misusing their ensign. I replied that it seemed fair enough for Britain's new *Mauretania* to flaunt the American Stars and Stripes for her disguise in the North Atlantic. We then parted, agreeing to differ and I left him in a daze of surprise at such politeness to a rebellious lieutenant of the Reserve.

I found an old shipmate in Operations Room, and I finally got the full and dramatic story. For the *Maiwara* case had become a *cause célèbre*, about which the Navy Office was very touchy: not about my disguising the ship, but about her later lack of disguise. After I left her she sailed under Captain McManus and the Red Ensign for Bougainville ports, calling at Nissan on the way, where there was no radio station at the time.

Two weeks later the ship had not appeared at Bougainville, so was declared missing, believed captured by a raider. She thus became the first ship lost in Australian waters from enemy action and the panic at Navy Office was really an education to the few who were privileged to witness it. My use of disguise was entirely vindicated, though of course they could hardly admit that to me and after all the panic the old *Maiwara* turned up again! She had run aground in the reef passage at Nissan, where they had to discharge all the cargo to get her refloated; then she had to be reloaded, and was therefore two weeks overdue getting to Bougainville, without being able to advise her plight by radio.

The *Maiwara* was later sold by the company and was running supplies for the Allies during the Japanese war in New Guinea waters. After the war she was sold to Chinese owners and I have heard no more of her. But my time in her both in peacetime and in wartime disguise certainly had its after effects.

Chapter Nine

From Navy to Air Force

CORDIAL RELATIONS WITH THE NAVY WERE EASY TO MAINTAIN in peacetime, but we fell foul of each other as soon as war broke out and we continued our private war for two and a half years. After that I was free to devote our offensives against the King's Enemies. What went on between Navy Office and myself might be better left untold, for it was neither creditable nor even credible.

After the affair of the *Maiwara* and her disguise had ended by the Navy calling me up, I got to Sydney with my family and took a flat at a rental of five guineas a week, as our house was still occupied by a tenant. Then I reported to the Naval Depot at Rushcutters Bay, only to be told that my services were no longer required. I pointed out that I had come all the way from New Guinea at the request of Navy Office and continued to report to them every day for a week without any change in their attitude.

Then I put a trunk call through direct to Navy Office in Melbourne, asked for the Director of Reserves and found him to be a four-stripe Captain and a friend of my earlier days in the Navy. He told me to ignore the local Depot and proceed to Melbourne by the first train. Then it came to light that the Sydney office had confused me with my cousin Willis Hilder, who was also a lieutenant of the Reserve, but whose company couldn't spare him at the time for naval service. I was told to go to Flinders Naval Depot for a couple of weeks to await appointment to a ship.

Reserve officers poured into a pool at Flinders, where we did some six-inch gun drill as a refresher course, because most of us were destined for ships with that sized gun. My letter of appointment to Flinders was dated " from date of arrival," so I immediately applied for the week's pay for my waiting in Sydney and also for my travelling allowance by train. I also found that although I was put on permanent rates of pay as a Lieutenant, I would not get a rise for three years, by which time I would be due for automatic promotion to Lieutenant-Commander in any case, after my eight years as Lieutenant.

The trouble was to keep my family on my pay, which was 18s. 6d. a day, or £6 9s. 6d. a week, plus nothing. Officers received no marriage allowance or anything for children, nor did my Reserve specialist courses entitle me to specialist pay. Later on I may have got an extra shilling a day if I had been appointed navigator of a ship, instead of the five shillings allowed permanent officers as navigators.

Fortunately I had about £200 in the bank, but that soon dwindled away on family expenses. The next blow came when I was appointed to a ship and had to call at Navy Office for orders. I was told to join the *Manoora* next day in Sydney, as a plain watch-keeping officer. She was an Australian passenger ship, about 10,000 tons, fitting out as an Armed Merchant Cruiser with six-inch guns. She had been given a naval Captain, and her Chief Officer was made Lieutenant-Commander although he was not even in the Reserve. This made him senior to me for the rest of the war, which was particularly tough as I was his senior in the Merchant Service, as a Captain and an Extra Master.

It appeared that I might be fourth or fifth in line of command, which was galling in the extreme, especially as my training and qualifications were enough to put me in command of an armed merchant ship. While these thoughts were arousing my Irish blood, I heard that some merchant officers were getting jobs in the Air Force to teach navigation. That seemed better to me than watchkeeping in the Pacific while the war was in the other half of the world and the " phoney war " at that. So I walked out of Navy Office with some hours to spare before I had to catch the train to Sydney, found a building with R.A.A.F. over the door and applied for a job. I was in plain clothes, being off duty, and was soon being interviewed by the Staff Officer for Air Navigation. Although I knew nothing about Air Navigation itself, my knowledge of navigation generally was possibly superior to that of anyone else in Australia. When it was settled that I should go to the Navigation School at Point Cook to lecture on navigation and naval co-operation, I pointed out that I was, at the moment, working for the Navy. This was no trouble to the young Flight Lieutenant in the Personnel Section . . . he would get my appointment to *Manoora* cancelled, and have me transferred to Point Cook. It looked a very faint chance to me, knowing the Navy Office as I did. So I went away to have lunch in the Navy Mess, keeping very discreet, for once, and when I returned I found that my appointment had indeed been cancelled, by a little co-operation between Air Staff and Navy Staff. But to get me to Point Cook was a much more difficult matter.

In the first place the Navy had no idea of releasing me; secondly there was no provision on the navy establishment or Parliamentary estimates for a Naval Liaison Officer at Point Cook; and thirdly, why had the Air Force picked on me? They tactfully replied that any officer would do, provided he had the same qualifications. Believe it or not, the Navy never woke up to the fact that I had disloyally gone and asked for a job when they had already appointed me to a ship. They would have shot me at dawn, and certainly would never have let me go to the Air Force. The negotiations went on for a month, which shows how the national effort is wasted instead of devoting it to the war against the enemy. In the meantime I was wandering around in Navy Office without a job or a post of any sort, or even a chair to sit on, as the new Director of Reserves had chased me out of his office after a discussion. I spent my time following up arrears of pay and possible allowances and hearing many items of interest which not only sickened me of Navy Office for life, but provided me with ammunition for later hostilities.

I finally went down unofficially to Point Cook to see the school and was told that, even if my appointment came through, the school would not be re-opening until after the Christmas vacation. After another casual glance at Navy Office, I went A.W.L. to Sydney to spend Christmas with the family, who were back in our own home by this time. Then at 9 p.m. on New Year's Eve the phone rang, with Navy Office wanting to know where I was. I replied that I was at home, and was ordered to appear at Navy Office in Melbourne at 10 a.m. next morning.

I flew down next day by plane, presented myself and was told to report to Air Force, as I had been lent to them. I was to continue to be paid by the Navy, who each pay-day sent the bill to the Air Force for reimbursement. On that same day I got a pain in my tummy, was ordered into hospital for removal of my appendix, and so took four weeks finally to get to Point Cook.

My career as lecturer started the first day, my subjects being aviation meteorology and higher mathematics, simply because no one else wanted to teach these subjects. This gave me a few weeks to catch up on air navigation, which I did at top speed, as I had so much to learn about it.

There were the mysteries of the bubble sextant to master, apart

from the whole subject of dead-reckoning navigation in the air and the art of wind-finding. All this involved a lot of chart plotting, far more involved than anything at sea, except in the Navy for problems of interception like torpedo fire and gunnery. The school was equipped with Avro Anson aircraft, in which I flew as much as possible, to get acclimatised.

I soon found out that my naval pay was lower than that of any possible officer in the R.A.A.F., and even my batman at the mess received more pay than I, as he was married with several children. After six months' more argument with the Navy, the R.A.A.F. was able to get my loan to them changed into a secondment; this put me into Air Force uniform as a Flight Lieutenant of no seniority, and my pay exactly doubled. Then followed a glorious six weeks during which I was paid by both Navy and Air Force.

When the Navy woke up they knew me so well they didn't ask me for their money back, but just bided their time. They still retained the right to take me back from the Air Force at any time. At the Navigation School were about five ex-seafarers, all experienced at teaching air navigation in civil life and collectively known as "Web-feet." None of us had any Air Force qualifications, so after a couple of months we were suddenly subjected to a spare-time course of studies and a series of examinations based on the specialist navigator syllabus. This qualified us as navigation instructors and I came top of the class with a pass of high distinction. The School became part of the Empire Air Training Scheme, changing its name to General Reconnaissance School for the rest of the war.

I was soon able to lecture on every subject, including all branches of air navigation and reconnaissance, which includes naval co-operation, ship recognition, signals, photography and the theory of map projections. These were mostly foreign to me, for at sea we only used Mercator's Projection and had to know something about the stereographic and the gnomonic. Yet on our highest course at the school we touched on about 36 different projections, as the Air Force had been influenced by landlubbers and geographers to despise Mercator, relying instead on absurd attempts to get equal-scale in a chart instead of orthomorthism.

The trouble was that air navigation started out by cross-country flying, which required more of a railway guide or Army Ordnance survey than an oceanic plotting sheet. They were even addicted to using miles-per-hour instead of knots and sea miles.

Nowadays, air navigation has at last switched entirely to knots and almost entirely to orthomorphic projections, the two principal ones being Mercator and the stereographic. We did quite a bit of research on different problems, for in Australia we were very short of suitable maps of the land and were forced to use anything we could get hold of for our overland flights. We even had to use a map of South Australia made on some strange projection for the agriculture department, which showed stock routes and suitable waterholes for cattle.

I also worked on the problem of whether Mercator could be developed from a true projection by having a moving point of origin. We succeeded in getting sights of Venus by sextant in the air and experimented in using the new bubble-sextant Mark IX by cutting out the bubble and taking a view of the sea horizon with one eye, looking at the sun in the sextant with the other. This didn't prove to be reliable at all.

By this time I had become Chief Instructor and, being hopeful of later becoming C.O., applied for a flying course, as all our C.O.'s were pilots and I wanted to become a pilot in any case. Most of my pupils and fellow instructors were pilots, so it need not have altered the set-up in the school. The Air Force refused to waste a pilot's course on me while the Navy had the power to recall me, so the matter remained in suspense. I used to get a lot of flying as instructor, to check the work of the pupil-navigators in the air and, of course, I soon got used to flying the aircraft on straight courses, making turns and climbing or losing height.

Before America officially came into the war we were joined by an American web-foot as a navigation instructor. His name was Pete Sawyer and he was a most lovable character. He came from a wealthy family in Boston, but spent his time at sea, getting a Master's ticket in the process. Before the war, he bought a 100-ton schooner named *Henrietta*, which had been built for fishing off the Newfoundland Banks and was later used for the making of the film

" Captains Courageous." Pete bought her after that, using her on scientific expeditions to Labrador and other Arctic lands in the northern summer.

In winter he served in the merchant service and there he met and married a girl from Melbourne. For their honeymoon, they cruised down the coasts of the Americas, through the Straits of Magellan and across the Pacific to Australia. They stopped for the birth of a daughter and the war broke out, ending their plans for a cruise around the world. So Pete joined the R.A.A.F.

The lovely schooner lay at her moorings at the port of Geelong and the Melbourne pilots thought of chartering her. One of the pilots took her chart of Port Phillip to bring it up to date and this had a disastrous effect when he failed to return it.

One week-end, four of us set out to sail the ship up to be docked in Melbourne; there was Pete, our C.O., whose name was Dal Charlton, an R.A.F. officer named John Archer, and myself. We boarded the schooner at midnight on Friday and dawn saw us clearing the port under the foresail and the engine, giving us a speed of six knots.

We all took a trick at steering and had to smell our way through the mudbanks by using a leadline, trying to keep in five fathoms, as she was drawing about 15 feet. I did try to keep track of the navigation, but we couldn't find the right chart, as the pilot hadn't returned it. Then the weather turned showery and squally and we steered for a ship we could see at anchor in the distance. We had passed Point Cook and the airfield, when we got a sounding of $4\frac{1}{2}$ fathoms. We were about one mile off the shore, but thought we

We all took tricks at steering

were more, when we ran on to a reef of rocks and stuck fast. That was about noon.

We tried to get her off by going astern, we laid out the anchors to seaward, and passed a message ashore by a launch for a tug to try to get us off at about 9 p.m. when it would be high water. In the meantime the wind increased to a gale, being part of a cyclone and the ship was driven further on to the reef.

About dusk she suddenly filled with water and the seas started

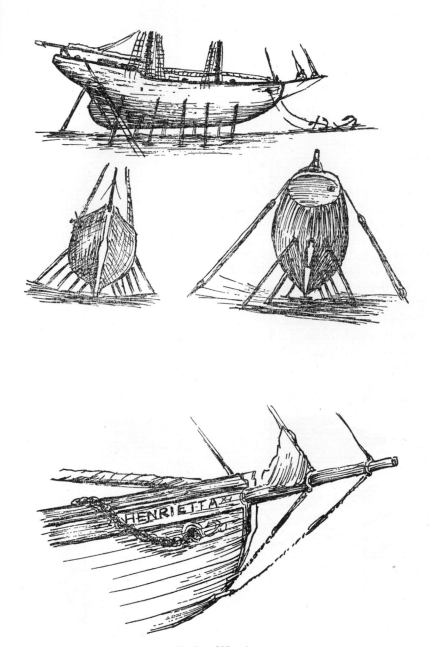

Sketches of Henrietta

to break heavily over her. It seemed likely that she would shake down her masts and spars as she broke up, so we launched the two little dories over the side and secured the painters. One of them broke adrift in the rising seas, and the other, which contained our good uniforms and cameras, was filled by a wave which broke right over the hull. I went over the side to save the gear and found the water nearly freezing, as it was midwinter. After the gear was saved, the dory capsized and broke adrift; both dories were picked up five miles along the coast, which was disturbing news for our waiting wives.

I was all for swimming ashore while we still had some strength, but we were failing rapidly from the cold, the lack of food, and our exertions. During the long stormy hours of the night we lit distress flares, but without any effect, and we finished the night in the main rigging wrapped in a sail to keep out of the freezing seas. We were finally picked off the bowsprit at noon the next day by the same launch we had spoken to the day before, manned by a stevedore from the explosives anchorage at Altona. We returned to work next day very sad at the loss of the ship, which was the apple of Pete's eye and he had to sell the broken hull for £10. Only three months later Pete was himself killed in a crash and, later, our C.O., Dal Charlton, and I had the sad job of scattering his ashes over the site of the wreck.

Unfortunately we had to get used to the sudden deaths of our friends and, as the Japanese came into the war, things took a very

Burning a distress signal at night

black complexion both in Europe and Australia. Our war effort had to be drastically extended, for England could offer us little help and, without the immediate aid of the American forces, our children would by now have been learning Japanese.

A lot of our exercises were arranged in conjunction with Operations Room to cover areas of the sea in searches for raiders, reported mines, missing ships and anti-submarine patrols for convoys. We had a difficult job to teach our pupils to identify ships from the air, estimating types and tonnages, so I used to take parties of them over the Melbourne docks and then back on the ground to actually visit the ships. I took a party to look over the Armed Merchant Cruiser *Manoora* one day and, when the Captain saw me, he asked " Why didn't you ever join this ship ? " This put me in a spot, so I replied: " Those bastards at Navy Office shanghied me into the Air Force ! " So he gave me his complete sympathy, which I thought might be useful to me in the future.

By this time I was getting an odd flight in different types of aircraft whenever the opportunity offered, even on short flights to do anti-aircraft target duty for the Navy and the Army. My flying hours as a navigator and observer finally got me the Civil Aviation qualification as 2nd Class Air Navigator and later a 1st Class licence, which I am very proud to hold with my Extra Master's ticket. One of my most hair-raising jobs was to adjust the compasses of an American aircraft known as a B-26. This was like a streamlined rocket, cruising at no less than 300 knots, with very short wings designed to hold it in the air only at high speeds. It had been nicknamed the " Flying Prostitute " because it had no visible means of support. The wings were later extended and it then became the Martin Marauder for medium bomber and torpedo duties with the Allies.

On the ground the B-26 rested on a nose wheel instead of on its

American B-26

tail, so that in the air this nose wheel retracted to a position just below the pilot's compass. I therefore decided, with the view of getting a flight, that the aircraft would have to have its compasses swung and adjusted in the air. This was easier said than done. The compasses hadn't been swung since the aircraft left the factory, yet it had managed to get across the Pacific safely. The rest of its fellows had, however, all come to grief and it was the only one to survive out of 29 which had set out. Our Flight Commander came with me to the plane, which the pilot prepared to start up, but neither engine would start and we finally flattened the batteries in the process. We tried again the same afternoon and this time the first pilot started up without any trouble. The other man turned out to be the co-pilot and they were both very hastily trained and very inexperienced, as America had just entered the war.

We taxied to the far corner of the landing field at Laverton, swung the compasses on the ground and adjusted them, so they would need less adjustment in the air. Then we tried to take off. Using the longest diagonal line of the field, we had reached over 200 knots with the aircraft showing no signs of wanting to take off at all. The pilot was using about 15 degrees of flap and a growing percentage of panic. When we reached the fence we were just able to lift over it and slowly climbed to 250 feet. Then the pilot released the flap and we dropped to just 50 feet, while my hair stood on end and stayed that way for an hour. The cloud base was low, about 600 feet, so we cruised around under it and checked the compasses against the long straight roads of the district, of which I had the magnetic headings. After half an hour we asked to be let down again and this was nearly our downfall. The pilot made a circuit of about 10 miles, then put down his flaps, put the two great screws into fine pitch, and pointed for Laverton like a bolt from the blue.

The trouble was probably caused by starting our descent from 600 feet instead of about double that height. The proper speed on the approach was 180 knots, the touch-down should have been 140 knots, while the stalling speed was said to be 120 knots.

It was therefore very disconcerting to run out of altitude on two parts of the approach, with a row of cottages in our path, and we staggered over them at 125 knots, just 5 knots above the stall, which would have meant a sudden flick into oblivion. The engines were screaming their heads off, with the throttles pushed through the gate, and then we reached the landing field. Our arrival was a sudden shattering crash, for we landed with a smack like a bucket full of nuts and bolts. I was quite sure the aircraft had been wrecked, but we continued to zoom across the ground with full brakes on until we came to a halt with a bit of field to spare. By the time we had taxied back, to anchor the furious monster outside the hangar, we had regained our breath and voice, though I never thought I'd be able to get my hair to lie down again. We staggered out and made for the bar of the mess with the two Yankee pilots for some triple brandies. When the first pilot, Lieut. Muller, regained his voice he exclaimed: " Gee, Gosh ! I only went solo on that kite on Thursday." Not knowing what day of the week it was, I just couldn't think of a suitable reply to the pilot, though I did silently talk to God.

Schooner Henrietta *under sail*

G

Chapter Ten

Flying adventures

AFTER A COUPLE OF YEARS OF INCREASING LABOUR AND mental effort our school had made quite a reputation for its very thorough training for all pilots going to operations in heavy aircraft. Air Force Headquarters thought so highly of us that we got senior officers as pupils, including two Wing Commanders at once. One of these brought his influence to bear on headquarters to grant me a flying course and on the Air Board to request Navy Office to give me a complete transfer to the R.A.A.F.

So one bright day I was told by phone that my transfer was through; I was appointed a Flying Officer, could start my flying training at once and that I was promoted to Squadron Leader the next day. Thus my battle with the Navy was over, after 2½ years. Air Board sent me two Gipsy Moths on which to learn to fly, but I didn't break either of them myself in the process.

Two of our pupils borrowed one on a Sunday to do some aerobatics, but finished upside down so close to the ground that they hadn't enough height to roll over; they just flew into the deck and wrote themselves off with the kite. Another day, two of the instructors were up for some unofficial stunting, taking it in turns to frighten one another; the Moth did a dive so close to the ground that they both pulled the stick back at once, only to find that neither of them had been in control during the dive!

My flying training had to be done in my spare time, of which I had to take full advantage to save the course lasting all the rest of the war. I managed to graduate to Ansons and finished all the official syllabus and tests in a year, the same length of time as full-time pupils at a flying school. The worst mistake I made was one night, doing circuits and landings solo, when I forgot to do any cockpit drill between circuits, and I found myself airborne when everything started to go wrong. I was lucky to avoid crashing and learnt my lesson permanently.

Most of the lessons in flying have to be learnt from other people's mistakes, particularly the fatal ones, and the close shaves. One of our pilots took off one day for a navigation exercise with all the controls still locked on the wings and tail. When he got in the air the aircraft, being a harmless Anson, did a very slow turn to port, finally returning to the aerodrome and by juggling the engines he landed it safely. Another took off at night with his artificial horizon not working, flew back into the ground with one wing-tip before seeing what was wrong, and was able to fly on out to sea not knowing why, at dawn, there was a tuft of grass caught in his aileron.

I had to be careful to complete all the bombing, gunnery, formation flying and other parts of my syllabus, so that there could

be no doubts about my course being just a backyard one. I then applied to go to operations on Catalina flying-boats, instead of staying on teaching navigation as was expected of me.

This annoyed Air Board, who kept me another year at the school before allowing me to go to the war. The flying I did in the 12 months, especially at night and in bad weather, was of great value to me later on. A number of our aircraft with pupil navigators used to get into trouble at times, getting lost over the sea at night when the wind changed, running out of fuel, and making unexpected landings. One finished up in a tree-top and the navigator had the nerve to write " landed " against the time. The crew had to be rescued with fire ladders from their perch.

The school had been moved from Point Cook to Laverton, then to Cressy, and later to Bairnsdale, all these places being in the State of Victoria. During my term, over 3,000 pupils passed through the courses and the school had been doubled in size no fewer than five times. We were constantly short of aircraft, short

of housing, short of equipment, but never short of pupils. This caused me tons of work and worry, which is worse, and I looked forward to getting to active operations for a holiday.

We had to keep in touch with the work of operational squadrons to keep our training up to date and used to visit the Operational Training Units for this purpose. Five of us spent a few days at Rathmines, where all the Catalina crews were trained, and got in some interesting flying there. I even went off on an operational flight in a Catalina to find a torpedoed Liberty ship, which had to be towed to Sydney with a great hole through her afterpart at water-level. The ship was the *Peter H. Burnett* and her position was 400 miles out at sea. We found her being towed by a Yankee destroyer and gave them an escort home.

A large salvage tug had been sent out from Sydney to take over the tow and our job, after locating the Liberty ship, was to find the tug and direct her to an interception. Finding these ships in the wide ocean was largely a matter of keeping a good lookout, as their positions were only approximate. We carried four 250-lb. anti-submarine bombs, to give the ships some degree of protection, as the tow was a sitting shot, being towed at only 5 knots. The crew of the aircraft, whose number was A24-29, were doing their final exercises before being posted to a squadron. The captain was Squadron-Leader Daniell, who had come fresh from a long period at headquarters and they were all lost a few months later off the Queensland coast. I was very pleased to be able to take part in a real operation in a Catalina; it was a typical one, as we were in the air for 19 hours.

After that, I returned to the school at Bairnsdale all the more determined to serve in Catalinas, as they were mostly operating in

New Guinea and all over the Dutch East Indies, and so providing a suitable sphere of activity for my knowledge of navigation, the coasts and ports of the area and of the salt water itself, on which the Catalina made its home. There was also the possibility of using marine sextants over the sea; they were not only enormously quicker to use but also much more accurate than any bubble-sextant.

It was always a source of surprise to me that our navigators made such good landfalls as a rule, after flying for hundreds of miles at sea, using dead-reckoning plotting and various methods of wind-finding. The average error of position after three hours was about three miles. This is an error of 1 per cent., or an average deviation off course of less than 1 degree of the compass. It is not possible to steer a better course than this, so that taking the fluctuating nature of the force of the wind into consideration, one must assume that a lot of errors must cancel each other out, especially when the aircraft returns to its starting point.

At sea in my early days we learnt the compass by points, based on the four cardinal directions of north, south, east and west. Later the method of dividing each quadrant into 90 degrees had to be learnt, but a direction of north 45 degrees east still gave a good sense of direction. In aircraft the compass is marked in three-figure notation, from 000 to 360 degrees and it must be much more difficult for a navigator to feel where he is heading

Navigator using marine sextant in Catalina

on a course of 315 degrees, instead of calling it north-west. The speed of the aircraft is also generally in three figures, so that the flight plan becomes a page of numbers like a page of lottery numbers; the track, course, airspeed, groundspeed and wind direction all being in three figures. It is therefore not impossible, as one of our pupils proved, to steer the airspeed as a magnetic course over the sea at night, without anyone being the wiser at the time.

We also had a pilot who managed to fly an opposite course to that ordered, as he mistook the north end of the compass needle in the dark and when the aircraft should have been back at base it was still somewhere over the dark and stormy waters.

Knowing that they must be somewhere in the Tasman Sea, they decided to fly west to find Australia, but ran into very intense thunderstorms when they must have passed over the only available point of the continent. When they were clear of the storm, and still over water, they steered north, assuming that they were somewhere in Bass Strait. This was correct, and they eventually sighted a coastal town with the glow of Melbourne in the distance. The static was too bad for them to get any bearings from our station, and they were running very short of fuel. They identified the town, then flew towards the nearest landing field, 100 miles away, but didn't make the distance. They were over a coastal bog when the pilot told the crew to bale out, and just as the engines died he saw a vehicle driving along a road. He glided down after it, but the road took a sudden turn around some sand hills, on which he stalled as gently as possible. Passing between two trees removed the wings and brought him to a stop, when he got out and walked the four miles towards the emergency landing ground. After an anxious night I was able to take off at dawn to pick up the pilot and crew, and had a close look at the unusual site of the crashed plane. By being able to walk away from the plane the pilot had fulfilled the definition of a good landing. Air Board were displeased at the plane losing its way over the sea, but I told them that they couldn't have acted with greater method and common-sense if they had found themselves in the same circumstances. The landing showed how difficult it was to hurt yourself in an Anson, and I was fortunate to go from them on to equally harmless Catalinas.

The only troubles I had myself were two occasions of engine failure and each time I managed to land on an aerodrome with the remaining engine. Our exercises took us as far afield as we could wangle, with off-shore searches and reconnaissance on the way to the three nearest States of Australia. This gave us a range of about

500 miles, covering an area as large as Europe, for the distances in this part of the world run into thousands rather than hundreds of miles. As we used Ansons, we had to stop overnight on the way to our distant objectives and we made use of every emergency landing ground to give the pilots experience.

One night, a plane on exercise missed the home strip in the blackout, due to a sudden change of wind, and flew on to a small town named Bacchus Marsh, set in a circular valley on the edge of grassy highlands. As the pilot circled the dim street lights, which he mistook for the landing strip, he kept at 1,000 feet in his circuit, but this was just the level of the surrounding hilltops. They suddenly felt the plane skimming the grass, though they didn't have the wheels down, and the engines were throttled back, allowing the plane to land safely in the dark. She came to a gentle stop when her nose caught in a wire fence; dawn showed that she was pointing over the cliffside, held only by the fencing wires.

The training schools with other aircraft weren't so lucky and I think that more aircrew were killed in training than in operations against the enemy. One of the worst schools in this regard was our nearest neighbour, the Beaufort Operational Training Unit at Sale in Gippsland, Victoria.

In 18 months they had damaged 100 Beauforts, the accidents ranging from taxi-ing accidents to the ten aircraft lost at sea without trace. These involved a total of 150 deaths. Their training was intense and simulated real operations, except that they didn't have any opposition. The Beaufort was a medium bomber of high wing loading, assembled in Australia from parts made in England. The pilots suspected sabotage amongst other things, while the instructors blamed the pupil-pilots. Then some of the instructors started to have accidents and everyone's nerves suffered badly. Finally one morning a plane crashed headlong into the ground from 1,500 feet without warning, with a pupil and a most experienced instructor, who had a D.F.C. and two bars.

I was assigned as president of the Court of Inquiry, with instructions to get to the bottom of all the trouble. The instructors gave me every assistance and one of them was made my colleague on the court. He was Flying Officer Cambridge.

The aircraft had been doing circuits and bumps and the exercise at the time was practice in " baulked approaches." This entailed being sent around again when just about to touch down, which put a great strain on the aircraft as well as the pilot. On the next circuit, the aircraft was flying straight and level on the downwind leg, cruising at 145 knots, when the nose was seen to go down in a sharp " bunt " and the aircraft dived vertically into a marsh with the engines at full revs. Several people, including Beaufort pilots, saw the accident, but there was a strong argument against the evidence.

The Chief Instructor and his pilots all swore that it was quite impossible to " bunt " a Beaufort in this way. It was therefore assumed that the " bunt " had been caused by some structural failure of the tail. The fragments of the aircraft salved from the swamp did not include the engines, but they gave us plenty to work on with regard to negative forms of evidence. Two drops of blood were salved from the remains of the instructor and sent to Melbourne for analysis. Cambridge and I worked through the records and findings of every crashed Beaufort, to classify them in search of clues to abnormal behaviour. One of the most incredible crashes, in which the two pilots survived, was a Beaufort which performed a series of " bunts " and vertical climbs immediately after take-off; the two pilots, by utmost effort, managed to crash safely on a golf course and stagger away. But they never could understand what had happened.

After a lot of work we managed to solve this two-year-old puzzle, finding in fact that the elevator trimming tab had been stuck in the hard-up position and put out of control during the pre-take-off cockpit drill. Then we found that this was not the cause of our crashed Beaufort and we did some tests to prove that it was really almost impossible to " bunt " the aircraft. The evidence of the eye-witnesses was so much in agreement, including even farming civilians, that we still thought that it might be possible.

Each attempt we made became more dangerous than the last, but each came a little nearer to success.

The drill was that Cambridge and I put on our parachutes and tested our safety-belts, then tested the window frames on each side of the cockpit, these being ejectable to allow for emergency exit. We took the plane up to 8,000 feet, put her into cruising trim and revs, and took a deep breath. The machine had dual controls, which we needed, for at the given word we both pushed the stick as far forward as possible. Then the world went mad . . . the revs screamed up, the altitude went down, the airspeed worked a couple of times around the dial, but the nose only got down to about 40 degrees of dive.

The acceleration tried to eject us through the roof, our legs came off the rudder bars, and we clawed back at the stick and the throttles before we died of fright. Once the stick was moved forward the speed increased so quickly that the controls became jammed with the stress and strain on the airframe. The only solution seemed to be to get the stick forward as quick as lightning, before the speed could build up. It was quite impossible to get the aircraft out of the dive without throttling right back to decrease the speed and this had been the cause of several fatal accidents in dive-bombing and air-to-ground gunnery exercises. Having landed safely and talked the matter over for the umpteenth time, we took off for a final attempt.

This time was much worse; the wings nearly snapped off with the sudden change of attitude, for which the aircraft was never designed. In fact the " bunt " was a forbidden manoeuvre in most aircraft. But this time we pushed the sticks forward so smartly that we dived at about 60 degrees, which proved the possibility.

Having proved that a vertical " bunt " was possible, we didn't know why it should ever happen until we tried baling out of the side windows (while the aircraft was on the ground). We then found that a pilot had to roll over on his side to climb out, kneeling on his seat on the way and that it would be very possible to kick the stick forward in one's haste to get out.

But why should this have happened? After two weeks' work we were just giving up the problem when the bombshell arrived. This was a report from the analyst that the sample of pilot's blood contained a lot of carbon-monoxide. This turned out to be over 25 per cent., just about a fatal dose, so that the cockpit must have been filled with exhaust gas, the pupil blacked out, and the pilot kicked the stick in his effort to get out. There was some evidence that he was half out of the window, either blacked out with gas or by the acceleration, when the crash occurred.

So we spent a further week testing for carbon-monoxide, and came to the conclusion that it had come through the wing-root into the cockpit, from the covered hole which was meant to provide exhaust gas for heating the cockpit in England.

My next big job was to do a course at the Staff School, to make Squadron Leaders into prospective Commanding Officers of units. No sooner was this over than I was called to headquarters to over-haul the subject of ship recognition training, including the writing of a 400-page book on the subject, but this was never published, as far as I know. That took about a month, as a lot of it was prepared in my notes and photographs used on the courses at the school.

My time in the Training Command was drawing to a close and

my prayers for a Catalina were almost answered. Then I heard that as the inquiry into the Beaufort crash had been so well done, they were making me permanent president of Courts of Inquiry. I ducked for cover and called for help from the heavy artillery of Training Command, as I had no desire to live in a world of crashed aircraft and carbon-monoxide poisoning.

So the new year of 1944 dawned and I went thankfully off to Rathmines and the salt-sprayed world of Catalina life.

Chapter Eleven

Minelaying by Catalina

SHORTLY AFTER STARTING A 2ND PILOT'S COURSE ON
Catalinas at Rathmines my promotion to Wing Commander was
announced. This not only made the regular Cat-men jealous, but
they were also afraid that I might be given command of a squadron.
Only the year before, several senior officers had arrived from
different headquarters' jobs, and their lack of flying experience,
through no fault of their own, had cost the lives of a couple of
crews and badly frightened some others. A Squadron Leader on
my course suffered with me the strong opposition of the instructors
and they even tried to get rid of us by having us grounded for
medical reasons. However, we fought back successfully, determined
to get into Catalina squadrons and stay there.

The actual course was a welcome change to me, splashing the
flying boats in and out of the water instead of landing on dusty
aerodromes. We had to practise the two types of landings, the
normal one in which the aircraft is flown close to the water until
the keel touches while the boat is still in flying attitude, and the
stall landing, in which the nose is held well up and the boat drops
on to the water in a stall. The latter could be done on a very short
stretch of water.

Then there were a lot of drills to be carried out on the water,
securing to buoys, coming to anchor and the difficult art of
manoeuvring the Cat with drogues while taxi-ing around.

Then there were cross-wind take-offs and landings and night
circuits and splashes, which can be very eerie as the water surface
is invisible in the dark. Finally we had full-load take-offs under
operational conditions of loading, in which the aircraft seems as
though it is never going to get up on the step, let alone take off.
After the first month the new captains chose their permanent crews

and all subsequent exercises were done by crews as they would later be flying together in squadrons.

These exercises included gunnery, bombing and minelaying, for the last was the special work of the Catalina squadrons in the East Indies. It was always done at night and was the most exacting work for both pilot and navigator. We were sent to coastal harbours to lay dummy mines in uninhabited areas at low altitudes, where the main danger lay in dodging trees and hillsides in the dark. Our biggest navigation exercise was to fly 400 miles out to sea and locate Middleton Reef at night. After bombing it from high altitude we strafed it down low, took photographs by flash, and then returned home. Quite a few crews failed to find the reef and we found that radar was invaluable for the purpose.

All our Catalinas were from California, flown out to Australia by spare crews resting after operational tours. One went missing near New Caledonia and we were sent to search for it. We flew a total of 36 hours 20 minutes in two days, landing at Noumea one night to refuel, but no trace was ever found of the aircraft or crew. After that we were posted to No. 20 Squadron, which was based at Cairns in North Queensland at the time.

Our main job of minelaying was top secret and could only be mentioned by code names. The civil population and the other branches of the Air Force believed that we were only engaged on ocean reconnaissance and convoy duties. I could never see the need for all the secrecy as all our mines were painfully obvious to the enemy, being laid in well populated and heavily defended harbours.

On my first operation as second pilot we went off to our distant base at Darwin, where we loaded two great mines under the wings and flew another 500 miles to a most secret re-fuelling base at Yampi Sound, known by the code-word " She-cat " Here we waited until 2 p.m. next day to take off for our first target, the port of Sourabaya in Java, a distance of well over 1,000 miles.

The code name for minelaying was " Courting " or " Flirting," so all our targets had nicknames of girls, some being respectable and others of easy virtue. Sourabaya was " Popsy." On the first night there were three Catalinas on the job, not in formation, but all staggering along with our heavy loads like Brown's cow. The first to reach the target was the C.O. and, after dropping his mines, he braved the ack-ack to strafe part of the military establishments with his poor armament. He was a definite " gong-hunter," after a D.F.C. for himself, and never mind the added danger for his crew or the native Javanese. He was badly damaged in the process and made for an " escape point " on Bali where it might have been safe to scramble ashore.   After dropping our own mines we went to Bali to look for him, but his aircraft had apparently crashed into the sea before he reached there.

Two nights later we had another similar operation, and as it became a memorable occasion I quote the story in full, just as I wrote it out a few days later:

NIGHT FLIGHT TO SOURABAYA: the story of a Catalina, A24-61, on an operation from 20 Squadron, on the 24th and 25th of May, 1944.

Time: late afternoon. Place: the Arafura Sea.

For some hours we have been flying northwards, away from our homeland, but so low on the water that we appear to be skimming the surface.

As the sun sinks lower, the sky and sea merge into one bright screen of many colours, the varied hues of the tropics.   Cerulean blue,   vermilion, lemon yellow, with the clouds of a powdery white, dusted here with warm brick-dust and there with the dull blue of approaching night.

The setting sun marks the direction of our distant goal, Java, but we are not flying direct to our target, the port and naval base of Sourabaya.

As the last daylight fades, land emerges from the haze and shadows, being the large island of Sumba or Sandalwood, where the natives are still pagans, worshipping animal gods, especially their hill ponies.   As darkness

Secret refuelling base at Yampi Sound

descends, lines of bright lights appear on the hills, where a large grass fire has apparently been burning, adding its smoke to the clouds and haze.

We pass close to the island and in a few minutes are off into the inky blackness of the night. We come to other islands, climbing to a sufficient height as we approach each one, to clear the tops of trees and hills. Here and there flickering lights show native activity and, as we get closer, hour by hour to our target, we see sharp pinpricks of light which come from Japanese rifles. To them we are a black shadow zooming close over their heads. We show no light and fire no guns.

We hope to achieve surprise, clinging close to the earth's surface to avoid detection by radar stations and can imagine the angry jabbering and profanity our mines must cause.

This night has been chosen specially, for there is no tropic moon to stare at us, or to light up the clouds to snowy white and silhouette us for target practice. Out of respect for the radar and airfield at Den Pasar we by-pass Bali, and leave her slumbering in the murk.

Time begins to drag. After the days of flying and preparation, we have already done seven hours in the air on this flight. We had done the final arming of the mines at our secret refuelling base, which was well camouflaged and given air cover by fighters.

While our aircraft are at anchor on the water it is very reassuring to see a squadron of Boomerangs overhead, and to know that there are some uck-ack positions on the hills nearby. Once we leave for a mission we get a cover of long-range fighters for the first 300 miles and the same on our return next day, in daylight hours.

In enemy waters the night protects us, for the Japanese have strangely neglected to develop night fighters. Our aircraft has a good captain, Flight Lieutenant Len Froud, called " Young Herc " because of his boyish figure. My job is second pilot and the regular second pilot is stationed in the blister, where he can watch the actual mine dropping and get a good view of the whole proceedings. I have the satisfying job of actually releasing the mines when the navigator gives the word. His station is lying prone in the bow, over the bombsight opening, to navigate us with great precision on to the target when it is identified.

All the crew have been shown the plan of attack, the target maps and photographs of the harbour and they all understand the part they each have to play.

With only ten minutes to go, we suddenly arrive at the east coast of Java and turn north along the shore, close over trees, beaches and rivers, with clumps of bushes showing black against the silver filigree of the paddy fields of the low coastal areas.

More flickering lights reminded me strongly of the Java of peacetime;

Night minelaying visit to Sourabaya Harbour

the strong sweet smell of this densely populated and fertile island is heavy in the warm air. But how much peace has Java been able to enjoy during the centuries? Waves of raiders, conquerors and oppressors have both despoiled and enriched the island, from the most powerful empires of each period: Malays, Chinese, Hindus, Arabs, Spanish, Portuguese, Dutch, English and French, and now the Japanese.

All this is hard to believe, with the land in darkness and only a few miles to go to our target. Here is the city of Sourabaya, where the River Kali flows into the sea, and where the harbour is formed by the strait, two miles wide, between Java and the adjacent island of Madura.

At last we are coming up to our datum point, intently studied for identification as we cannot afford to make a mistake at this stage. It is the corner of a wharf at the entrance of the naval base. We turn over it on our first run, the navigator counting the seconds with his stop watch over the intercomm. The pilot is concentrating on flying a perfectly steady course, airspeed and altitude, and we are only 250 feet above the water.

When the signal is given I pull the release and the blister reports, " Port mine gone! " as the wing is relieved of its heavy load. Then the navigator is counting the seconds again, for the second mine drop, when a shattering series of explosions and sparks come from the port engine . . . " We've been hit! " . . . and as the engine backfires violently all its power goes and the port wing drags in the air and falls lower and lower. The engineer puts the mixture into full rich, the pilot jettisons the mine, and opens up the starboard engine to help regain control. By the time he has the port wing nearly level again we have been very close to the water and just as close to the trees ashore as we circle around.

The port engine now begins to run smoothly at times, with intervals of backfiring when it seems to be running backwards. We increase power and try to climb away; by now we have got over the initial confusion and begin to realise our danger, when bang goes the starboard engine; just one single backfire, but how smartly it removes our remaining 10 per cent. of confidence !

As we turn away over open water other Cats are arriving over distant parts of the harbour, as we can see the searchlights and gun-flashes giving them the usual welcome. We have recurrent visions of being forced down and captured while still so close to Sourabaya and I imagine a diet of rice and warm water, if we are not decapitated as prisoners.

We are now flying east, climbing steadily, or rather unsteadily, with the port engine running one cylinder short; it is also losing its oil rapidly and might last for an hour. Finally we reach the incredible height of 8,000 feet and turn south, between the peaks of volcanoes, just above a thick layer of cloud which covers the valleys and volcanic plains of this area. At last we pass over the edge of the cloud layer, and see below us the fertile plains on the south coast of Java. We set course for Australia, 600 miles away. Our ears are attuned, and our hearts synchronised, to the roar of the port engine, dropping revs with it every time it backfires. Its oil has now run out and we shut it off before it seizes up. We feather the port screw, to reduce drag, and all our attention is transferred to the starboard engine, whining at climbing revs and boost. It is using twice its normal fuel. Can it carry on at this pitch for another 600 miles ?

We are now losing altitude and our speed is back to 65 knots, not much above stalling speed. We'll run right out of altitude if the aircraft is not lightened at once. The engineers start sawing and hacking at the auxiliary motor to jettison it, but the cables are armoured and very tough. The gunners are dumping all the guns and ammo, sea markers, flame floats, and yet we are still losing altitude rapidly. We are all glancing at the altimeters, needing no more encouragement than the moving needle to galvanise us into more furious wrecking and dumping of precious equipment.

Over go all the parachutes and harness, Mae Wests, personal gear, most of the radio and radar equipment, spare toolkits, all but two charts, the chart drawer, catwalks, engine-mounts, canvas screens, covers, stretchers, seats, and finally all our revolvers, spare clothes, shaving gear and writing gear. I am the most hated person in the aircraft as I ordered still more precious items over the side. The radio man hesitates with a black box of some marvel of electronics, the box in his arms and tears in his voice as he couldn't commit such sacrilege. I seize the box and hurl it over the side.

We keep the two rubber dinghies, with water, concentrated food, a first-aid kit and some distress flares, as we will probably be forced down on the sea and may have to abandon the aircraft. Another glance shows the altimeter still falling slowly, we are now below 1,000 feet, having sunk down from 8,000 feet. Our last contribution consists of all our boots and shoes, and at last we manage to maintain height at 600 feet.

All this has taken two whole hours to accomplish, armed as we were with only one hacksaw and one hatchet; the latter was unfortunately dumped by accident in the dark. We had to be careful in tearing out the fittings not to tear a hole in the hull, as that might have to be our floating home in mid ocean.

Just 400 miles to go . . . We have been tempted early in the emergency to jettison some of our fuel from the port wing but we now find that we'll need it all if the starboard motor will only keep revving for another five hours.

Looking back on those five hours now, they were deadly boring; our benzedrine tablets had kept us awake, but there was nothing to do but smoke cigarettes until we couldn't face another. There were 11 of us aboard, including an American naval officer who had come to see just how the mines were laid. His name was Sinderband, or something like that, so we called him Sinbad the Sailor.

As we neared home our speed slowly increased, and we were lucky to have only a slight headwind. Finally the coast of Australia showed up in the morning sunlight, like a dream come true. We still had 100 gallons of fuel left, enough for another 40 minutes' flying, when we landed back at our base at Yampi Sound.

Our aircraft had lost so much of its innards that it never again flew in operations. The time we spent on one engine was 11 hours 20 minutes, not quite equalling the record for operations. Our total time was about 22 hours.

My next operation was a bombing strike on a Japanese air-base at Ambon, with a different pilot and crew. We set out from Darwin and only took 13 hours for the whole job. This was a change from minelaying, as we rarely had time for mere bombing raids and it was certainly interesting to me.

When we got near the target area, which was called Liang, we found the land blanketed with low cloud. When we found a hole in the clouds we looked down exactly on the target area. We had to turn away to get ready for a bombing run, which gave the Japs time to prepare for us. On our first run over the target we

Catalina taxi-ing in water and taxi-ing " on the step "

Catalina in flight

were caught by massed searchlights and then by a barrage of five-inch shells; taking evasive action proved to be useless and spoilt the run, so we had to do it again. The next time we tried to ignore the blinding searchlights which held us all the time, but we could hardly ignore the red-hot shells which even passed between our wing and tail plane. Then there were strings of smaller shells which did not explode, being fused for contact, coming from some sort of Bofors gun.

Each time I looked down out of the window I looked right down the barrel of a five-inch gun just as it fired and I found this very disturbing. We made about four runs over the target, dropping two bombs each time, as we had orders to hit the actual runways if possible. The big shells were bursting above us, as they didn't have our altitude correct by radar; some of them burst well ahead of us because they allowed for a much higher speed than our average 100 knots.

The squadron's next job was a distant one, laying mines in anchorages in the Palau Group of the Carolines, due north from New Guinea. Most of northern New Guinea was still occupied by the Japanese, so we had to operate from the area called Hollandia, where the Americans had just landed. Immediately inland was a beautiful triple lake called Sentani, ideal for flying-boats, but only half the lake was in Allied hands. No one could tell us which end was which. To get there from Australia we had to fly right around the eastern end of New Guinea, refuelling at Milne Bay on the way.

After landing on Sentani we taxied towards the shore, where we anchored, but saw no signs of buoys or refuelling boats. Then we saw some amphibious " ducks " splash into the water towards us, and they came right alongside to give us fuel. We were alarmed and fearful that they might damage our fragile hulls, but the job was done without any accidents. Then we went ashore to sleep.

There were some dead Japs in the bush smelling badly and plenty of live ones only a mile away. The camp site was a recently used Jap camp, with shallow trenches for protection. We borrowed some American bell tents and found ourselves close to an R.A.A.F. wing of fighter aircraft. Fresh water came from a cool stream, in which we could lie in the heat of the day, when it was too hot to sleep and we flew every second night. Then we all got dysentery from the water, which came down from the Japanese in the hills. One of our men caught a Jap in our creek and made him a prisoner, both men being unarmed at the time.

Flights to Palau were shorter than usual, about 14 hours, and they were uneventful except for bad weather over the targets.

Our second flight was also an ordeal because of dysentery, and we all had to be doctored with medicinal concrete before taking off. When the job at Sentani was over, we flew back to Cairns, right around the mountains of New Guinea and arrived home very weak. The good food and beer soon gave us strength again.

My next three operations were just anti-submarine patrols on important ships going to New Guinea, one of them being my old friend *Katoomba*. By this time, the Allies had moved on from Hollandia to the island of Biak, which meant that we could refuel there and strike deeper into the temporary empire of the Japanese. We had to call at Milne Bay on the way, as we were heavy with mines. While making our approach to land there, one of the electric motors in the wing burnt out, damaging a lot of other wiring and gear, which would have to be repaired. So we dumped our mines in a barge for the day, wound up our engines by hand, and set off gaily for the lovely little island of Samarai, where there was an American base for flying-boats. Although we weren't even expected, all the repairs were done in less than an hour without any papers to sign. So different from the British way of going to war, fighting sets of papers in sextuplicate and yards of red tape. . . .

Then back to Milne Bay for our mines and fuel and all the way to the newly established naval base at Biak. From here we reached the Halmaheras, dropping our mines which were set to go dead after 30 days; this told us that the next Allied landing would be in that area. In fact it turned out to be Morotai.

To get home from Biak we decided to fly right over the top of New Guinea again, straight for Cairns. This would be much higher than our previous cross-country trip, but we were told that, if we could get up the mountains early enough in the morning, before the clouds formed and blocked the valleys, we could get through at 12,000 feet instead of climbing over the top at 18,000 feet. But we weren't in the race. Before we could get at the mountain valleys we had to detour around Wewak, still strongly held by the Japanese and halfway up the valleys we were blocked in by clouds. There was nothing for it but to climb in tight circles to some paralysing altitude, before setting a hopeful course for Queensland. I remember that we were above 14,000 feet for many hours and our aircraft was neither fitted with oxygen nor any heating system. We didn't bump any mountain tops and got right home in the rapid time of 12 hours.

The mines we laid were long black cylinders with blunt ends, of an average weight of 2,000 pounds, or one ton. They were so long that their noses projected ahead of our leading edge and their tails abaft our trailing edge, so they very effectively spoilt the airflow and lifting power of the wings. They were of several types, some British and some American, all highly dangerous and full of sensitive controls. These had to be set before we took off and, although they were not supposed to explode until they had been 24 hours in the water, some actually exploded when they hit the surface; this was very bad for the plane which had just dropped them.

To prevent this danger, the mines were each fitted with a big parachute in the tail, with the rip-cord fastened to the aircraft. On two occasions these opened up before the mines were dropped, wrapping around the tail-plane and endangering the plane. In each case the pilot was able to jettison them without losing the tail of his aircraft. The mines were both acoustic and magnetic and were full of traps to prevent them being swept up without being exploded. We always treated them with very great respect. I must admit that they never did me any harm, but they accounted for a very large number of Japanese ships and naval minesweepers.

About this time our squadron moved to Darwin, a depressing place compared with our camp on the sea beach at Cairns, which is a lovely town. This was done to intensify the minelaying effort and, instead of arrangements to work on moonless nights, we started laying mines all through each month. One lovely tropical night we were flying at 1,000 feet to drop some big mines without parachutes, in Macassar Strait, when a Jap night fighter appeared on our tail. It was full moon and when our gunners could see his markings we dived down to sea level where he was afraid to venture. We didn't see him again. The enemy was apparently short of fighter planes, as they didn't often molest a Catalina, even in daylight. We even flew past Timor, or right over it, every time in daylight, in spite of the six Jap airfields there with fighter squadrons.

Our nearest neighbours at Darwin were some " Cloak-and-dagger " merchants, who made landings and mischief behind the enemy lines in the East Indies. They used disguised fishing boats and rubber canoes and two-man submarines. Their work was so secret that no one else knew what they were up to at all, although we had sometimes to drop them at quiet spots by Catalina and occasionally pick them up again. The Port Naval Officer, for instance, used to get fed up with one of his juniors, who often disappeared into hospital for a few days without notice. The young man nearly got the sack, but couldn't divulge the fact that he had to pilot fast launches to land parties and stores on Timor under cover of night.

One day we had to take a party of five to an island called Seroea; this was small and exposed, so it was unsafe to attempt a night landing in the open sea. We therefore landed the party at high noon, remaining at anchor until they were safely ashore without seeing any signs of the enemy. The party had to set up a radio and weather station, but I didn't ever hear of them again.

One of my last mine-drops as second pilot was to Brunei Bay on the north coast of Borneo. The night was dark and stormy, but not too dark for some of our planes to sight parts of a Japanese task force at anchor. This called for a heavy bombing raid by Liberators from Morotai next day. Nearly all this American squadron were shot down or damaged, but the survivors came back with marvellous photographs of the enemy's manoeuvres at high speed. Unfortunately they could only claim one near miss on a cruiser, which was a great pity, as there were several big ships in the fleet.

At the time none of us realised that the war would be over in less than a year, with us flying our last operation from a base in the same Brunei Bay.

Chapter Twelve

The last year of the war

THE FIRST WEEK OF THE NEW YEAR OF 1945 BROUGHT me a posting back to Rathmines to do a captain's course on Catalinas. This was after the usual period of eight months as second pilot, during which time I had flown on 22 missions and a total of nearly 600 hours. For the first month at Rathmines, we went right through all the old exercises, doing circuits and splashes all over the lovely waters of Lake Macquarie. Then we crewed up, did night mine-laying in Port Stephens, and the many and varied forms of bombing and gunnery on all types of targets.

Our night navigation exercise consisted of flying 300 miles towards the centre of Australia at 8,000 feet, doing all the navigation by star sights with a bubble sextant. Then we had to turn and fly home and that's when the trouble started. For this aircraft, A24-62, had been used so much for short training trips that the outer fuel tanks hadn't been used for a long time and the fuel cocks couldn't be turned. The engineers reported to me that they could only guarantee another 15 minutes' fuel, so I tried to think of some patch of water we could sit down on, just 300 miles inland from the coast. We were near Parkes at the time, where there was an air station with concrete strips, but it was unoccupied and so was unlit.

There was a good moon, so I decided to land on the grass beside the runway, believing that the strong hull would take the wear and tear better than a land plane without its wheels.

At the same time I told the engineers to hammer and belt the fuel cocks even to the extent of shattering them. In this modern age of delicate scientific instruments it is marvellous what can be achieved by brute strength and perseverance together; the fuel cocks finally yielded and we flew on towards the coast. I regretted missing the opportunity to try the Catalina out as a sledge on the grass, but fate had decreed that I should never crash an aircraft, though I must have come perilously close at times.

Then we went to bomb Middleton Reef, at about 6,000 feet, taking photographs of the bomb bursts by means of the photo-flash, a parachute flare of no less than one million candle-power. Then down to sea level to strafe the sand cay on the reef, only to be un-expectedly illuminated by the photo-flash of another aircraft, as we were nearly hit by his bombs.

In conjunction with the local command of fighter squadrons, we had exercises in which one or more fighters tried to shoot down one Catalina at a time with their camera-guns. The fighters could never understand how we were able to turn circles inside them so easily. The secret was that a Cat was so harmless in a stall that it remained controllable in stall turns. These are done at very low speeds and although it may take a Cat longer to do any degree of turn or roll, because she is doing it so slowly, it takes up much less space or distance in the air. We could do steep, tight turns in small circles over the sea, with the fighters circling around outside, unable to get their sights anywhere near us. They had also learnt to be afraid of the sea.

Australian Second Pilot

One of the best fighter aces of the war, " Bluey " Truscott, was killed on an exercise with a Cat; they say he tried to pass below the flying-boat when it was keeping low on the sea. Our slow speed was our salvation, for we could dive steeply down at the sea without working up any speed, flattening out a few feet above the surface without any danger. One day two fighter boys came in my aircraft as passengers to see how we shook them off so easily. They brought a large F-24 camera with them, but weren't able to use it as our manoeuvres threw them about too much in the blister compart-ment. From these exercises we gained great confidence that we could shake off any Jap fighters which molested us, and this was borne out by the few Cats which had any fights with the Japs.

A different story was the exercises with the searchlight defences of the city of Newcastle, N.S.W. These home-town lights were very much easier to dodge than the Japanese, which were impossible to shake off. By this time the squadrons were being equipped with a later type of radar, which helped a lot with the navigational problems of minelaying. There was also the new toy, the radio-altimeter, which told your height above the sea or the ground down to a few feet, with flickering coloured lights, like traffic signals, to tell the pilot how he was maintaining his pre-set or chosen altitude. This was wonderful for minelaying at low altitudes; in fact they were making the game almost foolproof.

Another new exercise was the landing and taking-off of Cats on rough water. This meant the open sea, with wind, sea and swell to contend with. It proved to be possible to land a Cat on the roughest sea, using the stall-landing technique and then judging the right moment to drop on to the crest of the swell, as the Cat came to a stop before it could nose into the next swell. But the take-off was the opposite, for it was made down wind, or rather down swell for a start. The Cat's speed was similar to average swell, from 20 to 40 knots, so that it was possible to run with the crest of a swell, like shooting a breaker. As the Cat got up on to the step and increased speed as a result, she would have over-run the swell if she were not turned more and more diagonally towards it, finally getting flying speed and taking off along the crest of the swell. As the wind and sea were often from a different direction from the swell, it was best to turn more into the wind and sea at the last part of the run, rather than downwind. I found it most interesting, knowing a fair bit about the behaviour of the sea in any case.

When the captain's course was finished, there were no jobs vacant in the operational squadrons up north and we were posted to 11 Squadron, which was having a comparative rest at Rathmines.

We got sudden orders one night to take off for a secret job, but were given no details. On asking headquarters whether we should carry the usual depth-charges or anti-sub. bombs we were told definitely not. So we took a full load of fuel and set out in the dark, on a course of south down the coast.

Stall landing in rough water

Catalina on minelaying mission

We were to be given further orders by an unknown person next morning, by which time we would be off the coast of Victoria. On calling up the specified call-sign, on a given frequency, we failed to raise a reply. After an hour or two of trying, a stranger called us up and said that if we wanted to get in touch with that call-sign, we should try a different frequency. This seemed to suggest civil aviation stations and we were in the dark completely about what we had to perform. Finally we got a reply from our elusive quarry, who turned out to be an aircraft or two flying over Bass Strait. He told us to follow on his track, but we had no hope of catching up with him.

This took us right to Tasmania, where we were dismissed by radio and told to go home. By this time we had worked out that we had unknowingly been doing an air-sea rescue cover to the Governor-General, the Duke of Gloucester, on his way to visit Hobart. After that my crew called themselves, without the knowledge of H.R.H., " The Duke of Gloucester's Own." But the super secrecy had nearly defeated the whole purpose of our job.

The crews of our course were then put through a commando course to toughen us up, before being sent north to the war. My cobber McKinlay and I had one tough experience together, as our families wanted studio photographs of us before we went. The ordeal of the studio, with its concentrated lights, barrage of orders, and torments of being posed by experts, was as bad as anything the Japanese could do and qualified us for the Purple Heart at least. Then we went north, first to Darwin, then to the blackfellow's country of Melville Bay, in Arnhemland.

Here we joined the newly formed No. 42 Squadron, in which we served until the war came to a sudden end, by grace of the

atom bombs on the homeland of Japan. During this last phase of
the Pacific war the American forces, assisted by some Australians,
were island hopping through the East Indies and Philippines on
their way towards Japan. By this time we had virtually gained
command of the sea, and almost of the air, and so were able to
by-pass a lot of Japanese-held islands at each forward move.

One of the largest moves was to invade Borneo at many points,
including the ports of Balikpapan, Tarakan and Brunei Bay. Some
of these landings were opposite the large island of Celebes, which
was by-passed, including the Japanese naval base at Macasser.
The enemy still had a certain amount of air power there, which
may have proved troublesome to our landings, so it was arranged
that their airfields would be bombed by day. At night, to prevent
them repairing the damage, they would be harassed by a Catalina.
It was, therefore, a new type of mission for us, called harassing,
and we only hoped that it harassed more of the enemy than ourselves. I think the distance from Darwin to Macasser was only
850 miles. It was, therefore, assumed that a Cat could reach there
loaded with bombs and spend six hours over the airstrips before
making back for home. Thus it only would need two Cats to keep
three large aerodromes closed down all night, one Cat harassing
from dusk to midnight and the other from midnight until dawn.

This didn't work out in practice, as we found that we couldn't
spend more than four hours on the target and still get home. On
the three occasions on which my crew had the job we stayed as
long as we dared, but arrived back at Darwin with no fuel left,
the engines cutting out while we were taxi-ing to the buoy. We
had to arrange for the crash-boat to be ready to tow us in if we
couldn't quite make the distance to Darwin and fuel was a constant
worry for the whole flight.

A Catalina can only carry eight bombs on the wings, each
300 lbs., but that was not enough for four hours' harassing. So we
had a supply of smaller bombs loose inside the aircraft, to be dropped
by hand out of the blisters. This was quite contrary to standing
orders, as they consisted of 30 incendiaries and 30 anti-personnel
bombs or " daisy-cutters." This made a very dangerous cargo as
they couldn't be jettisoned quickly enough if we were hit. Then we
also carried a beer-case containing 48 empty beer bottles, each with
a razor-blade jammed in the neck, to make a screaming sound
like a bomb; these we handed out when we didn't want to waste
our few bombs to keep the enemy on their toes.

The aircraft was overloaded of course, over the permissible

military loading of wartime and this made it very difficult to take off. Fortunately we had a large harbour and used two or three miles of it before we groaned off into the air. Then for the first few hundred miles we were unable to climb, without wasting too much fuel and went most of the way to the target at a few feet above the sea. On this job the island of Timor was in our path, rising to a peak of 9,000 feet.

It was always broad daylight when we reached Timor and, rather than make a wide detour, we staggered up the valleys, assisted by a tail wind from the south-east trade. We ignored the danger of fighter patrols, but occasionally ran into heavy flak from lonely Jap positions. We used to get over the hills at 5,000 feet, then subside slowly to sea level on the other side, until we arrived at the target area. Being lightened by the amount of fuel used we could then climb to our safe height of 8,000 feet, which took us above the range of enemy rifles.

There were three aerodromes to harass and we went from one to another in varying order, giving each a few bombs or bottles as the occasion seemed to require. We kept our large bombs for the times when we caught the Japs laying down a flare-path to send off some night fighters after us. This was to damage the strip as well as to discourage the fighters, but the latter didn't give us any trouble. We sometimes saw their exhausts pass by, but they didn't have radar and couldn't see us in the dark. They had to rely on their ground radar to tell them where we were, including our exact altitude.

The airfields were difficult to see from 8,000 feet and the fires we started with incendiaries were generally out by the time we got back to them. Whenever we passed too close to the naval base at Macasser, up would come the searchlights and 5-inch shells and we sheered away again to the airfields. On these trips we carried 5,000 leaflets in the Malay language to tell the natives that Germany had surrendered and that the Japs would soon have to do the same.

By this time our three squadrons had used up all the mines available in Australia and we had to go far afield to get them for our last few jobs. We used the most forward American bases, where they would have a destroyer or mother-ship waiting for us with supplies of mines, fuel and the usual ice-cream, coffee, cigars and other PX stores. Some of our aircraft got as far as Manila in the Philippines; from there they mined Amoy and other ports on the Chinese mainland.

My crew were now to do what turned out to be our last mining job of the war and it took us a period of 15 days to complete. In this time we did two mine-drops, flying 9,860 miles in a total of 96 hours. We first flew to Leyte Gulf in the Philippines, where we obtained mines from the naval island of Jinamoc; thence to Labuan on Brunei Bay to refuel and off to Banka Strait on Sumatra to complete the last minefield. Our biggest trouble was that some headquarters' brain had decided that, as our striking distance to Banka Strait was only 900 miles, we would be able to carry less fuel and, therefore, three mines instead of two. So we had two mines on one wing and one on the other giving us an extra weight of one ton on the port wing, making it almost impossible to take off.

I had thought that it would be a good idea for me to do an operational mission without a navigator, so that I could do all the navigation myself and the chance turned up on our last mine-drop. For another pilot's navigator went down with appendicitis and, as the pilot didn't feel capable of navigating himself, I lent him my own navigator, much to the latter's disgust. I don't think he ever forgave me for it, as his plane failed to take off that trip.

We had great difficulty ourselves. We were lying at anchor off the remnants of the town of Victoria, on the island of Labuan, on the eastern side of Brunei Bay. There was no wind at all, nor any sign of sea or swell to ruffle the surface of the steamy sea. After lunch the heat was humid and oppressive and our engines didn't function well in such an atmosphere. We boarded the Cat, A24-365, and found it roasting hot under the burning sun. By the time we

Air Force camp at Lake Satani, Dutch New Guinea

were ready to cast off and taxi out, we had mostly stripped off our surplus clothes and equipment. I remember that I climbed into my seat for the take-off wearing only my shoes, underpants and a towel, tied around my neck to absorb the perspiration.

Our port wingtip was only held up by the float, which was under water with the extra weight of the two mines on that wing. When we tried to taxi I had to wind the ailerons hard a-starboard, with the rudder, to try to keep her straight. I decided the best way to take off was straight out to sea, where there might be some breeze or swell to take the shine off the surface, and allow us to become unstuck. The first attempt was abortive, for we groundlooped before we could get her up on the step and we had to throttle the motors right back to cool them off. The second attempt was the same, and the third, and then I tried to lift the floats before we got on the step to improve the lift. I believe we had about ten attempts altogether, each direct to seaward, with the second pilot and I pumping the controls like Greek wrestlers to try to get her up on the step. Each time the engines overheated or we groundlooped.

Finally there may have been a little swell, or the loss of weight caused by us using up 200 gallons of fuel during two hectic hours may have made the difference. But what did it matter? We were at last airborne and on our way, but I was an utter wreck. I handed over to the second pilot, Marsh Burgess, gave him a course to steer and lay down to recover. It was about 5 p.m. as we flew over enemy trenches and the burning oil wells of Meri, some actually out in the sea.

Then the whole mission had to be reconsidered, as we didn't have enough fuel to keep to the plan. So we cut over the town of Kuching, saving distance instead of going around the whole nor'-west corner of Borneo, and then steering for Sumatra.

We were late getting there of course, having lost two hours on take off; the navigation kept me fairly busy and the mission turned out to be so interesting that I made the following notes on it when we got back to base:

" Date: 26/27 July, 1945. It is nearly midnight, local time. . . . Just below the low cloud base the low coastline of Sumatra marks the limit of the visible world. To starboard lies the ever-nearer coast of Banka Island which we follow, keeping now about one mile off-shore. We have come down to 600 feet, and are aware of the closeness of the dull shadowy sea, that treacherous servant of man, the fickle mistress of flying-boats, for we can never trust

Shipping reconnaissance in Banka Strait

her changing moods. For it is still the sea of the Old Testament and the sea of Joseph Conrad.

"Points of land, breaking reefs, and large rocks or islets rush at us and pass quickly below, giving the feeling of speed which one misses at great heights. We have entered Banka Strait from the south and fly toward the narrows, where our mission lies . . . this is where our minefields are and this, we have been told, is the last mine-drop needed to complete the field. Owing to the imminent invasion of these parts by Mountbatten's forces no more mines are to be laid.

"'RADAR TO COCKPIT . . . Blip on the port bow, now four miles, looks like a ship.' Our eager Charles Lane has been reporting the shape and distance of the land ahead, while Marsh and I try to check with the objects we can see by eye and identify the blips by navigation. My usual reply to each report of a blip is ' That must be Lucipara Island.' But tonight there are too many Lucipara Islands . . . and being in mid-channel they can be nothing else but ships. These blips of ours are not a Japanese Task Force, but whatever they are they will have to wait until we drop our mines.

"We are now only a few miles from datum, as we fly like a bat into a low dark cavern; the soft murk is broken ahead by a line of radiance where the horizon ought to be. As we near it the heavens open up, the full moon appears in a dazzling sky and night is turned to day. The sea comes to life too, olive green with flecks of white, though the land looks blacker than ever.

" We turn across the strait to our datum, repeating, to refresh our memories, the courses to fly, the height, the speed agreed upon and, most important, the time in seconds between datum and each mine. Up comes the datum point, we turn on to course, get the speed and height steady, and the bow calls: ' Coming up to datum . . . on datum, GO ! ' and Norm starts counting the seconds, back in the light of the navigation compartment.

" During those hurried moments we have been aware of various black shapes around us, but what sort of ships they are will have to wait. More blips have been appearing in mid-channel, but they are never reported during the mining run. Soon we drop the first mine, half a minute later the second, finally the third, and the job is done.

" At last we are free to have a close look at the ships, and compile details for the people who arrange bombing attacks. We carry no bombs ourselves, nor any cannon or rockets and if we use our guns it will make us too definite a target. Although we must be fairly visible against the sky, I have a theory that once a gun's crew on a ship fire at us they will be too blinded by the flash to see us again. This turns out correct.

" Most of the ships were anchored in pairs, two by two like Noah's animals. I evolved another theory, that if we fly at deck level between each pair they might hesitate to fire for fear of hitting their mate. This proves quite incorrect, but it gives Marsh and me a good view of each ship, and we report the details for Norm to write down. Near the datum are two square masses of barges or house-boats in shallow water. Several canoes are tied up astern of them, but there is no sign of life. There is also a black shape just below the surface, perhaps a recent wreck due to our old mines.

" Now we are out in mid-channel, and pick up a single blip, which turns out to be a schooner under sail, making against the tide; she is probably of wood, and therefore safe against magnetic mines.

" Next we go to two ships at anchor, one ahead of the other. The first looks like a small tanker, but as we get close it appears to be a coastal vessel, with the funnel aft, about 1,500 tons. As I glimpse a pair of samson posts, which confirm the type, a stream of tracers squirt from her bows and another from the bridge. . . . Then a large yellow flash comes from the stern gun, probably a

3-inch model. We are closely surrounded by vivid violet streamers and I observe some wide shots skimming over the sea. By this time we are past the first ship and the second starts to welcome us with the same tracers, but no yellow flashes. This one appears to be a naval sloop or escort vessel, too good to be employed as a mine-sweeper and of powerful and modern design, also about 1,500 tons. Off we go to the next pair.

" They are at anchor like the last two and we steer between them. Marsh's ship opens fire before I can get a good look at her and we dive closer to the water, straight between them. My ship turns out to be a large tanker, about 5,000 tons, and Marsh's is no less. My ship opens fire belatedly and off we go. This is all very interesting to the crew. I duck my head into the cockpit each time to dodge the near misses. Norm is back at the W/T and very disturbed by the gunfire. Ted, the engineer, whose station gives him a good view on both sides, is wishing he had somewhere else to look, while our three watchers in the blisters are recoiling from port and starboard alternately.

" By this time we are closing the far side of the strait and a whole lot of blips show up. As we get closer we find four ships anchored in line abreast, and we steer past their bows. I assess them as large junks or small coasters, about 200 tons each, possibly minesweepers, as a stream of tracers comes from the second in the line. By this time we are suddenly tired of looking at ships and still more sick of being fired at, at close range. So I sheer away, and find we are flying up a small jetty to the land. There may be high posts around and there are buildings ahead, so we climb sharply and pass up the main street of a mining town, just over the rooftops. Even in the excitement I notice a man standing in a lighted doorway, apparently firing a revolver at us.

" As we clear the town and make for Cape Berikat, our departure point, the engineer reports that we have only 500 gallons left. So we have to cut across the corner of Borneo again, to shorten the distance, arriving home next day at about 9 a.m. with 50 gallons still remaining in the tanks. When we anchor off Victoria, to refuel before heading back to Jinamoc and home, we find a hole in the leading edge of the port wing, a few inches from the fuel tanks, made by a small bullet, about 0.3 inch, possibly from that man with the revolver ! "

That proved to be the last shot fired at us in the war, for the two atom bombs dropped on Japan brought feelers for armistice.

Our next two missions were daylight searches along the islands of the Dutch East Indies for Jap troops in barges. It was a glorious travelogue in colour, for the islands and coral reefs were like jewels set in a purple velvet of deep water and I took 50 feet of colour film. The Jap surrender came a few days later. Then we had to search again for barges, to make sure they all showed the white flag of surrender. It was clear that these troops had accepted the Emperor's orders to lay down their arms, the efficacy of which we were very doubtful. On our last search we passed the islands of Flores, Komodo and the Dragons, and exceeded our orders by going into Bima harbour on Sumbawa, just to have a look at the shipping and to see by daylight the island which we had so often passed in the dead of night on mining missions.

After that some of our forces had to go forward to take over the areas as each was surrendered by the enemy and others went south to be demobbed. I went on a courier flight to Timor, landing off the town just where Captain Bligh did after his long voyage in an open boat from the *Bounty*. Then a ferry trip from Morotai in the Halmaheras direct to Bowen, 1,900 miles with 15 armed troops as passengers for 19 hours. Two weeks later I reached Sydney and was demobbed myself, on 2 October 1945.

My service in the war had lasted for six years and I needed time to settle down with the family, for we now had four children, and a lot of lost time to catch up on. I hoped to spend six months ashore and this was made possible by my deferred pay which amounted to £536.

J

Chapter Thirteen

War-torn Malaya

BEFORE RETURNING TO SEA WITH MY OLD COMPANY I decided to go for the Sydney Pilotage Exemption, which would allow me to pilot a ship in and out of Sydney providing that I was her Master and that she was registered in Australia and not overseas. To qualify for the examination one has to go both in and out of the port three times while serving as Mate or Master of an Australian ship. I only had two voyages which counted for this, in the *Malaita*, so by the courtesy of a coastal company, I signed on a ship as Chief Officer for a week-end voyage to Newcastle and back. The ship was the s.s. *Mulubinba*, of 1,262 tons, Captain G. E. James. After swotting up all the details of the port of Sydney, including lights, beacons, depths, anchorages, wharves and the details of the bridges, I took a couple of trips around in the ferries to check up on the current information.

As most of the details would be forgotten long before they might ever be needed in our company, I learnt it all up in a week and went for the exam, passed it, and was then able to forget it all very quickly. Then I applied to Burns Philp for a job, having been six months ashore and, therefore, short of cash. The Marine Superintendent was a new man and did not favour any officers who had been trained as cadets. The company had lost half their ships during the war and were not happy about finding jobs for their old men returning from the war. After waiting three weeks for an officer's job of any sort, for I didn't expect to get a command at once, I went to head office and interviewed the heads. The chairman of directors, general manager, shipping manager and islands manager all told me sad stories, but a few days later I was appointed Second Mate of a ship newly built for the Australian Government, to be managed by the company. I spent a very interesting two months while the ship was fitted out and put through her trials. I was to serve at sea in her later, but that belongs to the next chapter; the day before she sailed on her maiden voyage I was transferred to the old s.s. *Mangola* as Chief Officer, the same job as I had had in her in 1938. Her new Captain had been junior to me before the war, but the Second Mate had actually been my Captain when I was Second Mate in the New Hebrides in 1932. I felt a bit strange after six years' absence from the company's ships, but there was better pay at sea than in any of the jobs available ashore. I did think of going into civil aviation, or the navigation department, or a navigation school.

But here I was with an all-Indian crew of Moslems, except for the two untouchables who swept the decks and cleaned the lavatories out. They were two bright lads, but darkly suspected of being infidel Christians because they spoke a little English. The Indian crew were not to my taste, a jabbering lot of schoolgirls after a good crew of Malays. The ship had won them in a lottery called a wartime shipping pool and their leader, a bearded Serang, had never done a day's work in his life.

We sailed for Singapore and our only stop on the way was at Bowen for a few hours, for coal; it took us a whole wearisome month to get to our destination. This was bad enough, but worse was to come. When we anchored off the dishevelled city of Singapore out in the Roads, we were told that we might have to wait a few weeks for a wharf! The whole of Malaya was still suffering a famine from shortage of food; here were we, with a full cargo of good Australian foodstuffs, denied a quick berth. There were a lot of other ships waiting in the Roads, but nearly every day a Blue Funnel ship arrived and got an immediate berth. After ten days I wrote a critical letter to the *Straits Times,* which they published next day, leaving out the paragraph in which I suggested that our agents might not be aware that bribery was rife in the port.

The agents took a dim view of me, but the same afternoon we were told to berth next day. The great port of Singapore was certainly in a mess, while economically and politically it was a mad shambles. Pilfering, looting, graft and blackmarketeering were rampant and involved every phase of activity. Banditry on land and piracy at sea were every day features in the papers.

The greatest shortage was rice, rationed by the Government at a lower scale than even under the Japanese occupation. The official price was 1½d a pound, and the blackmarket price 6s. The ration was about one pound a week, while the usual consumption was seven pounds of rice a week. Most of the workers, including tally-clerks on the wharves, got 2s. a day and so were fertile fields for bribes from the racketeers and bandits.

Our cargo went into large sheds or godowns on the wharf and the whole dock area was surrounded by high walls, guarded at the gates by British troops. There were also the port and city police, but what went on in sight of the ship was a complete travesty of law and order.

Every night, when work finished, the bandits and looters went into action. The dock gates opened to admit their trucks, the godown doors opened at their request and off went the items of cargo for the blackmarket. The trucks were British Army, the drivers also British, under orders from the head bandits, and every sentry, driver and godown caretaker received at least a banknote for 1,000 dollars ! To men of any race, with blackmarket prices to pay for most of their family needs, this represented no less than three years' pay. Money seemed to have changed as madly as the German mark in the 1920s. This was due largely to the wartime flooding of the country with worthless Japanese notes, so that people lost their respect for money, except in large denominations.

The blackmarket stretched for a mile along the main street of Chinatown, with shops, stalls and booths groaning under the weight of rolls of material and other scarce goods, while at the European stores in the city one could hardly buy a single handkerchief. Everything could be bought, anything could be sold, but only at black prices. A golden sovereign was worth £20, a cigarette tin of opium £150, and a plain white suit £15. Before the war, opium was £5 and the tailored suit cost only 15s.

The wharf and its jumble of cargo and humans was almost a stage drama. Now and again a coolie was seen to sneak away from a godown with an armful of textiles, away through the grass to the iron-railed fence topped with barbed-wire. Outside on the footpath were sitting runners from the blackmarket, always ready to pay spot cash for stolen cargo of any use.

The high spot of the day was when the leading gangsters took a walk along the waterfront to see what was available. A sudden hush descended on the wharf and the whisper: " Gangsters," preceded them from berth to berth. The two or three visitors sauntered along displaying disdain and arrogance and radiating a powerful aura of evil. They sauntered past the harmless police, like Japanese generals on parade, and everyone else minded their own business very thoroughly. Life was cheap in Singapore.

The wharf-labourers included gangs of either Hindu or Moslem Indians, displaced Javanese, sad and homesick, and smaller parties of good-natured Chinese matrons in wide hats and bell-bottomed black pants and bare feet. In the godown were jumbled heaps of broken and looted cargo, supposed to be tidied up by squads of Japanese prisoners-of-war, under the nominal charge of a Lancashire soldier. The Japs were happy and well-fed, picnicking on cases of Canadian salmon and precious Australian beer. It made my blood boil, after what our own men suffered as prisoners of the Japs.

We attempted to stop pilfering in the ship, though it seemed pointless in view of what went on ashore. By this time our crew of Indians had been exchanged for Malay sailors, Chinese cooks and stewards and Indians for the engine-room. This was exactly one year after the Japanese surrender and the troops at the docks were relieved by a Devon regiment. Things were being brought under control, according to the civil government, who had taken over from the military administration. One night we caught two pilferers red-handed on the ship, so I got our Malays to hold them while I went ashore to fetch the police. And this is what happened. The first man was an Indian military policeman asleep on a wire mattress, which had once been cargo. I prodded him into a sitting position, but as he slowly adjusted his turban I could see that he was drugged and still in a coma. When he eventually grasped what I was telling him, he said he couldn't help me, he had no power over civilians, let alone dangerous looters, so he sank back into his sleep. He was well armed, but showed no signs of offensive spirit except for his once-ferocious moustaches.

The next policeman was a Malay, of the Harbour Board, whose jurisdiction ended at his toecaps. He couldn't come to the wharf, let alone venture aboard a strange ship. Then a Chinese tally-clerk managed to get some sense out of a Japanese phone, and after speaking Chinese, Malay and finally English, he put me on to speak to a European officer of the city police. This man was sorry the matter was beyond his province; had I tried the Harbour Board police? So we rang the Harbour Board, which was a lucky number. A Chinese lieutenant promised to, and did, come along at once to the ship. The captives were still in custody, and were patiently interviewed by " Charlie Chan." He then waxed eloquent in Chinese, telling the looters their fortunes and their family histories. Then he committed them to the Malay policeman, to whom he spoke sharply on the subject of duty. The next day the looters got six weeks' hard labour each.

That evening at dusk I was intrigued by a wallaby coming along the wharf behind the heaps of packing cases. Then I saw that it was a small boy, doubled over the usual roll of cloth. I descended the gangway, seized him by the arm and gave him to the quartermaster to hold while I went off to try out the telephone again. This time the military police came in a jeep and took the prisoner to the nearby police hut, informing me on the way that it wasn't really their job. While the boy pleaded guilty and gave up his roll of cloth, a dishevelled ape-like creature was propelled through the door, his doubled-up form covered with blood and scratches. His wrists were tied tightly by a cord, held by a determined military policeman from Devon. Next entered a huge packing case, pushed on a hand truck by a small coolie, while the exit was covered by two stout men of Devon and their sub-machine guns. The looter had been trying to get this great packing case over the fence and h.d been damaged in the barbed-wire as he tried to escape. My surprise at this drama was nothing to the surprise of the men of Devon, when they found that I, a civilian, had taken the trouble and danger of bringing to justice one of the looters which the general public seemed to be taking for granted.

After two weeks discharging cargo we were an empty ship and had to go to Port Swettenham and Penang to load rubber. Both these ports are in Malaya, on the West coast; conditions in these ports were quite different to Singapore, but no better.

From Swettenham, where we moored to buoys, we were able to take a trip up-country as far as Kuala Lumpur, where we had a very pleasant day at the swimming club, part of the beautiful grounds of the golf club on the outskirts of the very Eastern town of K.L., which was the centre of the Malay States.

At Penang we anchored in the stream, for the harbour is formed by a strait between the Island of Penang and the nearby coast of Malaya. Strong tides run through the strait, which make boat-work difficult. Penang is a most attractive island, rising to a peak over the town called the Crag, where live the High Commissioner and the Chinese millionaires whose lives are in peril from the bandits of the town and sea coasts. For Penang was the chief base of the pirates of the Malacca straits, between Malaya and Sumatra. There was a lot of smuggling carried on from Sumatra, in fast sampans and Malay prows, but these craft were the prey of pirates in landing craft, who held them up and took what they wanted at the point of tommy-guns.

There were occasional raids by combined forces of police and

the armed services, but the piracy even occurred right in the port.
Fortunately we had no cargo to interest the pirates, as we were
only loading rubber, but an English ship just astern had a visit
from pirate craft nearly every night. She had a cargo of Australian
flour in bags, which was valuable as a substitute for rice. They could
be seen coming up to the vessel's stern to make fast, climbing aboard
and taking what they wanted. It paid the officers and crew not to
stand in their way, for their lives would have been of little account
to the thieves. When the ship finished her discharge she was just
short of 1,000 bags of flour.

The most impressive building in the town was the railway
station with its clock tower. Here you could buy a train ticket for
Singapore, or send your freight, but there was no sign of either
trains or of trainlines. But there was a fast ferry which took you over
to the mainland, two miles away, where you boarded the train for
Singapore in the south. The only kind of railway in Penang was
a cable track up to the Crag, an almost vertical line, which I
believe was the only means of getting to the top.

We loaded our rubber from large barges or lighters and at
night the crews of these, who lived and slept aboard them, were
loth to remain alongside the ship unless we illuminated them with
floodlights as some protection against pirates. One morning, we
found ten bales of rubber missing from one lighter, equal to a ton
in weight, and worth $5,000. Later I found that they had not been
looted, but short-shipped, as an attempt by someone ashore to
balance their books at the expense of the ship. Apart from the
banditry, I found Malaya teeming with interest as ever and felt
compelled to record my impressions by sketches of interesting items
and scenes.

We steamed back to Singapore to get enough rubber to fill
the ship. A lot of this rubber had lain in store all the war, or about
four years, and so was in a sticky state. As each tier of bales was
stowed we dusted them with white chalk powder, and laid covers
of native matting on them to prevent the next tier from sticking to
them. We had a total of about 6,000 tons aboard by the time we
had finished and the weight of the upper tiers proved too hot and
heavy for the chalk or mats to have much effect.

While we were in Singapore, the government decided to honour
the birthday of Sir Stamford Raffles, founder of the city, by replacing
his statue which had been deposed by the Japanese. The question
of whether his birthday was the fifth or sixth of July was hotly
debated. By the records he was born on the fifth, at sea (about

1770 I suppose). Diaries and other contemporary records of
Singapore show that he celebrated his birthday on the sixth, and
when he died, by a coincidence on July 5, his widow wrote that he
was one day short of his 45th year.

The clue to the answer was that he was born at sea and in
those days the Astronomical Day was used at sea; in fact it did not
go out of use entirely until 1925. The day was reckoned from noon
to noon, that is from one transit of the sun over the meridian to the
next. When the navigator, with his sextant, announced that the
sun had gone, the Master ordered eight bells to be struck, the
clocks or sandglasses to be turned, and a new page and new date
to be used in the logbook.

Captain Bligh's account of his voyage in the open boat puzzles
readers because of his references to the forenoon as " the latter end
of the day," and the afternoon as when " the day began. . . ."
Similarly, Cook's Journal shows only a few hours between " Thursday the 23rd, in the morning " and " Friday the 24th, in the
morning." Students of maritime history must bear this in mind
when reading original log-books which have not been translated
into the modern civil time, the day now being reckoned from midnight to midnight.

The Government decided that the fifth was the right day, but
held the ceremony on the sixth, because that was a Saturday. As
the Irish would remark, the Government only does things right
by accident !

After thankfully leaving Singapore and its heat and smells,
having spent a total of six weeks in Malaya, we started on the long
wearisome road back to Sydney: that meant a whole month at sea,
broken only by a few hours' call at Bowen for coal. I tried to occupy
my spare time in practising Malay on the crew, sketching the more
interesting ones, and then in writing articles for publication on the
surprising state of affairs in Malaya. This writing of articles became
quite a hobby of mine, and I keep it up for many reasons, the least
of which is the financial reward. On arrival in Sydney the ship
and I parted company, without any regrets on either side, for I
was sent to another ship and missed the trouble of trying to dig out
the congealed mass of 6,000 tons of rubber !

PART THREE

Adventures

of Peacetime

1946-1960

Chapter Fourteen

The iron ore trade

FROM THE *Mangola* AND THE MALAYAN TRADE, I WAS transferred back to the ship which had been fitting out six months before. She was the s.s. *River Hunter*, of 5,025 tons gross, 2,877 tons nett, but capable of carrying 8,000 tons deadweight. My company were her managing agents, although they did not run ships around the Australian coast as a rule. This ship was to enter the dusty cycle of the iron ore trade, in which we had no experience. I found out what the trade was like in the first week and then the palm fringed isles of the South Seas became part of a heavenly dream.

I joined *River Hunter* in Newcastle as Chief Officer. She was lying at the coal wharves, surrounded by acres of railway lines, coal trucks, and clouds of coal dust. She was being loaded with 8,000 tons of coal, a process which took about 30 continuous hours. Each truck of coal was lifted by a crane over a hatch, the pins knocked out and the coal vomited down into the hold. The coal dust blew everywhere and I didn't like it at all. The ship was down to her marks before she was full and I had to take care to get her on an even keel at the last minute. The crew had been ordered to turn to at about 4 a.m. to cover up the hatches and secure the derricks for sea. This took a few hours, by which time they had sobered up somewhat, and the grey dawn brought us a pilot and tugs.

Newcastle is 60 odd miles from Sydney, but we only called at our home port for fuel oil, which took about four hours. Then we were four days at sea on the coastal route to South Australia and it took most of this time, which was often a week-end, to get the ship reasonably clean. On arrival at Adelaide we berthed at Osborne to discharge the coal; this was done by large grabs held by cranes. They grabbed the coal in mouthfuls, spewing it all over the decks and the dock, and into the wind, until it went into a conveyor to the nearby gasworks. This phase of our dusty cycle took about 36 hours, as the last part of the coal had to be trimmed by infernal machines out of the tween decks and corners of the holds.

As soon as the ship was secured again for sea we were off, empty except for our ballast tanks. Then the fun began.

Rollicking, rolling, rollicking, rolling, the empty ship steams into the Spencer Gulf. We are bound for the port of Whyalla, the bane of all ship-lovers' hearts. The Gulf shoals and narrows to the north, but the land is that same flat, dry and biscuity crust which extends for a thousand miles to the north and the west. Between her and Western Australia is the Great Australian Bight, where the dead centre meets the great Southern Ocean, though that doesn't help either rainfall or vegetation.

Out of this dry powdery sheet of sedimentary crust rise occasional hills of metallic rock. Bold and dark, they look like seals' heads above the sea, while others stand like the age-old monuments of ancient Egypt.

The whole landscape is in pale pastel shades. Coarse yellow sand, glittering salt pans, white accumulations of gypsum and limestone, and the pale blue-green of saltbush and spinifex. The dark outcrops of igneous rocks stand out all the bolder and, ever since a dilapidated hill turned into the wealth of Broken Hill, most of the others have been prospected for ores.

The most recently fossicked ore is that of uranium, while the first was gold and there seem to be few important metals which are

Discharging iron ore at Newcastle

not found in this central slice of Australia. Of the known deposits of iron, the Monarch is the most striking, a hill which was originally estimated to contain 20,000,000 tons of ore. To see the trains of ore rattling down from the Monarch to the sea in a cloud of red dust, leaving a red smear on the land, is to imagine that a fire-belching dragon had passed that way. And if you follow the track 30 miles to the port of Whyalla, you'll surely see the animal itself!

The red track of the railway doesn't stop when it gets to the sea, for it curves around Hummocky Hill and then out over the shallow waters of the bay on a long serpentine jetty. The trucks empty into bins and the bins on to conveyor belts which take the ore in stages out to the waiting ship. There are several pumping stations to connect the stages and these crests give the jetty an undulating form above its centipede legs.

The red dust blows out and stains the waters around as the serpent swoops to the five-fathom line and here it rears up on ugly squat legs to squirt the ore into the victim ship.

The jetty-end is marked by a single green navigation light, like a green-eyed monster, pouring its indigestible stream of ironstone and ore-dust down a spout at the rate of 1,000 tons an hour. Every day of the year there is another ship to load, taking at least 6,000 tons of ore, making a total of 2,000,000 tons a year.

But what of the poor ship? We secure her with her main hatch under the spout; all hatches are open and ready for their turn. Into No. 2 hold goes 2,000 tons of ore and the wonder is that it doesn't go straight through the double-bottom of the ship. Then the ship is shifted along the line of dolphins to get No. 3 hold under the spout. When 1,500 tons are in, it is time to shift again. Now the centre of the ship is sagging under the weight while the two ends are empty and buoyant, so the hull has a tendency to turn up at the ends like the toes of old shoes. She does indeed bend somewhat, but she is built to take the strain, as a ship has to do in a big sea when her extreme ends are held up by waves and her middle droops in the trough between. Next, we haul her to get No. 4 hold loaded, then No. 5, and then all the way back to No. 1 to finish the job. At low tide there is a chance of her stern digging into the mud while she is still by the stern; this is my job as well as seeing that she is not overloaded and that she finishes up on an even keel.

The ore in unbelievably heavy. It is about the same weight as lead-ore and so puts the ship down to her marks when the holds are only one-tenth filled. The ore piles up in a pyramid or heap in the hold but doesn't even touch the sides of the ship.

Having so much weight in the bottom certainly makes for stability and there is no chance of the ship turning turtle. But too much stability can be almost as bad as not enough. For when a wave rolls her over to one side she flies back so violently that severe stresses are put on the hull, the masts, the boats and the weary crew. Ships loaded with iron ore roll so quickly and continuously that it is hard to believe it possible and as they roll their way along the coastal routes their cargo is very obvious to any other ships in sight. The Iron Ore Roll is unmistakable. And unforgettable. For the degree of roll is not only greater than usual, but at least twice as rapid, so that it is difficult to keep on your feet without holding on to some support.

While the ship is being loaded at Whyalla there isn't much rest for the crew. Every hour or two the ship has to be hove into a fresh position under the spout and then the last loaded hold covered up and secured for sea. All the time the roar of the ore pouring into the hollow holds is accompanied by the mechanical groans of the loading machinery and the dyspeptic rumblings of the ore coming along the jetty in a constant stream. The ore pours over the decks, till they are a foot or two deep, the dust blows over the whole ship, right to the mast-tops, and into the bay to settle on the bottom and reduce the depth all through the years, until it is dredged up again.

Night and day the work continues, until the last ton is on and the ship is able to struggle away from the jetty and the temporarily silent loading monster. As we get down into the open Gulf the rolling suddenly starts and never stops for the next four days. The ship is hosed down from the masts, funnel, samson posts and upper decks, while the excess ore is shovelled off the main deck over the side into the sea. Then all the superstructure is hosed down and washed, but nothing will remove the red stain of the trade from the ship, crew, or their clothing. All the ropes and canvas are permeated with the fine hard dust, hastening their disintegration. Our clothes and

The iron ore roll

our bodies are ingrained with iron, but why should we try to get ourselves or the ship clean ?

Four days later we reach Newcastle again, to go straight to the steelworks wharf to be discharged, this time with huge grabs which take 15 or 20 tons of ore at a time. They are capable of biting whole pieces out of the ship at the same time, including the timbers of the holds and any steel ladders they find in their way. In an hour the ship is buried under red dust and silted around the decks a foot deep in ore; thus passes the next 30 hours of the dusty cycle.

The ore taken from the ships forms a line of coastal hills between the wharf and the steelworks, where the blast furnaces burn day and night to make the steel of progress and industry. As soon as the last grabful of ore is out, and the worst of their ravages repaired, the tugs appear and we are off around to the coal berths again, to start the cycle all over again. Coal and iron ore, iron ore and coal, and no respite for the ship.

This went on for the worst part of a year, with a few short spells on other types of cargo that were very welcome as a change. We were sent once from Adelaide to Wallaroo for wheat in bags, a good clean cargo for Brisbane, when Queensland was short of its wheat harvest. The newly bagged wheat was hot and dry, full of golden sunlight; loading it was clean and pleasant, taking about a week and discharging it in Brisbane was also a pleasure after our usual dusty ports. It rained quite a lot in Brisbane, but the weather was warm. The loose grains of wheat which collected on the decks, mooring lines and wharf all burst into leaf after the first two days of hot-house weather, so we had emerald green grass to make a gay and colourful scene.

Twice we took full cargoes of coal to Western Australia and from Fremantle we were ordered to the lovely little port of Bunbury to load full shipments of wheat in bulk for Sydney. This was all too good to be true, after our usual fleeting visits to Sydney for fuel oil. The grain trade was quite new to me and so was Western Australia. The golden harvest of this state is drawn to the western seaboard, to the three ports which are equipped to handle wheat in bulk for export; Geraldton in the north, Fremantle in the centre, and Bunbury in the south. The mechanical loaders at these ports enable ships to be fully loaded in three or four days, instead of a week or more, apart from the fewer men required. Each port has its zone of wheatfields and wheat comes to Bunbury from points up to 250 miles away in the interior.

We were in Fremantle when we got our orders to prepare the

ship for wheat in bulk, which meant that we first had to clean out the holds of every trace of coal and iron ore. Removing the " traces " took nearly a week, for the iron ore had penetrated every pore and detail of the ship's anatomy; in fact the cleaning process lightened the ship by about 50 tons.

As each hold was cleaned we had to erect fore and aft bulkheads in the centreline to prevent the grain from shifting in a heavy sea, for this had caused the loss of many a ship in the bad old days. As the ship is not completely full of wheat when she is down to her marks the loose grain tends to settle and, if it shifts to one side during a heavy roll, the ship may take a permanent list to that side and eventually capsize.

The actual loading of the wheat is done by conveyor belts and spouts, like the iron-ore loading. The silo at Bunbury holds 8,000 tons of wheat and our cargo under the regulations works out to 7,400 tons. It is a mile from the silo to the ship, because of the shallow water of the bay, and the wheat is sent down to us in trucks. Astride the railway lines on the jetty stand two long-legged loading gantries, which can move about on their own wheels and so load the ship both ends at once, without the ship having to shift up and down the jetty.

The grain is poured out the sides of the trucks, through gratings in the wharf and down into bins below. From these it is scooped

Loading grain

up by a bucket dredge in the gantry and fed on to the conveyor belts to be run into the ship through the spout. The rate of loading is from 70 to 100 tons an hour.

These machinations are not achieved without some noise and dust and the air becomes full of the wheat husks which blow through the rigging like snowflakes, gathering in drifts around the deck when they have no better employment. The wholemeal dust, so full of vitamins, is trampled into a fine gruel on the deck after each rain squall, while those grains of wheat which refuse to go down the hold are turned into " poor man's porridge " by the same process.

The noise of the loading is mostly the whirling of the electric motors and the swishing of the grain, which also makes a pitter-patter as it turns each corner on its way down to the hold. From the sunlit decks to the scene below is like a change of pictures from Van Gogh to Rembrandt.

From the lower hold a beam of light comes through the small opening in the upper hatches and mixes with the stream of golden grain, which is itself little more than concentrated warmth and sunlight; both the light and the grain diffuse as they fall, and both are confined by the walls of the trunkway and the shifting boards of the bulkheads. The grain is a few carats more golden than the sandy beaches of Sydney and holds a living warmth, while its movements are as lively as quicksilver.

The liquid stream pours down pulsating with energy and the pulses appear as waves when it sprays out from obstructions. When the stream hits the surface of wheat in the hold it turns into a gently heaving mass of living grain that has no landslides, but only undulations like the muscular movements of abdominal breathing.

When the hold is filled to within six feet of the deck beams, it

Wheat pouring into the hold

K

is time to get the trimming machines into action. These take the stream of wheat and turn it into a horizontal jet, which travels at such speed that it can reach to 120 feet. These trimmers are worked by electric motors, handling 60 tons an hour, filling up the furthest corners of the hold with tightly packed grain. They are controlled by men in the hold, like a gun's crew training and elevating the jet, but they have to wear masks to avoid breathing the dust they produce.

When we got to Sydney the bulk wheat had to be discharged by grabs, just like coal or iron ore, for although there were mechanical loaders for wheat, they could not unload it from ships.

On our next visit to Fremantle we were there in mid-winter. Our cargo of coal had just been removed and the ship lay empty at the wharf on Saturday morning while the crew got paid and went up to Perth to sample the beer. I was up town myself to see an old Air Force friend and returned in the last train. Then I had to walk about a mile to the ship and, being in a heavy coat, I got quite hot. So I turned in after midnight with nothing on but a towel. The weather had been squally and threatening and, after a storm-warning from the harbourmaster, we had doubled up our ropes and wires to hold the empty ship safely to the low wharf.

My sleep was shattered by a loud bang and, as I looked through the port hole at the driving rain, I saw the lights of the wharf start moving past. As I dashed out of my cabin I met the Captain and Third Mate and ran right forward to the forecastle in the driving rain to let go an anchor.

The Captain started blowing the ship's whistle for a tug, while the Third Mate let go the other anchor. We found that all the lines had carried away from the forward part of the ship, but the sternlines were still holding. Across the other side of the narrow harbour was a line of ships, including our old *Marella* on the Singapore run; if we had blown into them we would have rammed and sunk the one we hit. Our bleary eyed crew, those few who were aboard, hardly had time to sober up before they needed something to warm them against the wintry storm. After some hours we got a tug or two and secured back again to the wharf. The remainder of the Sabbath passed quietly.

Our next cargo, when we got back into the coal and iron-ore trade, was a full cargo of limestone from Rapid Bay in South Australia. This is used in the making or iron, or rather in its conversion from the basic ores. It takes a ton of coal to turn a ton of ore into iron and the limestone is also cooked in the same blast

furnace to help get rid of the surplus oxygen. South Australia
has both iron ore and limestone, but no coal, while New South Wales
has the coal but no iron ore or limestone. As a result the coal has
to be shipped to the blast furnaces at Whyalla and the ore and
limestone to the two main coaling ports of Newcastle and Port
Kembla in N.S.W. where the steelworks are.

This bulk handling of such basic needs is very cheap, only
£1 or so a ton, thanks to the mechanical handling at each end. The
limestone, though a rough and dusty cargo, is at least a clean one
and not as heavy as the iron ore.

Because it's not half as heavy, it fills the lower holds up, but leaves
the tween decks empty. So we don't roll so badly, and we can often
get a cargo of motor-car bodies to fill the decks and leave us a day in
Sydney. Another break from the iron ore was a half-cargo of steel
and iron products for Brisbane and on one rare occasion we even
got a general cargo from Adelaide to the west.

One of the worst features of the iron ore trade was the type of
crews we used to get from Newcastle. There were generally a
couple missing at sailing time, so we always had replacements
standing by, if the agent could arrange them. We had frequent
desertions by men who were ashore drinking and just couldn't be
bothered returning to the ship and her obnoxious trade. The bosun,
who had the trouble of getting the men on deck to work, was only

s.s. River Hunter

paid £1 a month more than the A.B.s, and it was no wonder the ship had five different bosuns during my first six months there. They were mostly driven to drink, and got the sack. Then the trouble was to find another man to take the thankless job.

After nearly 12 months in the ship my leave fell due, and I started to plague the company to send me in some of their island ships where I could get some up-to-date knowledge of the various island trades, instead of being smothered in the iron ore trade, in which neither the company nor myself had any interest.

While I was on leave our senior captain died in harness, at the age of 76, which gave me my chance for a command again, the first since 1939, which was eight years past.

Chapter Fifteen

The brave little ship *Muliama*

IT IS A GREAT SATISFACTION TO GET COMMAND OF A SHIP: to be her Master under God, as the old legal phrase has it. And there generally seems to be a long period of waiting for promotion to Master. In this case my new ship was the baby of the Burns Philp Line, the motor vessel *Muliama* of 689 tons gross, built in Hong Kong in 1937 to work in New Guinea waters like my old *Maiwara*.

She was now running out of Sydney, which was a promotion for her, though she was rather small for the run across the wide ocean to Lord Howe, Norfolk Island and the New Hebrides. She had taken this run over temporarily for the *Morinda*, which was undergoing her post-war refit. I was very pleased to see the islands on this run again, after an absence of 14 years, though that didn't make the navigation to the large number of small island ports in the Hebrides any easier.

The ship was very seaworthy for her size, very buoyant and very manoeuvrable, but she did roll most enthusiastically in the open sea. She carried white officers and a crew of about 20 wild and untrained natives of the Hebrides, but she was a happy ship, as most small ships are. We carried half a dozen passengers and had two or three Chinese cooks, who overfed us if anything. Their cooking was also rather rich for a badly rolling ship.

I found that I had forgotten most of the island ports and anchorages, my memory having been worn out during my years of work in the Air Force. So I had to do plans and sketches in a notebook to remind me of the bearings to clear dangers and the bearings on which to anchor the ship safely. We still called at Havannah Harbour for fresh water, where we had collected it in surf-boats in the old days.

During the war, the Americans had started to turn Havannah into a naval base, by marking it with beacons, laying mooring buoys, constructing air-strips, erecting buildings and constructing some small jetties for fuelling and getting fresh water. They put a cover over a fresh spring, with piping and pumps to supply it to ships, which could either lie alongside a small jetty or tie up to mooring buoys nearby. By the time I got there the Yanks had long since left and only ruins remained. Most of the mooring buoys were sinking and, being anchored with huge chain cables to 40-ton blocks of concrete, they became a hazard for our anchors.

Before they had time to develop Havannah Harbour, a new admiral had arrived and shifted base to the Segond Channel at Santo. That became a huge base for the invasion of the Solomons and at one time had no fewer than five main wharves, six picture shows, and nearly half a million men in a permanent camp. They threw bridges over the rivers, built 100 miles of good roads and made a big airfield as well as some fighter strips. Santo slowly declined as the American forces retook the Solomons and moved in steps from island to island on the long road to Tokio and the final surrender of Japan.

When the Pacific war was over all the surplus equipment which couldn't be sold was ordered to be dumped in the sea. This was done at Santo from a low point of land since known as Billion Dollar Point, because of the vast amount of valuable material they pushed into the water from that spot. Hundreds of new vehicles, jeeps still in their packing cases, cranes, bulldozers, electrical equipment, miles of wires and chains and stores of all kinds, all went into the drink, some in deep water and some in shallow. On the shore were left hundreds of planes, mostly brand new fighter planes which had never flown, their engines still in their waxed paper wrappings and cases, stacked high in sheds which were soon overgrown by the jungle. Most of the roads were soon covered by the rapid tropical growth, trees grew up through the sheds, while most of the Qanset huts were pulled down and rebuilt by local residents on plantations.

Very few people or island Governments had the money to pay for any equipment, although it was going very cheaply and the American business interests were apparently afraid that a glut of cheap wartime vehicles in the world would spoil their market for many years to come. The only item I was able to come by was a dust-covered old typewriter but, after cleaning, it turned out to be a 1939 model and I am typing this chapter with it at the moment. Various large firms and syndicates bought the salvage rights and shipped away vast quantities of metal and vehicles and most of the planes have since been melted into ingots of aluminium for shipment back to the United States.

The impressive wharves of Santo were only built of oregon and so made a happy meal for the boring worms of the sea. We soon had only two wharves intact out of the five and, between the dry-rot of the decking and the eating away of the piles below, we eventually had no wharves left at all.

We called at most of the other islands of the Hebrides in the *Muliama*, mainly to drop cargo and collect copra in return. Some of these islands had long and interesting histories and some had special products for trade. Aneityum in the far south produced a beautiful timber called kauri pine, which we loaded in logs for Sydney. Then there was sandalwood from Erromanga, where a sheep station bred Merino sheep from Australia, both for the wool and for the supply of mutton chops.

The island of Tanna has its volcano, only 600 feet high, but erupting every day of the year since it was first sighted by the illustrious Captain Cook. We used to anchor barely a mile away, at a place called Whitesands, to distinguish it from the other beaches round about, which were of black volcanic sands. Only three European houses stood at Whitesands and they were inhabited by people of opposing camps. One was the home of an English trader,

Volcano at Tanna

Yankee crane at Santo

named Bannister; the next was a French trader named Vigeroux; the third was the home of the Presbyterian missionary who regarded all traders as " blackbirders " and agents of the devil. The other camps on the island included the two Government officials, French and British, who seldom saw eye to eye, and the mass of natives, some 6,000 strong, who kept the fires of opposition burning by continuous intrigues and tale-carrying between the camps.

Tanna has always been like that and so has the volcano. I climbed it several times, latterly to get photographs of the crater, which was a compound assortment of several apertures. From some of these issued smoke, from others steam, and the two most dangerous ones gave forth sulphur fumes, sharp pieces of broken rock and liquid strips of the froth from boiling lava. But they all made a point of erupting together, about every five minutes, so that on our way up the steep slope of the volcano we were subjected to ever greater shocks as we neared the top.

It took nearly half an hour to climb, after which the scene was so interesting that we didn't want to leave. We could see the nearby islands of Erromanga, Aniwa, Futuna and Aneityum. Below us was the sea coast, with the ship at anchor almost hidden by the high cliffs of volcanic tuff. Between us and the high mountains of the interior was a lovely lake of fresh water, reflecting the mountains, cut off from the sea by a plain of volcanic ash which had interrupted the lake's natural fall to the coast and also killed the jungle for a mile around. We ran down the volcano in about five minutes and got a lift back in a truck to Bannister's, where we were served with a breakfast of cold beer. For we had started out at dawn, before the sun got too hot, as the volcano itself and the job of climbing it were hot enough without the heat of the sun.

Another interesting call was on the island of Aoba, called the Isle of Lepers by Bougainville, who said that the natives there were dark and dirty and covered with a skin disease. This is far from the truth today, as the natives are lighter than the rest of the Hebrideans, have no skin disease, and are noted for their cleanliness. They all swarm down to the sea every few hours for a swim, a remarkable thing amongst Melanesians, to whom the idea of personal cleanliness is completely foreign as a rule. In fact the native girls of Aoba have always been the first choice of traders who wanted a native wife, anywhere in the Hebrides.

Towards the eastern end of the island is a pretty little port called Lolowai, headquarters of the Anglican Melanesian Mission. On one side is the valley of Vureas, containing the native boys' school, and on the other is the mission hospital, with the home of the Venerable Archdeacon Teale in the centre. Beyond the hospital, over a ridge, lies a valley forming the eastern extreme of Aoba. This fertile area is known as the Valley of the Virgins, for here is the mission school for native girls, run by mission ladies. It was previously run by Anglican nuns or sisters, of the High Church of England, but they got a little too high and went over to the Roman Catholic Church in a body.

The Valley was guarded by a ferocious dog, like the Hound of the Baskervilles, who went into action as soon as a visitor topped the distant rise. He roared up the hill with tremendous strides, with teeth bared for the kill, but I never heard of him doing any harm. The schoolgirls wore only short skirts, and nothing above the waist except on special occasions; they grew their own fruit, vegetables and flowers in the valley, so the scenery generally was very attractive and natural. There was a rain-filled crater in the grounds, but well out of sight, where the virgins could have a swim in private, but they kept it a fairly good secret.

On my second trip to the Hebrides in the *Muliama* we ran into big trouble. It was January, well in the hurricane season. As we left Lord Howe Island the first warnings reached us of a blow which had started near Santo, swept past New Caledonia, and was now on its way to Norfolk Island. And so were we. But we changed our minds and headed south towards New Zealand, as it would be unnecessary to call at Norfolk during a hurricane.

The glass soon started to fall and we slowed down to become hove-to and await developments. And I must say that things did develop quickly. We were soon heading about south-east, steaming into rising seas, wind and swell, and slowed down to bare steerage-way, to avoid hitting the seas too hard.

It was then announced that the cyclone was now heading for Lord Howe instead of Norfolk. This was better news, for it meant that things might improve after a few days. But they had to get worse before they got better. On the second day, the swell had got to what should have been its maximum height, about 40 feet from trough to crest. This was higher than our bridge and each fifth swell, larger than the rest, appeared half as high as the foremast when we started to climb.

Every now and again a sea would break on the top of a swell just over the bow, which flooded the fore deck, swamped the launch which was lashed on No. 1 hatch, and drenched the whole ship. Our lifeboats were turned inboard, fortunately, but we had two surf-boats hung from davits on the poop, which were in danger from the wave crests as they swept past at furious speed. The wind wound up to hurricane force, which is 65 knots and above.

The wind was much less in the troughs than on the crests, so that the most difficult moments for the ship were when she had to climb over the sharp crests just as the full force of the wind struck her. If she was not heading directly into the wind at this moment her bow would blow away and the wheel had to be put hard over to get her back into the wind before she came to the next crest. Now in any cyclone or tropical revolving storm the winds tend to spiral towards the centre of low pressure, while the swell tends to spiral outwards, as it prefers to run in a straight direction rather than a circle. The wind, therefore, and the sea which goes with it, is generally not from the same direction as the swell. So if the ship heads directly into the wind and sea, she is not heading directly into the swell. This is the usual state of affairs, but it means that the ship is liable to roll badly at times as well as pitching into the seas. The danger arises when the ship rolls and her low side is broached by a breaking sea, but that just cannot be helped.

During the second night the swell rose so high in front of the bow that it almost came to the level of our masthead light, which shines out horizontally ahead of the ship. When a crest was topped by a breaking wave, the breaker was illuminated by the light, so that the anxious watchers on the bridge saw a white line of breaker high over the bow, halfway up the mast; this was most alarming. The high wind had forced salt water into all the accommodation, through every crack of the woodwork and into all the electrical conduits and wiring, with peculiar results.

I had to leave the bridge every hour to bale out my cabin. Most of the native crew were unable to get back into the fo'c'sle and were sleeping in the alleyways awaiting a watery grave, for they and several of the Europeans had given up all hope. The four passengers had done the same and the radioman, whose cabin and sets were doused with seawater, only hoped to get out a last message of the position in which we would sink, so his sorrowing family would be able to have a wreath dropped on the spot marked X. By the third night, some of the floodlights for cargo work lit up, flooding the decks with light, in spite of the fact that they were switched off. All the watertight deck lights were half-full of water and many lights went out when they were still switched on. These included the navigation lights, so that we could no longer be threatened by illuminated breakers bearing down upon the bridge.

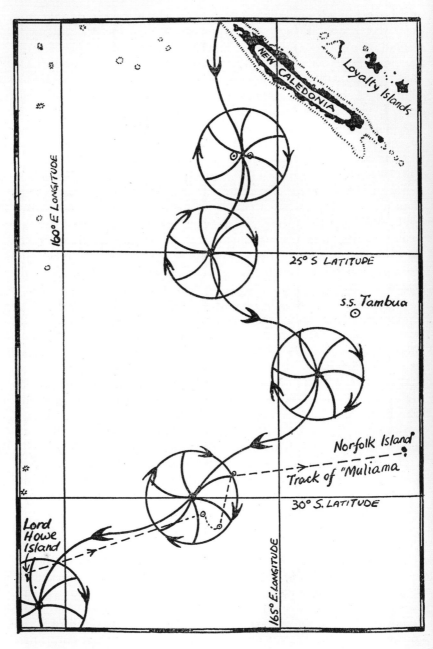

South-west Pacific hurricane of January 1948

The small junction boxes and other electrical fittings gave forth blue flames as they expired, but the weirdest thing of all was the light over the charthouse table. This was on a long arm, and as the ship rolled from side to side some pipeful of water changed in resistance and caused the light to glow dim when we rolled to port, and bright when we went to starboard.

It would have been ghostly and unreal if it had not been for the vital force of the wind and the very real cold sea so close and full of violent life. There were other vessels in worse trouble than ourselves. One large empty freighter was drifting helplessly off New Caledonia, broadside on and carried about 200 miles off course. Our company's schooner *Resolution* was blown from the New Hebrides to the coast of New Caledonia; a yacht, which was taking part in the ocean race from New Zealand to Sydney, was blown off course, dismasted, and then so badly crushed by the heavy seas that her deck beams were split.

Our speed through the water was two whole knots, though our speed over the chart was only half of that. As the storm increased and the swell grew higher and steeper we ran into the most disturbing trouble of all. For what use is a ship when her engines stop? We were just at the top of a swell, balancing on the crest, when the bow descended and the stern flew high in the air, taking the propeller out of the water and allowing it to race madly in spite of the engineer on watch throttling her back. Then the automatic governor cut in, stopping the fuel and therefore the whole engine! The bow blew away as the wind got her and our hearts stopped beating until the engineer got her started again and we steered into the next swell. From then on, for 24 hours, the engines cut out at least once a watch. That night the centre of the hurricane had changed its mind again and made straight for us.

By 2 a.m. next morning we were at our nearest to the eye of the storm, the wind and sea at their worst, with the glass down to 29.04 inches, the lowest I had ever seen it. The wind was well over 100 knots, possibly nearer 200 in gusts. The sea was getting rather confused, as the centre was so close, and one wave struck the port surf boat on the poop and knocked it askew in its lashings. Then a great sea crashed on the port side of the bridge, tearing away part of the light deckhead and breaking a lifeboat davit adrift. The time was 2.30 a.m. and the engines were stalling every hour. The big Second Mate and I secured the loose davit and whatever we said in the emergency was overheard by the passengers in the nearby cabin and taken to be the end of everything. So they solemnly shook hands and said goodbye to each other, though we didn't know anything about it at the time, nor had we any idea of what was said between the Second Mate and myself against the screaming of the hurricane. After that, things improved rapidly. The centre of the blow went off to Lord Howe after all, not abating in fury at all. The machine recording the force of the wind at the Meteorological Station there was scribbling the graph with a shaky hand, with gusts up to 100 m.p.h. The moving finger writes, and having writ, moves on. In this case the recording pen finally moved right off the paper and the rotating drum, leaving a record of 111 m.p.h. and a large question mark on the further increase.

A day after we passed the centre, we were able to resume our course to Norfolk Island, though high seas were still running. Soon after midnight the next night a valve spring on the main engine broke and the engines had to be stopped for 17 minutes while it was replaced. When we did reach Norfolk Island, battered and weary, it was too rough to work, but we were glad at least to be able to anchor.

Next day it was still too rough and our anchor cable parted which cost us one anchor and 35 fathoms of cable. So we set off for the other side of the island close to the cliffs. On our way around, the ship suddenly turned towards the shore and refused to come back on to course. The steering gear jammed and we only avoided the rocks by going full speed astern.

After that little contretemps things settled down to normal for a few weeks. We got our next fright as we anchored in Bushman's Bay on Malekula. After dropping the anchor and ringing for full speed astern to pull us up, the engineer on watch put the engines full ahead by mistake; our repeated ringing only made him run the engines faster. By this time we were running out of chain cable and also running directly for the breakers on the reef. When we got a message down below and got back into a safe anchorage I found that it was the Chief Engineer himself who had made the mistake. When he appeared before me, with tragic face, I just burst out laughing, while he went on to tell *me* that it was no laughing matter.

After a few more trips to the Hebrides, the *Morinda* took over the run again, and we were given a new run to the Solomons, the first regular post-war service to that group of islands. On the first run up the coast of New South Wales we were overtaken by a storm, which we tried to run before, with great seas towering down on us from astern. The worst came about 2 a.m., as usual and, as we rolled badly to port, one wave broke down on us, filling a surf boat in the davits and tearing one end of the boat clean out. That left the remains of the boat hanging over the side by the falls, so I decided to turn to starboard and stop the ship, to try to recover the boat. Before anything like that could be done I was amazed to see a sea break over the ship at bridge level, over the lifeboats and around the funnel, so that my head was just above the foam. We went full ahead, resumed our course and cut away the remains of the boat before anything worse happened.

After running to the Solomons for six months, on a fast monthly service, we had to do a recruiting trip to the Gilbert Islands, to gather natives to work on the company's plantations in the Line Islands, another 1,600 miles further to the eastward.

This trip had to be done about every 18 months and at the same time the workers who had completed their contracts had to be returned to their individual Gilbert Islands. These are a chain of coral atolls, on which life is quite different from that on any other islands of the South Seas. They are well described in the book *A Pattern of Islands* by Sir Arthur Grimble.

Gilbertese maiden

At the end of each voyage in this company the Master has to submit a report of the voyage to the general manager and it may be of interest to the reader to read the report just as it was submitted after our voyage to the Gilberts.

M.V. Muliama *22 January* 1949. *Master's report for Voyage* 141*; to the General Manager, Sydney.*

Sir,—We sailed from Sydney on Saturday the 16th *October, leaving No.* 7 *Walsh Bay at* 9.46 *a.m. and, after dropping the pilot, cleared the Heads at* 10.45 *a.m. The passage to the Solomons was generally slow, with adverse winds.*

SOLOMONS. *The ship arrived at Honiara (the capital) on Sunday the* 24th*, berthing at* 9.27 *a.m. Sufficient water was taken to fill the ship's* *tanks and the spare tanks on the fore deck. We loaded 10 tons of fuel and sailed at 3.13 p.m.*

TARAWA *(capital of the Gilberts). After another slow passage we sighted Betio Islet at dusk on the 29th, and found anchorage outside the lagoon at 7.40 p.m. Next morning the ship entered the lagoon and anchored for* pratique *at 7 a.m. Owing to the slow arrival of the Senior Medical Officer, and the searching of the ship for traces of malarial mosquitoes,* pratique *was not granted until 9 a.m.; the ship then shifted closer to the beach-head.*

The discharge of cargo to Betio began at 10 a.m. and continued until 10 p.m. The next day was Sunday, so there was no work, and I took the opportunity to have the resident commissioner, H. E. Maude, and his family, off to lunch. On Monday the discharge was resumed and arrangements completed for the two recruiting trips. We sailed at 7 a.m. on Tuesday the 2nd November with William Reiher, the recruiter, and Mr. Turbott, for the Government.

TABITEUEA. *We reached this atoll at 9 a.m. on the 3rd, but the re-cruiting got away to a slow start for three reasons. The recruiter had made no previous arrangements, the Government man was inexperienced, and the natives were very difficult and argumentative. After recruiting the 80 men for Washington Island, of whom the required two-thirds were single men, it proved impossible to obtain single men for Fanning Island and 28 married men were signed on. This was done by sundown, but the embarkation took all the evening and through the night until 10.50 a.m., owing to the long drag over the tidal reefs and shallows. The trouble of getting single men may be due to Government policy of maintaining family life for the production of brown babies, but the atolls are already so overpopulated that the village policy was to have whole family units recruited to ease the food shortage on the islands. We sailed at 11 a.m. on the 4th, making a slow passage of 10 days to the Line Islands.*

The Commissioner at Tarawa had insisted on the return of Mr. Turbott to Tarawa and Reiher was anxious to be dropped at Abemama. As these diversions would have delayed our now overpopulated ship for a day or two, I arranged for the trade-scheme ship Tungaru *to do the work for us, as she was in the area. She called a week later, striking very bad weather at both Abemama, and Tabiteuea, so that she lost two days on her way to Tarawa. She is rated to cost £67 a day, and I was glad to settle for £100 for the service, as it would have cost us about twice that sum. At this time we were carrying 270 deck passengers and I thought it better to make a quick passage.*

FANNING AND WASHINGTON *(two of the Line Islands). The ship stopped off the entrance of Fanning atoll at 7 a.m. on the 14th, when Mr. Palmer, the manager, boarded us with his assistant, Hugh Greig, who acts as local pilot.   We entered the lagoon into English Harbour, moored with one anchor and two lines to the shore, in a comfortable berth, despite the constricted area of the lagoon.   The recruits for Fanning and their gear were landed with 32 tons of cargo.   At 4 p.m. the ship left the lagoon on the turn of the tide and stopped outside to take the two large surf-boats in tow, proceeding at 6.20 p.m. for Washington Island.*

Here we spent the next three days, landing the recruits and embarking the repatriates and their gear and making a start on loading the copra.   On the third day the weather went from bad to worse and the copra, after 38 tons were loaded, was postponed until the following trip.

Next morning the ship re-entered the Fanning lagoon at 7.50 a.m., and moored with the stern close enough to the jetty to get a water hose aboard.   The watering proceeded all day and night, with a further 22 tons of copra to make a total of 50 tons of ballast.   This was necessary as the ship is tender when light, and we were encumbered with extra boats and 200 very unstable deck passengers.   The next morning we shifted out the passage at 6.30 a.m. and sailed at 7.05 a.m. for the Gilberts with 124 repatriates and their 89 dependants.

GILBERT ISLANDS.   *After a fast homeward passage of seven days, which included crossing the equator, the magnetic equator and the date line, we arrived at Tabiteuea on the 26th November.   That afternoon and the next day were spent in landing the repatriates and their gear over the miles of reefs.   We sailed at 6 p.m. and arrived at Abemama at dawn.   The arrangements for the second recruiting trip were that, after embarking half the recruits at Abemama, we should proceed to Tarawa for the rest, sign them all on there, and depart once more for the Line Islands.   The beauty and simplicity of this plan were marred by the usual imperfections of the recruiter, the government, and the natives.   We entered the Abemama lagoon and anchored off the government station at 7.16 a.m.; embarked the recruits and William Reiher, and sailed at 11.30 a.m.   This day was Sunday.   As it was by this time impossible to reach and enter Tarawa before dark, we anchored at Maiana for the evening.   Mr. Palmer hoped to land his re-patriates there, but the tide was out and it was impossible for the boats to enter the lagoon.   We sailed at 2.30 a.m., and anchored inside Tarawa lagoon at 7.40 next morning.   The recruiting, medical inspection and signing-on proceeded all day, but in the evening Reiher reported that as it had been impossible to recruit enough single men for Fanning, he had signed on married men, instead, without any authority.   Next morning Mr. Palmer had these men's contracts cancelled, at the cost of a day's rations, and we decided to try Kuria atoll for single recruits.*

We sailed from Tarawa at 10.43 a.m. on the 30th November, anchoring at Maiana in the afternoon to drop repatriates.   Next day we called at Kuria, but were unable to get any recruits owing to the lack of warning, this atoll being without a radio. We moved over to Abemama in the afternoon, anchoring in the lagoon at 2.30 p.m. A few men were obtained here, the ship moved out before dusk, with the boats following, and we sailed at 7.42 p.m. for the Line Islands. The passage eastwards was again slow, taking ten and a half days this time.

FANNING AND WASHINGTON. *We arrived off English Harbour at 4 a.m. on 11th December and the ship entered and moored as soon as the tide served. As the weather reports had been continuing good at Washington Island we decided to make all speed there to take a load of copra, postponing our intended visit to Christmas Island until later. The 11th and 12th were spent at Fanning discharging all the copra ballast, the Christmas cargo and recruits, and filling the fuel tanks from the drums in the hold to make more room for copra.*

The spare lifeboats were landed, and the ship generally prepared for the rigours of cargo work at Washington. Mr. Palmer gave us enough men to work the ship and boats, with Mr. Greig as overseer, two large surf-boats, and a small submersible launch to assist in the work on bad days. We loaded copra for the next four days and while the weather was classed as " workable," and proved to be so, it would not have been regarded as workable in any other place.

The ship returned to Fanning to discharge on the 17th and all the copra was landed by the next afternoon. On Sunday the 19th we left Fanning and spent the next five days loading the rest of the 600 tons of copra at Washington. During this period the weather was dangerous for boat-work and the large surf-boats got out of control several times in the breakers. One of them was

Loading copra in surf at Washington Island

Boat-work at
Washington Island

carried on to the western reefs and washed right ashore without any crew but without any damage. It was dragged along the beach to the passage and launched again into the work. Apart from minor delays the work was only stopped on one occasion, for two hours on the 22nd, when the surf became impossible at high tide. The ship's launch was several times caught under breakers, but managed to make the surface again each time because it was kept bow-on to the breakers.

The success of the copra-transfer was due to the manager, Mr. Garrett, and the way in which Hugh Greig kept the natives at work in the boats in the face of difficulties and danger. There was also a great deal of good luck in the operation, for past records of Washington Island show an average of 25 tons a day for loading, and only half the days of the year are workable. We averaged 60 tons a day, as the 600 tons took a total of ten working days.

We sailed from Washington on Christmas Eve, and called at Fanning on Christmas Day. We re-loaded the recruits and cargo between 9 a.m. and noon, and sailed for Christmas Island.

CHRISTMAS ISLAND. This island was reached at midday on Boxing Day, when the recruits and cargo were landed, and also a government officer to relieve Harold Markham as manager of the island. During the night *the repatriates were loaded with their gear, which amounted to about one ton per man, either food saved from their rations or gear salved from the American air-base. This was completed about 2.30 a.m., and Mr. Markham joined as a passenger for Sydney with 80 dozen tern eggs for our breakfasts.*

FANNING ISLAND. *After stopping off the atoll at midnight, we made the passage at dawn and entered the lagoon at 6.35 a.m., mooring again close enough to get the water-hose aboard. The next two days were spent in discharging the 267 tons of copra from Washington, watering and fuelling the ship, and loading the empty drums on deck. The ship shifted outside the lagoon at dusk, completed the loading of drums and repatriates, and sailed for the final run to the Gilbert Islands at 7.43 p.m. We made the run in seven and a half days to Tarawa, which gave a speed of nine knots.*

Submersible launch

TARAWA. *The ship entered the lagoon and anchored at 8.27 a.m. on the 7th January. The repatriates and their gear were landed in the boats, and 13 tons of fresh water were loaded into the ship's tanks. The empty fuel drums dumped here earlier in the voyage were filled with salt water to serve as 20 tons of ballast. Owing to the ship's good behaviour on the run from Fanning and the fair weather now obtaining, I decided to proceed on the voyage without further delay. It was unfortunate that we were prohibited from taking Washington copra as ballast, particularly as none was available in the Solomons. We sailed from Tarawa at dusk and made a good passage to the Solomons.*

HONIARA. *We made this port at 4.52 p.m. on the 12th January and started by landing all the empty drums. Those containing water had to be emptied. The fuel remaining in the hold in drums amounted to 14 tons, of which 7 were poured into the fuel tanks, and the remainder put ashore as a reserve for next trip. Our reserve of 20 tons at Yandina was not touched. We loaded 250 tons of scrap metal and then the empty drums, which filled the remaining space. The ship sailed at 7.35 p.m. next day.*

Carrying copra

During the voyage the Chief Officer proved more than usually difficult and obstructive. I regret to report that his advice, when proffered, was of a nature to deter my navigation, slow up the cargo working and generally delay the ship. His tactlessness and abject pessimism brought us no goodwill from the shore people and tended to poison the otherwise happy atmosphere of the ship. The only serious trouble with the natives arose when he pushed one out of his way, and was promptly assaulted and knocked down. I placed the native under " house arrest " on the fo'c'sle, and on our arrival at Fanning charged him before the district officer, who fined him £5.

The ship's main radio transmitter has been out of action since the early part of the voyage, as the motor-alternator broke down on the 29th October. The Teleradio set, only installed on this trip, was therefore of great value, and made possible the co-operation needed to effect the transfer of copra from Washington to Fanning. The time saved by its use in making detailed arrangements before arriving at the island ports must be counted in many hours, amounting to a day or two for the trip. On our next voyage, to the New Hebrides, our calls will be greatly facilitated by the Teleradio, and I trust that the set will be retained aboard for future voyages.

The ship is due to arrive in Sydney on the 22nd January, after a voyage lasting three months and six days, and entailing a distance steamed of 13,200 miles. The time we saved was partly due to taking the ship inside Fanning atoll, which she had not done before. The nine passengers for Sydney include the wife and two daughters of Mr. Palmer of Fanning, Mr. Markham of Christmas, Mr. Tregenza and two sons of Fanning cable station, and the two sons of Mr. Lawson, our agent at Honiara.

Trusting that this voyage will meet with your approval,

I remain, Sir,

Yours faithfully,

Brett Hilder,

Master.

The voyage did indeed meet with the approval of the company, and we all got a bonus as a result and to compensate us for the added discomforts of the voyage with the ship overloaded with the natives. My bonus was £100 and this was the only occasion that I have had a bonus from the company in my 33 years of service, so it was really an historic end to the Gilbertese trip.

During the remainder of 1949 the *Muliama* and I paid visits to various other unexpected places, in addition to our regular ports of call in the Solomons. In my spare time I did all sorts of strange jobs, including scattering people's ashes in the sea. The first instance of this was when old Captain Bayldon died in Sydney. He had been a Master in our company from about 1905 and he had

made a name for himself by doing hydrographic work in the uncharted parts of the islands. He left the sea in 1910 to start a navigation school in Sydney, which he gave up 40 years later, just before
he died. The League of Ancient Mariners asked me to scatter his
ashes in the Solomons, over the Bayldon Shoals which he had charted
just outside the harbour of Tulagi. The Chief Engineer and I
opened the tin of ashes and we had a round of drinks, giving the
ashes one to damp them down and so prevent them from blowing
all over the ship in the wind.

The next occasion was the death of Richard Swinburne, a
nephew of the poet. His unfortunate ashes were scattered in the
sea near Santo, where I had known him years before. I'm sure he
appreciated the final drink we shared with him in farewell.

During this year my researches into obscure branches of navigation had borne some fruit. After becoming a member of the
newly-formed Institute of Navigation in England, I spent part of
my annual leave in Sydney gathering a similar crowd of men together
to form the Australian Institute of Navigation, which has since
grown into a society of repute. We were lucky in getting the
immediate support of Dr. E. G. Bowen, who had been an early
worker on cosmic rays, then the assistant to Sir Robert Watson-Watt
who invented radar and developed it during the war; afterwards
Dr. Bowen had become the head of the radio-physics section of
the C.S.I.R.O. He has been in the forefront of the new science of
radio astronomy and several subjects dealing with air navigation.
Quite a number of important developments have been made in
Australia in navigational science and Dr. "Taffy" Bowen has
been in charge of most of them.

The sooty tern of the Line Islands

Chapter Sixteen

Old mail coach of the South Seas

AFTER TWO YEARS IN THE *Muliama* I WAS PROMOTED TO MY old steamer *Morinda*, in which I had served as Third Mate 16 years before. She was still on the run to the Hebrides and she had not improved with age. She was getting on for 40 years of age and, during the next two years, we were to do ten voyages together, including her last famous voyage, without getting into too much serious trouble. After the little *Muliama* the *Morinda* seemed to have neither power nor any manoeuvrability to speak of. Her speed was still as uncertain as ever.

On our first two voyages we arrived at Lord Howe unexpectedly in the middle of the night, after fixing her position at dusk by the stars and being sure that she wouldn't get us there till morning. We had neither radar nor echo-sounder and the only radio-aid on the island, as at Norfolk Island, was a radio-range for the use of aircraft. This was on a wavelength that we could tune into from the ship, to get an approximate bearing after some manoeuvring and would have been useful in bad weather when we could neither get astro-sights nor see the island by eye. But fortunately it never came to this sad state. Her behaviour in the small rocky anchorages of Lord Howe and Norfolk was not at all reassuring to a new ship-master. When the wind blew hard and the sea rose, we had to beat out of the anchorage like an old windjammer on a lee shore, for her bow just wouldn't come up into the wind. So I had to redouble our precautions, by anchoring with more elbow-room, and being ready to move out before the weather made a move too dangerous.

Even leaving the port of Sydney the old ship could misbehave and on one occasion, with a strong gale from the southward, she wouldn't steer properly, or even normally. On this occasion the bow was well down in the water and the superstructure on the poop was caught by the wind-pressure, so it was the bow which kept coming up into wind. Passing each point of wharves or headland she would steer straight, but as we passed each bay her bow turned right into wind despite the helm being hard a port.

By performing a kind of waltz we sidled out to sea, though we were heading in all directions for a time and caused some anxiety in the harbour. Another time we put to sea into heavy weather from Sydney and, before we had gone five miles, we had the fore deck flooded and the deck cargo adrift from its lashings. So I put her right back into harbour and we stayed the night at anchor after re-stowing and re-lashing the deck cargo.

After calling at Lord Howe and Norfolk Islands we made the usual calls in the New Hebrides, then made back for Sydney. The produce of the New Hebrides is mostly copra, which is all sold to France, as no other market will take such poor and ungraded copra. We were always short of return cargo for Sydney, which we needed as ballast as well as freight-earning cargo.

On some trips we only got about 30 tons of produce from Vila and Santo, mostly cocoa and sandalwood; the only other cargo available was timber in logs from Aneityum. This depended on the weather, as wet weather made the logging roads impassable, so that there were occasions when we got no logs at all. I had suggested to the company that the ship should extend her run to the Solomons,

s.s. Morinda

Morinda loading logs
at *Tenaru*

where we could get a return cargo and this finally was decided upon. Our last two calls at Aneityum rather forced this decision.

On one voyage we got very few logs and the ship was so light in the bow that she pounded heavily in a cyclone we struck, although we had hove-to in plenty of time. Some of her bottom plates were dented, which was a bad sign in such an old ship.

On the following trip we were still in the centre of the Hebrides when a hurricane formed near Santo and started bearing down on us from the nor'west. We made for Aneityum with all despatch, to get some logs as ballast before we had to face the force of the storm. We had a day or two to spare for the job but, when we anchored in the open harbour at Aneityum, the swell from the hurricane was coming through the entrance and the ship insisted on lying broadside onto it, as there was no wind as yet.

She was rolling very badly to the swell, which slowed up the loading of the logs. Most of the logs were big ones, up to eight tons, and therefore had to be loaded at our main hatch by the " jumbo " derrick. We wanted to get her bow down as much as we could, so the lighter logs all went into the fore hatch.

On the second day of loading, the swell was causing the ship to roll so badly that the heavy logs would first crash into the ship's side when they were hoisted out of the water, then they swung across the deck and over the far side: on the return roll they were dropped as they passed over the hatch and went down below with sickening bumps into the coamings and other parts of the old ship's structure. The work was highly dangerous and the main hold and its tween

decks were nearly full. As dusk got close I decided to finish off
loading and put to sea while we could and the last log broke the guys
of the jumbo before it settled into the hatch, completely filling the
last space in the coaming.

The beams and hatches were hurriedly fitted and covered with
tarpaulins, which were battened down, before hoisting the boats
and the launch. The local manager had lit the two leading lights
to guide us out safely, but by the time we were all secured for sea,
and for the hurricane, night was falling fast and one of the leading
lights had blown out. We picked our way out the passage between
the reefs, with the last dim twilight, and found ourselves safely at
sea to fight out the storm.

The wind was now strong from the north, and the swell about
nor'west. The centre of the blow should pass over Aneityum, so
I decided to run south with all speed to get as far away from the
centre as possible before we were forced to heave-to.

Running before a storm can be quite a thrill. The swell was so
great that the old ship was making feeble attempts to " shoot the
breakers," but she only succeeded in wallowing and surging forward
alternately, at an average speed of eight knots.

The ship, unfortunately, slid sideways down some of the waves,
which shook the logs about in the tween decks. All the logs there
were lashed with wires and tommed off with timber, but these
precautions proved too weak for the eight-ton logs under the very
violent accelerations and decelerations. Once the logs started to
move in their lashings, nothing would hold them. The wires tore
out of their shackles and the shackles tore out of the beams and
frames of the old ship. The tween deck was full of narrow stanchions
and these bent and fractured when the logs leant against them too
hard. Finally the logs had nothing left to restrain them except the
sides of the ship, and they weren't of unlimited strength. Several
times the crew had to re-lash the logs and they used up all the wooden
hatches in the decks, but to no avail. After running before the
storm for 20 hours the time had come for us to heave-to while it
was still safe for us to do so.

So the engine-room saved up a good head of steam, we picked
a calm patch just after two large swells had passed us and put the
helm hard a-starboard. It seemed to take ages for the ship to turn
and we seemed to be broadside on to the swell for a long time, but
luckily no great waves assailed us. The wind had risen to gale force
by this time, so it was difficult for the bow to turn into wind, but
eventually we made it, then eased right down to slow revs. We

could now concentrate on keeping the ship as calm and quiet as possible, to minimise the violent actions of the waves, and save the logs from wrecking the ship.

In the lower hold were four large stanchions holding in the heavy logs and nothing could have bent them, or so the builders thought. The strange thing about the logs in the square of the hold was that they had originally been piled right up to the deck beams, so that the beams could just be fitted into place. But now we found that the logs were six feet below the beams, and where had the lower ones gone to? Perhaps into the double-bottom tanks. At least they were still with us, as they definitely had not gone right through the bottom.

The logs in the tween decks took all our attention, for they played up every time we turned our backs; one of them went from No. 2 tween deck to No. 1 tween deck, ploughing through some cargo on the way, as well as ploughing up the wooden deck like a rogue bulldozer. The rest of the stanchions by this time had all been either bent or had snapped like carrots. This meant that the tween decks were no longer firmly attached to the upper deck, which carried the weight of the winches above, and I was getting more than anxious for the general integrity of the old *Morinda*.

Apart from the more alarming moments, when a big log would get adrift and try to batter its way to freedom through the ship's lean side and hungry ribs, there were some lighter moments. One of our passengers spent 24 hours trying to soothe his wife's nerves with tots of whisky which she declined, so he had to drink it himself. About one every five minutes, just " as the doctor ordered."

After 24 hours, hove-to waiting to see which way the blow would pass, it apparently recurved to the eastward and the seas eased off.

The eruption of Ambrym Island, 1951

We were supposed to call at Norfolk Island, but as work would be impossible there for perhaps a week, we by-passed the island and only called briefly at Lord Howe on our way to Sydney. There the ship was surveyed and repaired and as our voyage was extended to the Solomons we saw no more of Aneityum and its logs.

About this period the island of Ambrym in the Hebrides started a period of violent eruption, covering the neighbouring plantations with ashes and finally driving away most of the local natives to other islands. One result of the eruption was to form a thick haze of the finer dust, reducing visibility near the island to barely 100 yards at times, while clouds of dust travelled around at various layers of the atmosphere for hundreds of miles.

Another result of the volcanic activity was the emergence of a new island, formed by a small cone of pumice building up out of the sea as a volcano. It got to about 250 feet in height before it stopped and we steamed close by to get bearings to fix its position accurately on the chart. One of the first men to land on the island called it after a girl-friend, Karua, and that is the name the Admiralty used at our suggestion, when it was added to the official charts. I don't know if it is still there, as the seas may have eroded it away since then. Previously there was an island in the same place for a year or two around 1900, before it sank beneath the waves again.

During 1950 one of my hobbies suddenly took a serious turn. This arose from my drawings and paintings of the natives of the East Indies which I had started in Malaya after the war. The natives of the East are very colourful, but it was their racial types of features which caught my interest and started me drawing and painting them in watercolours. When I got back to the South Seas

Karua Island erupting out of the sea in 1949

I kept up the practice, painting all shapes and shades of natives from yellow to blue-black. These paintings amounted to a complete catalogue of the racial types of the western Pacific. It was suggested by the President of the Royal Art Society that an exhibition of my work in Sydney would be of general interest, particularly as I had had no training in art.

It just happened that some publicity for my paintings turned up at the right moment and the exhibition was quite a success, leading to others in the following years. These have been held in Melbourne, Port Moresby in New Guinea, Honiara in the Solomons, and even one in New York. I had also been making drawings of the traders, planters, officials and missionaries of the islands, which are published one a month with a short biography, in the *Pacific Islands Monthly*. Quite a number of my characters have appeared in the books by James Michener, who made his name by writing *Tales of the South Pacific* and *Return to Paradise*. Indeed he wanted me to illustrate the latter book with sketches of typical islands people, but the publishers wouldn't agree to any illustrations at all.

My next unusual job was to design a series of postage stamps for the small territory of Norfolk Island. The designs covered the island's colourful history from the discovery by Cook in 1774 to the building of the air-strip in 1943. Unfortunately they were not accepted by the Australian Stamp Printer, who used photo-

Sketching the control tower on Henderson Field

graphs instead, for the new set of stamps. The Government are
still holding my designs and there is still hope that they may yet be
used for Norfolk Island. On top of this came an open competition
for designs of Solomon Islands stamps, with prizes of £25 sterling for
any designs accepted. Out of eight new stamps, three of my designs
were used; they were issued on March 1 1956.

One of my Solomons designs showed Mendaña and his ship
and I had a very difficult job to find a picture of Mendaña; the
only picture ever used is a German one, no doubt painted from pure
imagination and I could have done without it, by using myself
and beard as a model. This design is on the five shilling stamp and
I could only afford to buy one for my collection; had it been something like 1½d., I could have bought a whole sheet.

During the last year of the *Morinda's* life we carried no doctor and
the Second Officer, a sensitive young bachelor, had to act as medical
officer. He used the prescribed text-book, the *Shipmaster's Medical
Guide*, which is worth its weight in gold. When he couldn't find a
particular ailment in the index he used to seek my advice, like
consulting a specialist.

He came to me one day to ask what was dyspepsia. I asked
first who was complaining of it; when he replied that it was a stoker
from the engine-room I told him that dyspepsia was only permitted
to the upper classes and that the man must have some much more
common complaint. After he had gained some more confidence
in himself and the textbook he made a mistake which caused him
great embarrassment. A lady passenger reported to him that she
was suffering from " pilitis." He took it to be another item in the
index, as " pilitis " is not shown there, but " piles " are shown of
course. Poor Paddy was too shy to attempt to examine the lady's
anatomy and finally gave her some medicine mentioned in the
book as good for piles and she went away and never came back for
more. Perhaps she was disappointed in the handsome young
medical officer, but she might have had worse befall her.

At last the *Morinda's* time was coming to an end. She was to
do two more trips and then be sold, as she was due for a big survey
by Lloyd's and this would have proved too expensive. She was
nearly 40 years old and had a rough life in the island runs, having sat
on many a coral reef and once was burnt out in a fire in her cargo
of copra, when she had to be scuttled in Sydney Harbour to put the
fire out. It was only by good luck and great care that I had been
able to keep her out of trouble myself.

What was intended to be her second last voyage turned out to be her last and it was full of troubles and other incidents. The voyage included Christmas and New Year, which was perhaps the excuse for some of the crew breaking into the special cargo locker and stealing some whisky and cartons of beer two days after leaving Sydney.

We had to search all the crew's accommodation and found some of the loot in an engineer's cabin, though he was brand new in the ship and only an accessory after the act. He had to be logged and promised the sack when we got back to Sydney. Then the Third Engineer fell sick and had to be landed at Norfolk Island.

A day after leaving Norfolk we ran into a hurricane, but as it was only just gaining strength we were able to carry on, eat our Christmas dinner, and still make for the island of Efate, where we got some shelter and came to the port of Vila.

We were crawling along towards the port at 4 a.m. on Boxing Day when the Chief Engineer reported that he was having some trouble with the old boilers. We were only just moving through the water, at about four knots, but we entered the port and anchored at exactly 6 a.m. I was just going for a bath when a tremendous hissing roar arose from the innards of the ship and vast clouds of smoke and steam billowed out from the funnel, ventilators, fidley-hatch and stoke-hold. All the decks and passages filled with cloud, as I listened for any sound of injured men down below.

Fortunately all the watch in the stoke-hold were up out of the way and when the steam subsided we found that one of our two main boilers had come down in the furnace; it was therefore out of action for the rest of the voyage.

This meant that we were very short of steam, which was needed to generate electricity, drive the water-pumps, run the refrigeration machinery and blow the whistle, as well as to operate the rudder and, most important of all, to turn the old propeller around sufficiently to get us to the Solomons and back to Sydney. As the one boiler couldn't manage all this we decided to cut out all the refrigeration. This meant selling all the frozen cargo for ports beyond Vila and eking out our frozen meat as long as it would stay cool in the chambers.

Of course we couldn't expect to break any speed records, but we did succeed in making an average speed of six knots, and that had to drop to almost nothing each time the furnaces were cleaned. My main consideration was to get a safe speed for manoeuvring and we had to bear our infirmity in mind both coasting along the islands and in passing through reef passages and anchorages. We got full co-operation from the crew, particularly the stokers, so our main discomfort in the tropics was the lack of cool drinks.

During the voyage there were some complications of the usual shipboard romances and the pursers and officers had their work cut out to keep the passengers actively engaged in all sorts of entertainments. We had run out of fresh meat and vegetables by the time we left the Solomons and the company had arranged to send us some supplies by the *Muliama*. We met her at sea and, as the weather was calm, we were able to use our launch and boats to collect some live sheep and crates of vegetables. While the two ships were stopped in company in the Coral Sea I took the opportunity to go aboard the *Muliama* and take a photograph of the *Morinda* on her last voyage; perhaps the only time a shipmaster has been able to do this himself, from another ship at sea.

Chapter Seventeen

Voyages of trouble

CAPTAINS OF SHIPS TRADING AROUND THE SOUTH SEAS OFTEN have the unfortunate experience of stranding on coral reefs. And I must confess that I am no exception to the rule. There are many more reefs than there are ships and it is not regarded as so culpable if your ship decides to sit herself on a reef which no other ship has sat before. It is inexcusable to run on to a reef where there is already a wrecked ship in occupation and there are quite a lot of these in the Pacific, largely due to the exigencies of the Pacific War.

The best one can hope for is to be able to prove that your particular reef is not shown on the charts; another means of expiation is to get your ship off the reef again and complete her voyage without further incident. In spite of my share of bad luck with reefs I have become more proficient at getting ships off coral reefs than in stranding them there. At present my account is in credit on this score and I hope it will remain so.

My worst stranding was committed in blissful over-confidence, while I was doing one relieving voyage in the *Mangola*. Early one morning we were approaching the southern coast of New Guinea, making for the entrance in the barrier reef which protects the fine harbour of Port Moresby. There was some moonlight, lighting up the sea in patches between the clouds, which made it difficult to sight the line of breakers on the seaward edge of the reef.

The lighted beacon at the reef entrance came into sight on our starboard bow, just where it had to be, and the lights of the town also showed up by the time we saw the breakers on our starboard beam. Our course appeared to be keeping the breakers about one mile distant and we were only a few miles from the entrance when the unbelievable occurred. The ship was fully laden, displacing about 8,000 tons, and making about 10 knots, when a low rumbling and series of bumps suggested that we were running aground. I rang " full astern " on the engines, but we were hard and fast before they could have the slightest effect.

Some rapid cross bearings showed that we were ashore on a projecting ledge of the reef where there were no breakers at the time, owing to the calmness of the sea. We were in 17 feet of water amidships and in a dangerous position if the wind and sea arose with the normal trade wind. By dawn, we had sounded the ship to make sure she wasn't taking any water and also sounded around the ship to find that we had over 100 fathoms under the stern and therefore no hope of heaving her off with anchors.

We pumped out all the water possible, to lighten the ship, and called for assistance from the local shipping. On the fore-deck we had a lot of heavy cargo vehicles which we transferred during the day to various small ships. After an abortive attempt at getting off at high water, about 11 a.m., we carried on with the lightening of the ship and made arrangements to try again at midnight. The sea remained calm, but the gentle motion caused the ship to groan and strain in an agonising way and at low tide the strain caused some buckling and tearing of the double-bottom tanks and part of the bunker hatch, which was very weak.

At 11 p.m. we got a couple of small ships to take our lines, ready to help us to drag ourselves off the reef. As the tide rose we felt the ship getting more lively in her motion and sure enough we were able to get her off by going full astern on the main engines.

Under the turtle ensign of the Solomon Islands

We proceeded into port and managed to complete the whole voyage around New Guinea and back to Australia. On our return to Sydney the ship was dry-docked after discharging all the cargo and she was then surveyed and repaired.

The repairs were extensive and expensive, for most of the old ship's bottom from the bow to the engine-room had to be completely rebuilt. The cost added up to £38,000, and took two months to complete, so that she missed a whole voyage. This was all very serious and it was in great trepidation that I went to see the general manager to hear what he had to say. This was indeed something quite unexpected. For his first words to me were, " Well, it's no good crying over spilt milk ! " and I could have fallen on his neck and kissed him.

About three years later, when the *Morinda* had suddenly gone out of action, I was sent on another relieving trip, this time in the *Malaita*, also to New Guinea. This was my best command, a fine passenger ship of fairly modern vintage, and having passed the dangerous age of 40 myself I thought that I had settled down to a quiet life. After leaving Brisbane, our first port of call was Samarai. We reached the port at night on April 1, entered by a safe passage and anchored for the night.

We had run into a cyclone in the Coral Sea and all the deck cargo had broken adrift in the heavy seas. The ship had also rolled badly, much to my surprise, and we had to heave-to to get the deck cargo safely lashed again. When dawn broke in Samarai it was April 2 and the 21st anniversary of the wreck of the *Malabar*. We got a signal from the local manager to say which way the tide was running at the wharf, where it is unpredictable. Then we blew a loud blast on the whistle to clear the small craft away from the wharf and fairway; they all got clear except one small yacht at anchor, which had no crew aboard.

This forced us to make our approach at a bad angle, to go starboard side to the wharf. As we passed the yacht and got close to the wharf we found that the tide was running with us, instead of against us, and we had no hope of getting alongside.

The tide swung us past the wharf, as it turned us around, and I decided to swing the ship completely around and go alongside port side to. This had only one objection, a small shallow patch of coral somewhere about where we were swinging. All the water is shallow enough for the coral bottom to be visible and it is therefore difficult to see the shallower patch on which there is 19 feet of water. There was once a beacon on this patch, for all our ships on the New

Guinea run had bumped it at some time or other, the last one being the *Montoro*, which knocked the beacon down and it was to be replaced at a later date. Now, 15 years later, the Government had just voted the funds for its building, when our stern stuck on it and stayed there. We were drawing about 20 feet aft at the time, so were only just fast on it by a few feet of the keel. We were still so close to the wharf that we were able to run two headlines to it, but our attempts to pull the ship off were unsuccessful. We waited for high water, about 2 p.m., when we tried again. After about an hour she slid off very much ashamed of herself and meekly went to the wharf to be tied up. The damage was negligible, just a couple of dented plates from our efforts to get her off by having the bow towed from side to side.

My next three voyages were in the *Muliama*. The first of these was a short run to Port Moresby and back, which took only three weeks, but there was a lot of minor engine trouble which entailed a few stoppages at sea.

On the second trip we were bound up the Australian coast on our way to the Solomons when our troubles commenced. After the first 24 hours of gentle steaming we were just passing the Solitary Islands with their neighbouring rocks about 8 p.m., when our main engines ran hot and had to be stopped for repairs. After 3½ hours we got under way, but had to stop again before the night was through. So we made for the anchorage in Byron Bay in the morning, and did what repairs might suffice for the rest of the voyage. We left the bay at about 3 p.m. and at dusk we were just passing the reefs of Danger Point when we had to stop again. I decided that we would call at Brisbane for repairs, instead of setting out with sick engines across the Coral Sea.

After two days in Brisbane things were fixed for the trip, by an emergency arrangement of the water-cooling system for the main and auxiliary motors, but this had its limitations.

We got to the Solomons without undue incidents and secured to the decaying wartime wharf, in the sheltered port of Tulagi, the ancient capital of the Solomons. While we were discharging our cargo here for two days the auxiliary motors played up, one giving up the ghost altogether, and another behaving " in a manner unfitting " to a piece of diesel machinery. These little troubles delayed the cargo work, so that it was dark before we were ready to sail, and we had to organise two hurricane lights to be placed on the leading beacons to enable us to get out of the port safely through the surrounding reefs.

We left the wharf at 8 p.m.; a minute later, the Chief Engineer arrived on the bridge to ask me to return to the wharf as there appeared to be something seriously wrong with the main motor. It was indeed making a heavy thumping sound, but instead of returning to the wharf we anchored off. For several hours we pulled pieces of engine adrift, put it together again and tested it, then started pulling another piece adrift. This went on till about 2 a.m., without any trace being found of the trouble.

By this time the lights had gone out, but the moon had risen and we made our way very gingerly out of the harbour by the pale light of the moon and checked our position continuously by means of cross bearings. Taking a calculated risk like this doesn't generally get a ship into trouble; perhaps because so much care is being taken at the time. On other occasions when there appears to be no risk, trouble is likely to arrive without any warning. The result is very shattering to confidence and the effect is very lasting on the nerves.

The 55 mile run across the Ironbottom Sound from Tulagi to Yandina produced no further knocking in the engines; in fact the cause of this was never discovered. But at Yandina another problem presented itself. Some of my officers have been heard to mutter "Never a dull moment" but I'm sure it's not all my fault. In this case a schooner of 100 tons, the *Matoma*, had run on a reef

Trading schooner Miena

three weeks before and, despite all efforts, she was still sitting there, about three miles from Yandina.

A radio from Lloyd's agents in Rabaul, who happened to be also a branch of my company, asked me to attempt the salvage. They did this without reference to head office, who were my real owners, but the matter was arranged with the owners of the *Matoma*, who were Lever Brothers, the soap people. This big firm owns a lot of copra plantations in the Solomons and there has always been a lot of co-operation between them and my company.

The *Matoma* was sitting in a precarious position on the edge of a reef, where she had been badly battered by two storms. Although she was in about 10 feet of water, the reef dropped away so steeply that 100 yards away it was over 100 fathoms; in fact the nearest sounding on the chart showed 161 fathoms. The difficulty about this was that it would be impossible to anchor the *Muliama* at a safe distance during our attempts to tow the *Matoma* off.

The skipper of the *Matoma* was my well loved friend, Ernie Palmer; he and his devoted crew had been working themselves to shadows in trying to refloat the lovely old schooner and I was determined to make the utmost efforts to help them.

After inspecting the *Matoma* underwater and surveying the neighbourhood, I had to work out a plan for keeping the *Muliama* from bumping the reef in the long process of making fast to the *Matoma*. Once the attempts to tow commenced, the danger of having no freedom of manoeuvre would be all the greater. When my plans were ready, we held a council of war aboard the ship, to plan the details. As it would call for extra effort by the main engines, whose health was doubtful, the Chief Engineer had to carry a big share of responsibility. Levers had to provide the help of a ketch, the *Cape Torrens* and also a small launch for inter-communication, while our launch would stand by the bow of the *Cape Torrens*, while she in turn had a line from our bow to help us to keep in position.

When all was ready, we left the wharf at Yandina and stopped off the scene of the wreck. We lowered one anchor down to 60 fathoms; the other was left in the hawsepipe and the cable from it hove out of the chain locker and ranged the full length of the deck and out over the stern for the towing. This gives a much stronger towline than anything else available and, when the weight comes on it, the strain is taken by the anchor in the hawsepipe, the strongest part of the ship.

We could not hope to anchor the ship near the wreck in 60

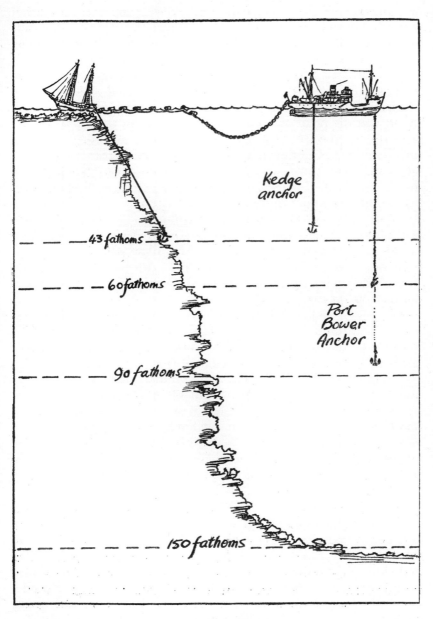

Salvage of schooner Matoma
by m.v. Muliama, 1952

fathoms and still be clear of the reef, so we hung a kedge anchor over the quarter, by the mainmast, on 40 fathoms of mooring line so that the ship could lie alongside the reef without actually bumping on it. It took about an hour to connect our cable up with the tow.

The *Matoma* had been filled with empty drums to ensure her floating and not sinking when we got her off and a double strop of wire ran right around her hull to a big shackle under her stern, which was the point of towing. From this point some heavy wires were run out towards us, buoyed at intervals to keep them near the surface instead of getting foul on the reef. These wires were shackled on to our chain cable, which was then veered out to its full length, so that the heavy bight of the cable would provide an elastic connection between the two ships.

A set of signals had been arranged for all the important stages of the attempt and when the tow was secured we all took a deep breath and moved into position. The *Cape Torrens* had a line from our bow, as we moved away from the reef. There was a strong tide running past, which would have carried us around and dumped us on the reef as we were helplessly secured by the stern to the wreck and therefore unable to steer ourselves. The *Cape Torrens* had to do this for us. If things went wrong we were ready to drop the tow by unshackling the cable, but this may have taken too long and was therefore a calculated risk.

At last we were in position and commenced to tow, but soon after we had really taken the weight of the *Matoma* she signalled to stop, as the wire strop had parted at some portion of the tow. We managed to get back into our anchored position while the tow was all unshackled and by the time this was finished it was getting on for dusk; there was obviously no time for a further attempt that day. So back we went to Yandina to load copra and arranged to make another attempt next day at high water again.

By the next afternoon we had loaded all the available copra, which gave us some useful weight in the water. The abortive attempt had been a valuable experience and had given us all a lot of confidence. The *Matoma* had been girdled by a much stronger strop and there were no weak links in any parts of the tow. One added complication was that there was a coral rock or " nigger-head " under the stern of the *Matoma*, so she would first have to be slewed clear of this before she could be towed off.

Everything was done as before and after an hour we were ready for the main attempt. So we pushed out from the reef, taking the strain of the cable and increased speed to maximum power ahead.

I could see that this hardly took the droop out of the cable and there-upon decided to try to increase the pull by sudden jerks. This is contrary to accepted practice and might break the towline, but I had to try everything I could think of.

The actual pull of the main engines was only about five tons, which is strange but true. So I stopped the engines and allowed the ship to drop astern until the tow was slack. Then a sudden burst of full power ahead gave the ship a good start before the weight came on with a sudden jerk. We managed to slew the *Matoma* round, ready for towing off. Then we backed towards her again and gave her a bigger jerk. Each time we did this we put more weight on, until the jerk must have been close to the breaking strain of our cable and, as it pulled us to a sudden stop, the towing cable actually pulled so tight that it came right out of the water. Finally, after backing as close to the wreck as I dared, we gave one God-almighty burst which pulled the cable five feet out of the water and should have broken something, but instead produced shouts of joy as the *Matoma* shuddered off the reef into deep water. Then we had to hold ourselves in position for nearly an hour while the tow was hove in and unshackled and handed over to the *Torrens* to take the *Matoma* away to a safe anchorage at her home port of Lingatu.

This adventure resulted in salvage money being paid by Levers, my share being £100. It was also written up in Lloyd's Calendar for 1954 and 1955, together with a later salvage success of the same kind. We finished the trip without any more excitements.

My third voyage in the *Muliama* was also a memorable one. We got to the Solomons and back to the Australian coast without anything more than the usual engine trouble. We had just passed Brisbane on the way to Sydney, with less than 500 miles to go, when we had an unexpected shock. It was 1 p.m., a sunny day with a calm sea, just the weather we sign on for, when the long-suffering Chief Engineer, Jock Burnett of Aberdeen, appeared with anxious face. " Come and have a look at this," he said, and we both went to the engine-room skylights to look down at an amazing scene. For the engine-room was flooded to the floor-plates and small wavelets were breaking as the ship slowly rolled in the gentle swell !

The water was apparently coming from some broken pipe in one of the pumping lines, but as all the pipes were now under water and under the floor-gratings, there wasn't a hope of seeing which pipe had sprung a leak. To stop the inflow of water we stopped all the pumps, which meant we had to stop the main and auxiliary motors and everything came to a standstill, including the ship. The inflow then apparently ceased, as the waterlevel didn't rise.

The next question was how to get rid of the water without starting up any pumps. We had no time to lose, because the water was already splashing into the electric generators, which don't like salt water in their innards. So we had to call all hands on deck, and form two chains of buckets to actually bale out the engine-room! That this could be necessary in the year 1952 was incredible, but there was no other way. One line of buckets was passed from hand to hand up the steel ladders to the tweendecks, where the buckets of oily water were poured down the ladies' lavatory; another gang pulled up buckets with heaving lines and emptied them on the main deck. After four hours' bailing, the water was down sufficiently for the engineers to get at the pipes: the broken one was located, and then all the other pumps and pipes and motors could be got going, and we were on our way once more. The broken pipe was not between the hull and a pump, but fortunately on the inboard side of a pump, or otherwise the water would have continued to flood the ship even after all the pumps were stopped. This was later the cause of the loss of the *Joyita* out in the mid-Pacific, in October 1955, when she was abandoned as sinking but stayed afloat while all her crew and passengers were lost without trace. This caused all sorts of wild rumours, including suggestions of Japanese piracy, Russian submarines, atomic dust, and even a visitation by the men of the Flying Saucers.

After our experience in the *Muliama* we knew only too well how unexpectedly disaster can strike a ship, and how quickly the position can get out of hand if the usual precautions are not taken. Disasters are adventures of the wrong sort.

Chapter Eighteen

Adventures of the *Malaita*

IN 1942 A JAPANESE SUBMARINE TORPEDOED THE *Malaita* JUST as she emerged from the harbour of Port Moresby in New Guinea. Her escorting destroyer was astern of her, but rushed into the attack and was able to find and destroy the submarine. The *Malaita* was taken back into the harbour safely, but she had been hit just forward of the bridge and was down by the head from the flooding of her forward holds. She was found to be almost broken in two and her hull had to be stiffened before she could be smuggled back to Australia, being towed behind the shelter of the Barrier Reefs to Cairns. Later she reached Sydney and was laid up for the remainder of the war.

In 1946, she was repaired and returned to her lawful occasions in the New Guinea trade. Her tonnage was 3,310 gross and she carried about 60 passengers. She had been built in 1934 for the Solomons trade, where she had run regularly and without undue incident until the Japanese reached the area in 1942. I had been Third Mate in her during her first year, later returning as Second Mate, and as Chief Officer in 1938. Starting in 1953 she touched the bottom three times in four successive voyages, a dreadful run of bad luck after all her years of good behaviour. Two of these bad voyages were under my command. On the other voyage, under her regular captain, she reached her first port of call, Lord Howe Island, in bad weather. When the sea improved enough for boat-work, she anchored off Ned's Beach and commenced discharging cargo. Then she swung to the tide and sat heavily on a pinnacle of rock, which made a hole about a foot square in her bottom.

She was quickly hove ahead on the anchor and shifted out to safety. In all our 50 years of trading to this island we had not known of the existence of that rock in the anchorage.

What has to be done in a case like this ? After the damage was inspected a diver was flown over from Sydney to put a patch on the bottom, like mending a puncture, and a mass of concrete was put on the inside, like a poultice, to keep it watertight. Actually the ship may have been able to continue her voyage safely without the patch, but being so close to Sydney it was deemed better to make a good job of it. On her return to Sydney she was repaired in dry dock and then I joined her as Master, to continue on the run to the New Hebrides and Solomon Islands.

My first voyage passed without accident, but the next was much too eventful. We were steaming through the central Solomons one night, passing through an area reported to contain two submarine volcanoes. These two positions were marked on the chart ten miles apart, so we steered to pass between them, five miles from each.

A late report said that a new volcano had emerged from the sea, to a height of 15 feet, but no position was given and we had to assume that it was one of the two reported positions on the chart. As we were due to pass between them about 11 p.m., I told the Third Mate to call me before we got there, so we could see if anything was visible. The previous submarine activity had consisted of masses of smoke and flame, only seen on rare occasions and presumably caused by inflammable gas welling up from the depths.

I lay me down to relax and, soon afterwards, an hour before we were due at the trouble-spots, the Third Mate called me with . . . " Breakers on the port bow." The breakers were about a mile off and, as we passed them in the moonlight, we weren't able to see what they were breaking on. We fixed the position exactly and found that the volcanic islet was right on the track we had laid down. I felt very relieved that we hadn't run on to it in the dark, as sitting on a hot volcano might be much more embarrassing than a comparatively cool coral reef.

Only 36 hours later we were entering the port of Kieta from the eastward, through a passage between reefs marked on the German charts as one mile wide and there were no other charts of the area. The passage was three miles from Kieta and we were still travelling at full speed when we suddenly saw the coral bottom under the ship, as we slid up on to a submerged reef. I rang " full astern " on the engines, but that couldn't have had any effect in the few seconds. We found ourselves fast for most of the ship's length, with reef extending all around except under the stern, which was over deep

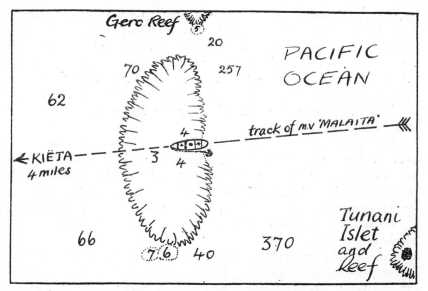

Gero Reef

20

70　　　257

PACIFIC
OCEAN

62

←KIËTA
4 miles

3　4

4

track of m.v 'MALAITA' ↞

Tunani
Islet
and
Reef

66

7 6　40

370

From German chart No. 431 (soundings in metres)

water.　Our momentum had been expended in running uphill towards the shallow centre of the reef and this meant that we were some feet higher in the water than before.　We would have to lighten the ship by about 1,000 tons of cargo, water, or fuel before she would be tempted to float.　There is no tidal information about this part of the islands and I was afraid that we had run up at about high water, and would therefore get no help from the rise of the tide.

We sent out radio messages for small ships to come and take some of our cargo and we prepared to discharge some in our own boats as well.　I sent a message to head office in Sydney with the bad news and they took a very pessimistic view of the situation. I felt so bad about things myself that even all the activity wasn't sufficient to allow me to forget my personal worries.　I went around in the launch sounding the reef with a leadline and fixing its position and extent, so that it could be charted.　I also got hold of a civil engineer from the Government to verify that our stranded position was shown as clear water on the charts.　The local authorities assured me that it was low water at the time and that high water would occur about 2 p.m.　This was really heartening news, if it were true.　We pumped out 200 tons of fresh water, but the discharge of cargo was likely to take anything up to a week.

By lunchtime the tide was definitely rising and as I sat down to lunch with the passengers in the saloon the ship was starting to grind on the reef, a sign that she was getting lighter, although it made me feel very uncomfortable. The ship had no serious damage or leaks, but the bottom was probably very badly dented and corrugated. We had taken the port bower anchor and cable right along to the stern, where we dropped it over the edge of the reef. This might help us to heave off and also help to keep the ship straight as she came astern, instead of turning and bumping our stern on to the seaward edge of the reef.

At 2 p.m. we were just ready to start discharging cargo, but belayed that while we made an attempt to get the ship off while the tide was high. We hove on the anchor and went full astern on the engines, in fact " double-full-astern," and after a few minutes we felt the ship come afloat and move off and away from the reef.

I could hardly believe it true and as we steamed around to the northern entrance to Kieta I lit up a big cigar and paced the bridge with thanks to the Almighty. I sent an immediate radio to Sydney and received the reply, " delighted your message." We also cancelled our calls to the small ships coming to our rescue and settled down to the rest of the voyage and the large amount of paperwork which follows a stranding.

At Rabaul and at Samarai divers went down to inspect the damage, but they could only find minor scratches. This was too good to believe, but when we docked in Sydney we found that it was really true. Docking and repairs only took a short time, but we had Christmas and New Year at home before we set out for our next voyage. This proved to be just as eventful, but in a much happier way.

We got through the Hebrides and Solomons according to timetable, but things started to happen while we were in Rabaul, ready for a quick return to Sydney. Our cargo ship *Mangola* had run ashore on the island of Kar Kar, near Madang on the northern coast of New Guinea. The liner *Bulolo*, flagship of the company, was in Madang at the time and promptly went to the rescue, so it seemed that we were not being invited to the party.

During the next few days the *Bulolo* made several attempts to tow the *Mangola* off the reef, without any success, while I was wishing that I could try my luck with the *Malaita*, fortified by my success with the schooner *Matoma* in the Solomons.

After leaving Rabaul we set course for Sydney, and next day I sent a message to head office to say that we were at our closest point to the *Mangola* at noon, just 400 miles off, if our services were required. Back came the welcome orders to divert to the help of

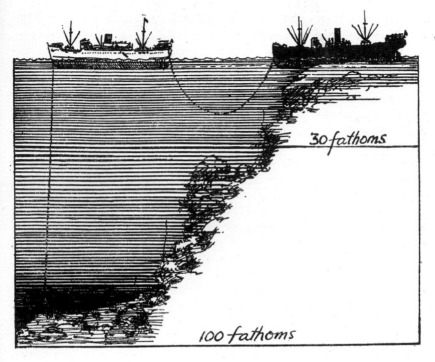

Salvage of s.s. Mangola, 1953

the *Mangola*. . . . It took us a day and a half to get there at full speed, during which time I coached the officers in salvage procedures, including the use of the anchor cable for towing and my own method of applying jerks to the tow to increase the pull. We got the port anchor cable up out of the locker and ranged it along to the stern ready for towing if we got the chance.

We reached the scene of the wreck on a dark and squally night at 11 p.m. and there were no charts of the coral reefs in the area. The *Bulolo* had spent four days in making vain attempts at salvage and in the process had sounded the area, finding very deep water with patches of shallow reef between.

The *Mangola* had run into Kar Kar island at night in a heavy rain squall, turning hard a port to avoid collision. She nearly got clear, but was caught by a submerged spit of reef carrying 16 feet of water. Half the ship had got over the spit, on which she stuck on her engine room. Her water tanks had been pumped out, but as she was lightened the swell had pushed her further up on the spit, so that she was stranded in 11 feet of water when we saw her. One of her anchors was veered from the bow on a wire, but the reef was so steep-to that the wire was almost vertical.

The *Bulolo* had found herself an anchorage only a ship's length away to the northward, where she hung on precariously in between her attempts to tow the *Mangola* off. We spent the first night taking copra in our boats from the *Mangola* and the next day transferred copra from the *Mangola* to the *Bulolo*.

We just drifted up and down the coast, trying to keep handy, as we had been unable to find an anchorage for ourselves. After two more days the *Bulolo* decided to give up her attempts, which had been very risky among the reefs and had resulted in nothing but broken wires and shattered nerves. She steamed away to carry on with her interrupted voyage, while we took over the job with great hopes and high spirits.

Lowering our starboard anchor down to 90 fathoms, we steamed towards the shore until we hooked up the bottom. Then we paid out the remaining few fathoms of cable and ran a rope to the bow of the *Mangola* to prevent our stern from swinging into the breakers on the shore reefs. In the meantime the *Mangola* had been persuaded to jettison some of her bunker coal and also some of her copra. This was to lighten her more quickly than we could transfer her copra into our holds by surf-boats and launches.

When we were safely in position we lost no time in starting the heavy work of shackling our towing cable on to hers, which took about an hour. Then we went ahead on our engines, giving severe jerks to the stranded ship, in the hopes of getting her moving. We were just warming up to the job when her cable parted under the strain. We had to get back into position and start all over again. Our anchor cable had an official breaking strain of 64 tons and the *Mangola's* was much heavier; it should have been able to stand up to 120 tons of direct pull. Her cable must have been fatigued with age, for it was certainly weaker than ours. We then joined up our towing cable with her second cable and went ahead again with ever increasing jerks and pauses.

This succeeded in slewing the *Mangola* around through about 60 degrees and we were just getting the towing cable clear of the water with the force of our jerks, when her cable parted once more. As it was now getting dark, we decided to try again at 9 a.m. next day. We had lost our anchorage during the hectic manoeuvres and so we put out to sea to have a night's rest.

At dawn we moved in again, hooked our anchorage, ran a rope

from our stern to the *Mangola's* bow, and found that there was just too great a distance between the two ships to be able to join the heavy cables up again. Our anchor cable was paid right out ahead, so we couldn't slack away any more. The only alternative was to heave on our sternline as hard as possible to get the ships closer. We led the rope from one winch to the next so they were heaving with a total strain of about 10 tons. This was equal to the breaking strain of the rope and we were hoping to get the cables shackled up for another attempt within the hour when shouts arose from the distance. The *Mangola* was afloat and making straight for our stern.

She seemed to be nodding slightly like a horse on a halter, as I leapt on to the bridge and rang the engines to "Stand-by" and then "Half ahead" to dodge the *Mangola's* bow and lead her out to open water. At the same time we ran two more ropes to her bow, to get her under some control. She was so light that she was at the mercy of every gust of wind and eddy of current and her erratic movements soon broke our three ropes. The next few hours were full of frantic manoeuvres, as the *Mangola* did her best to escape capture, or to drift right back on the nearest reef. This was all quite a surprise to me; I thought the only job was to get her safely afloat.

With the help of a small local vessel, the *Josey*, we were at last able to relax clear of the land, while the engineers of the *Mangola* struggled with the task of lining up her engines and tailshaft in the badly bent hull. This took four hours, after which we escorted the *Mangola* to the port of Madang, instead of having to tow her. She entered the port at dusk and secured to the wharf, while we

Japanese wreck on coast of Guadalcanal

N

waited at anchor until the next morning. Then we had to go alongside to give her fresh water and that evening the successful salvage was suitably celebrated by all hands. She had been exactly one week fast on the reef, which had been a very exhausting and nerve-wracking period for all concerned. Then we left her in Madang and proceeded on our way homewards, feeling quite pleased with our efforts. I felt that my share in the company was once more in credit.

About this time, the company had been threatening to omit our calls at Lord Howe Island and Norfolk Island. Owing to the lack of shelter at these rock-bound islands, we had often been delayed up to a week to do two days work in unloading cargo. After striking rough weather all one winter at Lord Howe we ceased to call there but continued to call at Norfolk Island.

Sometimes we had to call at an additional port which was not on our itinerary. One of the most unexpected of these was on a sudden request at Santo to take a British District Agent and some police boys to Port Patteson in the Banks Group. A report had come in that a Japanese fishing vessel had called there illegally, but we weren't able to catch her. I hadn't been to the Banks islands for 20 years and we had no chart aboard, so we had to rely mainly on my memory. We made sure of getting there in daylight and left again at dusk, resuming our course for the Solomons.

Another extra port was in New Guinea. This was the port of Kavieng, on New Ireland, reached by a couple of hours steaming through the maze of islets, reefs and wrecks of Steffan Strait. The wrecks were Japanese, mostly transports and small warships, all of which had been sunk by magnetic mines laid by our own Catalinas during the war. The final approach to the wharf is made narrower by a Jap wreck on each side, one with decks awash and the other showing only her masts.

A similar hazard in the war-time ports of New Guinea, the Solomons and the New Hebrides is the quantity of war materials

Japanese ship sunk by mine at Kavieng

dumped by the American forces at the end of the war. This consists of sunken mooring buoys, wires and cables, motor vehicles, cranes, barges, pontoons and ammunition of all sorts. Anchoring in these waters always includes a danger that the anchor may foul the scrap and be difficult or impossible to heave up again. This happened to the *Morinda* two or three times in Havannah Harbour. Twice the anchor picked up a bight of a very heavy cable, moored by sunken mooring buoys and 40-ton blocks of concrete. It was just possible to heave the anchor to the surface with the old steam windlass, which threatened to pull the *Morinda's* bow under the water in the process. The cable then had to be stoppered off to get the anchor clear, so we could proceed, and not remain permanently at anchor. If we had caught up something a little heavier, we would have had to slip the cable.

The last remaining American wharf at Santo, built of oregon for use during the assault on the Solomons, had got to the crumbling stage. It had also been damaged by different ships cutting into it with their bows, but it was still better than no wharf at all. On our last occasion of berthing at the wharf I dropped an anchor to steady the ship as we crept gently alongside, for otherwise the wharf would have collapsed completely at the first nudge. There were holes in the decking of the wharf where loaded trucks had broken through and it was even dangerous to walk across it.

Our cargo had to be carried by man power over the wharf to trucks waiting on *terra firma*, which took a couple of days. When we cast off from the wharf and hove up the anchor we found it foul of a whole group of heavy steel hawsers. We were still so close to the wharf that we would have bumped it with our stern if we hadn't charged at full speed into mid-channel. We were still held by the hawsers, which had to be cut through by oxy-acetylene burners before we could get the anchor clear and proceed on our way. Another troublesome spot has been Yandina in the Solomons. There is a good wharf at this place, but when a northerly wind is blowing it is difficult to get away from it safely, owing to shallow reefs at either end of the wharf.

On these occasions we drop an anchor well away from the wharf before berthing, so we can haul off to the anchor against the wind. Just off the wharf, in deep water, is a lot of dumped war material, bulldozers, pontoons and heavy vehicles, so we try to drop the anchor clear of this rubbish. On two occasions we have picked up ten-wheel motor trucks with the anchor. The first time we were able to free it by dropping it hard on the bottom, but the second one had the anchor right through the chassis and we had to tow it, half-submerged, over a mile to our next port.

It took several hours to clear the anchor and to drop the un-wanted truck where we wouldn't foul it again. Some of our so-called ports would scare a deep-water shipmaster, but they make life much more interesting for us. We call at over 20 ports on each voyage of six weeks, most of them in different islands and territories and very different from each other. And I must admit that we are given a very free hand by our head office, especially when we are in real bother, such as being stranded on a reef.

Passengers and tourists relish any unscheduled ports and excitements and the cruise of the *Malaita* through the islands must be about the most interesting available in the Pacific.

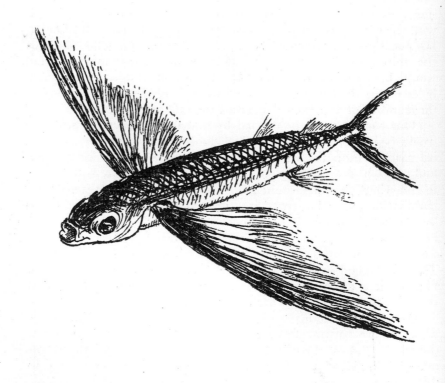

Chapter Nineteen

Underground navigation and other hobbies

APRIL 25 IS HELD SACRED TO AUSTRALIANS AND NEW
Zealanders because it commemorates the landing at Gallipoli in
1915, when our troops made their name under fire and brought
nationhood to their two Antipodean countries. The day is called
Anzac Day, and on this day in 1954 we sailed across Ironbottom
Sound to Nggella Island. This may be pronounced by first swallow-
ing hard, then saying Gaila. The island was called Florida by
Mendaña, but the local natives paid no attention to that. An arm
of the sea divides the island into two unequal halves and forms a
fine port at each entrance to the passage, which is known locally
as Mboli Pass. The official purpose in calling there was to get
fresh water in a part called Port Purvis, which is a beautiful and
spacious harbour. The only inhabitants live in a few native villages
nearby, subsisting on fishing and their vegetable gardens.

Getting fresh water into the ship's tanks calls for an unusual
type of seamanship. The watering point stands in a small nameless
bay under a jungle-smothered mountainside marked on the chart
as Egan Bluff. We steam into the bay, drop the starboard anchor
and swing on it to starboard, then drop the port anchor.

At this moment we go full speed astern, to get the ship to travel
tail-first into the corner of the bay, paying out the anchor cables
as we go. Sternlines are then run by the launch to the shore and
these heave the ship into position, when the stern is about 40 feet
from the actual water hydrant. The cables are then hove taut,
so the ship is held safely against the chance of a squall blowing the
stern on to the reefs which lie submerged around the bay.

The hydrant stands in about six feet of water and mud and is
the end of a pipeline which runs from the shore; it is supported by
a line of sticks and piles. The pipe is six inches in diameter, and

runs up the hillside to a cave in the cliff 200 feet above. This cave is full of water and mystery and had never been explored. So we had to do something about it.

The shores of the bay are hidden by mangrove trees, with their countless roots hidden in the muddy salt water, and forming a favourite haunt for crocodiles. One afternoon there were four of these implacable amphibians circling the ship like a pack of sub-marines. To get ashore we pushed off in a boat and, when it stuck in the mud, we waded ashore warily through the fringes of man-groves and started climbing up through the jungle.

The pipeline is anchored and secured to rocks and trees, climbing up almost vertically in places and a great help to human climbers. We were wearing shirts and long pants as some protection against stings and scratches from insects, plants and rocks. We wore good shoes, though we were soaked to the armpits getting ashore to start with. The jungle is always damp with dew, or rain, so our copious perspiration made no difference.

When we got to the water-cave, 200 feet above sea-level, we jumped into the pool of cool fresh water to refresh ourselves before facing the unknown interior of the dark cave. I had tried to swim into this cave two or three times previously, but had come to a curtain of stalactites which hang down from the ceiling into the water. I thought we would have to swim underwater to get any further but fortunately our electric torches allowed us to work our way, swimming, between the stalactites, and we soon found our-selves in a larger cave, later to be called the Cave of the Snakes for a very good reason. We waded out of the water, gazed in wonder at the arched ceiling of snowy crystals, saw the water-course leading further into the mountain and felt that our discovery was as much as we had dared to hope for. The water-cave might only have been a spring from a hole in the ground.

Full of excitement, and not knowing how far we would be able to go, we set off at full speed, slithering on muddy patches, stumbling over loose rocks and broken stalagmites, wading through pools and having to swim in the deeper parts. We carefully followed the water upstream so we wouldn't get lost, and only stopped at times to draw breath and admire our newly found wonders of architecture. Most of the walls were draped with stalactites like choir stalls, while some of the upper galleries had rows of little stalagmites like figurines of saints. Sometimes a large cluster hung like a chandelier from the ceiling, while the larger caves were as big as old parish churches.

The height of the biggest caves was about 70 feet, as well as we could judge from the small light of an electric torch, but we were too busy watching where to put our feet and hands to look around properly. On later trips we were to see new wonders every time and were to spend a lot of time taking photographs under great difficulties.

On our first visit to the caves we were thrilled with every new passage and cave and with the facility with which we were getting through them without the use of ropes or ladders or any of the gear which serious speleologists would take with them. We were the first humans to enter this hidden world, which had taken nature many thousands of years to excavate and decorate.

The whole mountain mass was limestone, old coral reef which had grown in the seas about 10,000 years ago, according to the geologists. The local folding of the earth, raising chains of islands out of the sea, has lifted the mass about 1,000 feet above sea-level; the volcanoes had put a layer of stones, mud and ashes over the top to provide soil. The nearest active volcano at present is the island of Savo, 20 miles away. No doubt the earthquakes had made cracks in the limestone mass, allowing water to seep through and dissolve some of the limestone, forming caves. At the same time, infinitely slowly the limestone deposits of crystal were formed by evaporation. Most limestone caverns of this sort are of much greater antiquity and the experts are amazed at the size of some of the formations we found, some of the stalagmites being five feet in diameter. The most famous caves in Australia are those of Jenolan in the Blue Mountains and their age, by contrast, is officially given as 400,000,000 years or more !

Never before had any light penetrated these caves of ours; we were the first to see the limestone since it was a growing reef in the sunny coral seas. Although there were living things in the caves, there wasn't even a glow-worm or any phosphorescence to light their hidden world. The first living thing I saw looked like an insect from a nightmare. Its body was about the size of a matchbox, and it had about eight legs, the front pair carrying many large hooks. From where its head should have been extended two long feelers like radio or radar antennae and these measured no less than $13\frac{1}{4}$ inches from tip to tip when stretched out straight. It was not an insect, but a whip scorpion, belonging to the arachnid order which includes spiders and scorpions. His family name or species is phrynus, mentioned and illustrated in the best books, but none of these say whether he bites or not ! I finally caught a large one in my handkerchief and wrapped him up to carry in my shirt pocket;

the scorpion later found a home in the British Museum in London.

We next became aware of little gusts of air past our ears and this encouraged us to think that the caves had a ventilating system, for otherwise there was a danger of running into foul air or some poisonous gas. Then we found that these gusts were the slipstreams of bats flying down the passages in the dark by means of radar, or rather by supersonic asdic. They were covering some of the ceilings in hundreds, fast asleep hanging from their toes, until we disturbed them into a scramble to take off in squadrons. We estimated that there were about 2,000 of them in the caves and, when I later caught one, I got a bitten finger as well as the specimen.

We went about a quarter of a mile into the mountain, though it felt like a lot more, and there the stream came from a heap of loose stones at the bottom of several vertical shafts like lift-wells, or chimneys. After some perilous climbing up loose and balancing rocks we finally saw daylight above our heads and we were able to lift our purser up until he could manage to climb out. He went up bare-footed and managed, much to my relief, to climb out of the valley and over the mountain back to the entrance of the water-cave where he had left his camera.

When we got back to the entrance ourselves, battered and exhausted, we spread out to rest awhile, tired but still thrilled with our discovery. Then the purser arrived, and prepared to take a photograph of us at the entrance. One moment he was standing on the edge of the rock near us, the next moment he was gone, and when I dashed to the edge and looked down at his inert body I was sure he was dead. His head was jammed between two coral rocks and blood was seeping over his face; his eyes were open but unseeing. He came back to life slowly, as we carried him down to the boat and a few days later he was over his concussion safely.

On later trips to the caves we found the final passage had suffered a fall of loose rocks and we could no longer get to the top. We took black and white photographs and later a series in colour, in order to prove the wonders of these new caves. I also took a pocket compass and made a survey of the caves, measuring the distances by paces when walking and by strokes when swimming. Several waterfalls made things difficult, but I finally got the plan completed, with all the caves and main items of interest.

We had given names to quite a lot of the caves and the more striking formations. By this time I had been made a member of the Sydney Speleological Society and I gave them a lecture on the caves, at a joint meeting with the Australian Institute of Navigation,

*Discovery of the limestone caves
of Mboli Passage*

on the exploration and surveying of the caves, under the title of
" Underground Navigation."

On the very same trip that we discovered the caves at Mboli,
which I called the Caves of King Solomon, we had a passenger
going around the islands on business, whose ambition was to make
his fortune at pearl-shelling. He had had experience at pearling
and had been running small craft around the islands including some
for the Air Force during the war. His name was Bill May and
from him I caught the malady of conchology, and learned a lot
about the behaviour of living shells in the coral seas.

We used to take the ship's launch, or borrow a dinghy or canoe,
and go exploring and fossicking on the reefs awash at low water,
swimming underwater to search the reefs a fathom or two deep.
Here we could wander through colourful gardens of living corals,
with their colours competing with the vivid tropical fish and the
amazing variety of underwater life. I don't think that I have ever
gone reef swimming without seeing some new form of aquatic
life which I could only recognise from the pictures I had seen in
the text-books. A lot of the beautiful shells are very well disguised
in their surroundings and there are very few shells really compared
with the large numbers of fish and corals. The animals which make
the shells are very interesting forms of primitive life, though not as
primitive as some underwater growths which are halfway links
between the animal and vegetable kingdoms. Most of the shell-
creatures have a very uninteresting sex-life compared with humans,
some being bisexual, so they never have to be married, while others,
like oysters, change their sex with the seasons.

Most shells have the capacity of continually increasing the size
of their shells, without changing their shape, which would baffle
most architects in designing extendable houses. The insides of shells
are mostly hidden from view, except when the shell is broken open,
or sawn in half to show the internal structure. The nautilus is the
most intelligent and interesting of all shell-creatures, being a type
of squid and related to the cunning octopus. The nautilus shell
contains a series of small compartments, the animal living in the
outside one and building himself a new and larger one every year
·or so, cutting off the old one by building a pearly bulkhead only
pierced by a thin pipeline. This apparently enables him to fill the
old compartments with gas to adjust his buoyancy as required for
diving.

Its submarine skill was known to the ancients, and its name
was given by Jules Verne to his fictional underwater ship in

20,000 *Leagues Under the Sea*. It was also chosen for the name of the first atomic submarine, built in America. The name nautilus comes from the Latin word " nauta " meaning a sailor.

All the inside of the shell is made of mother-of-pearl in delicate colours, while the outside is clay white with russet stripes. This exterior can be cleaned off with muriatic acid to make the shell completely mother of pearl and the shell is then known as the pearly nautilus.

The main dangers in swimming around coral reefs lie in the stings and poisons of both plant and animal life. Even the harmless looking cone shells include two species known to have stings fatal to humans. There are also the stone fish, whose back has spines with fatal poison, the butterfly cod or lion fish, striped coral snakes, sting-rays, conger eels and a few vicious fish with sharp teeth. The greatest danger is threatened by sharks, groper and the larger octopus.

The large clams which could close on a man's foot and drown him generally close their massive jaws when they see or feel a man getting close, as they are really very shy. They are greatly prized by the natives for food and clam-chowder is made from them in some parts of the tropics. The wary octopus has only one weakness in his make-up and that is his horror of the harmless sea-slug called trepang, beche-de-mer, or holothurian. The octopus hates, loathes, detests and abhors the slug, which may grow as large as a loaf of bread, but is more harmless than a caterpillar. When one is placed at the entrance of the octopus's favourite cave he just can't get out fast enough. When the natives catch an octopus they kill it by biting it smartly in the brain, just between the eyes.

Most people swimming underwater use goggles, so that they can see clearly, for it is impossible to focus the eyes underwater for some reasons of optics and refraction. A lot of spear-fishermen use

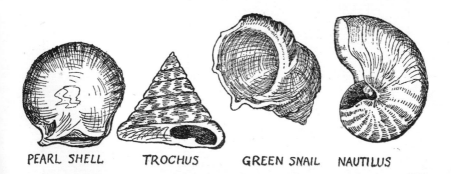

PEARL SHELL   TROCHUS   GREEN SNAIL   NAUTILUS

rubber flippers on their feet to enable them to swim fast without using their arms, but we always use strong shoes or sandshoes to avoid being scratched on the coral or stung by stone fish. Some of the living coral is poisonous, but almost any scratch in tropical waters will fester and turn into a tropical ulcer unless great care is taken to sterilise it.

Having collected a number of living shells, the animals in them have to be killed by immersion in fresh water for a few days and then extracted by various means as carefully as possible. Then the outside is cleaned to show the pattern of the shells, unless the outer brown skin is kept on as part of the collection. Cone shells have the toughest brown skin and this can be removed by soaking in caustic soda, a slippery process and a dangerous one, as the growing edges of the shells are as sharp as razors. Then comes the difficult job of classifying the shells, for which several text-books are required, as well as endless patience. For most people, like myself, it is sufficient to class the shells in very general groups and not to worry about the finer varieties and the Latin names of the species.

Before we finish with the shells, there are many attractive articles which can be made from them, apart from the commercial production of pearl buttons for clothing. Of course only the common shells are used for shellwork, the rarer ones being kept in the collections as specimens; the rarest of these sell for as much as £300. The best use I have made of any shells was the construction of a galleon from nautilus shells, one shell for the hull and others cut up for the bellying sails and pennants, all in a mother of pearl finish, and worthy of any art gallery.

Chapter Twenty

Science and seamanship

RADAR CAME TO US AS A BOON IN 1953, AS A RESULT OF THE stranding of the *Mangola* on Kar Kar Island early that year. All the ships in the company were fitted with it, even the *Muliama*, baby of the fleet. To the harassed shipmaster, radar has been the greatest blessing since Mercator, in my opinion. For while Mercator's projection, the sextant and the chronometer put the navigation of the open sea on a sound basis, for inshore pilotage and coasting the mariner had to rely on his eyesight; this has been almost imitated for dark or dirty weather as though it were always a clear sunny day. Though radar does not see, or make the scene visible as clearly as eyesight, it has one very great advantage over human eyesight in that it can judge distances very much more accurately.

I have found that most experienced navigators and captains think that they can judge distance fairly well, to the nearest mile of course. Since we have had the radar set to check our guesses by I have found that our estimates of distance are not very good at all. In fact when passing a reef or rocks one mile off, one man will estimate the distance at half a mile and another at one and a half miles. This might not always be good enough for safe navigation. The advent of radar, once its habits and temperaments are known, has meant a saving of a lot of grey hairs and ulcers in the badly charted parts of the western Pacific. It has also turned out to be very useful for survey work of the type which pretends to no great precision or accuracy. But such sketch surveys are much better than nothing.

On the very same Anzac Day as we discovered the Caves of Mboli, we finished watering ship, disconnected the hoses, cast off the ropes to the shore from our stern, hove up our two anchors and all their cables, and proceeded to the next port. This was the open anchorage of Tenaru, on the coast of Guadalcanal, at the exact spot where the great assault by American troops was made to capture the Henderson airfield, before it could be completed and used by the Japanese. The anchorage is off the mouth of a river and the coastal shallows of sand and mud are liable to change from time to time by the effects of tides and the flow of the river.

We usually anchored in nine fathoms of water, exactly half a mile off-shore, but on this occasion we ran in a little too far, and the bow apparently stuck in a submerged mudbank for 15 minutes before the ship gathered sternway and was anchored safely in deeper water. I thereupon decided to make a plan of the anchorage and mark on it the soundings of the area at the time, with a warning to avoid the area at the mouth of the river. We had recently been fitted with radar, the set being a Marconi radio-locator mark IV. This turned out to be very useful in making a quick survey for the plan, for it enabled distances to be measured rapidly instead of the usual laborious method of taking vertical sextant angles and then calculating the distances by trigonometry and logarithms.

As each sounding was taken from the launch a bearing of it by compass and a radar distance from the ship was all that was needed to enable the sounding to be placed on the plan in its right place. I made a sketch of the foreshore on the plan, to enable the place to be easily identified. We also made a plan of the anchorage at Lunga, a similar place five miles along the coast. This is a port for two of Lever Bros.' copra plantations and is only complicated by the number of stranded and sunken barges and ships from the wartime operations of both Japanese and American forces. These two plans were drawn on one sheet, which the company had printed for the use of our ships. We also made plans of the ports of Arigua, Numa Numa, Teopasino and Soraken on the badly charted coast of the large island of Bougainville and these were similarly reproduced, and copies sent to the Hydrographic Service for their

Wreck of El Retiro *on Billion Dollar Point*

information. These plans were similar to the one of Nissan appearing on page 74 and are a sample of what can be done by merchant ships without any special equipment or loss of their time from their lawful occasions.

A few trips later we arrived off the port of Arigua after dark and with the help of our new chart and radar we managed to enter the reef-infested port and anchor safely in the right spot. Most of these ports are very small and it is necessary to anchor in the exact centre to have safe swinging room. When the weather is squally it is often necessary to drop a second anchor to reduce the radius of the ship's swing and the chance of the anchor dragging.

In two or three of the ports we had to lay a buoy to mark the position of a coral patch which lay submerged near the anchorage and was too difficult to see in poor light, or when the muddy water from rivers nearby clouded the sea water. To lay a buoy we took an empty 44-gallon drum, an old oily wire from a winch and a piece of scrap iron from the shore to serve as an anchor.

The next problem that arose to keep me busy was one of unusual scientific interest and complexity. It is still unsolved, and seems likely to provide us with occasional headaches for some time to come. This is the mysterious illumination of the sea commonly called phosphorescence, though the scientists would prefer us to call it bio-luminescence. This has been observed by sailors and travellers from very early times, though it used to be received with some scientific reserve, along with the other incredulous stories from distant lands.

Since the war of 1939-45 the reports of phosphorescence at sea would suggest that it was occurring more brilliantly than ever before and there are official reports of the phenomenon reaching alarming degrees of brilliance. In one ship the man in the lookout panicked and left his post; in another ship the helmsman left the wheel in fright of the supernatural light. I hadn't seen these reports, published by the Meteorological Office in their magazine for mariners, *The Marine Observer*, but I was soon to find myself deeply involved.

Perhaps I should first explain that, *as far as we know*, all forms of marine phosphorescence are caused by light emitted by living organisms in the water. Some of these are large, such as sting-rays and eels, others just visible to the naked eye, but most of them of only microscopic size, like bacteria or microbes. They are of various species, not necessarily related, nor evolved from one another, but most of them are now known to science and listed in the catalogues and text-books on the subject. All the smaller ones come under the general name of plankton, and are studied by fisheries research stations, because they are the food of many important kinds of fish and also of some types of whales.

The light produced by phosphorescent plankton is a " cold " light, having no measurable warmth transmitted with it and this makes it different to any light made artificially by man. It belongs to the same class as light produced by glow-worms, fire-flies and luminous fungus on a dead tree. The light is very weak compared with daylight, but on a dark night it can easily be seen for miles, as the smaller organisms, especially the microscopic ones, stay in large colonies or clouds in the sea and can flash their lights in unison. They light up on being stimulated by any outside disturbance, which may be of several different kinds.

Firstly they are stimulated by a breaking wave, a bow-wave from a ship, the splash of an oar, or the movement of fish. This is called mechanical stimulation. Another form of stimulation is that from other lights, either from a ship, or from other organisms. The third known form is stimulation by sound waves, either from a ship's engines or propeller. We don't know whether heat waves would trigger them off, as heat is not easily transmitted in water.

Finally we come to the growing belief among seamen that the waves from a radar set can stimulate marine phosphorescence. This belief is opposed by the scientists, who say that the electro-magnetic waves from a radar transmitter are too weak to sink to any depth in the sea, although they are of the same nature as light rays, but of a different wavelength.

The night of 5 September 1954 was dark and overcast by low rain clouds. The *Malaita* was steaming southwards through the islands and reefs off the eastern end of New Guinea, on our way to the China Straits and the port of Samarai. As we were passing some of the Hardman islands a loom of light appeared on our starboard bow, like the diffused light from a ship in rain, or from a distant town. The illumination resolved itself, as it came over the horizon, as a long bank of phosphorescence in apparent co-incidence with some submerged coral reefs. We passed them two miles off, about 2 a.m., and they disappeared astern.

A few minutes later a similar loom appeared on our port bow, also beyond the horizon, but as we got closer it came over the horizon as a brilliant streak in the sea, stretching from fine on the starboard bow to well on the port bow. The streak later became defined as a series of what looked like sandbanks in an estuary, illuminated by neon lights. They remained fixed in position and brilliance, apparently a few fathoms below the surface and it became obvious that we would run foul of part of the display. This might not have mattered except that there were reefs in the same direction, and we had to alter course to starboard before we got to them. If the phosphorescence was in coincidence with them it meant that our navigation was about two miles out.

The radar set was working continuously and we could also see the nearby islets, so we checked and double-checked our bearings and distances off to make quite sure of our position.

Just as the ship was about to enter the area of luminosity, I noticed that there was a large echo on the screen of the radar similar to that produced by a rain squall; it was two miles square, in exactly the same position as the bands of light in the sea. This was not due to a rain squall over the area, for we could see beyond the lighted area to some islands three miles away, and there was only faint rain falling as we passed through the area of light and the echo on the screen.

When the ship's bow cut into the nearest cloud of light, which appeared to be about 30 feet below the surface, the breaking bow wave showed as a dark lace silhouette against the unearthly light from below. The screen still showed the echo when we were passing through the lighted area and then we had to alter course away to the west. Our nerves slowly quietened down, for the very brilliance of the light had been disturbing and in our tricky circumstances of navigation it had been positively alarming. Next morning I painted a picture of the appearance of the sea at the nearest approach to the centre of the phosphorescence, and this was reproduced with my report in the *Marine Observer*.

After this experience we read up the subject and were very surprised to read reports of men who believed their radar had actually stimulated phosphorescence. On the night of our own experience I would not have liked to switch off the radar for even a few minutes to see if the light decreased. But six months later we got a chance to test it out and found out other facts as well, to complicate the subject and thicken the plot.

Our second experience was off the coast of Guadalcanal in the Solomons, about 3 a.m. on a dark and cloudy night. We were three miles off the coast, in about 400 fathoms of water, when a patch of light showed up ahead of the ship, followed by a few more, until the ship was passing through a sea of flashing patches, each about 50 feet in length, and oval in shape. They appeared to be two or three fathoms deep, just glowing clouds of light, without any individual points of light being visible. The patches flashed about every second, as described in the textbooks, but they did not flash in time with each other. When I tried to time the flashing by counting seconds, I found that each patch was flashing faster than one second, and to my surprise, their speed of flashing was exactly in time with the beat of the ship's engines ! This rate was 94 revs. per minute at the time. Each patch we timed was the same, but their independent flashing meant that they were like a lot of soldiers marching at the same speed but all out of step, and suggested that they were each keeping time with a different cylinder of the engines, rather as though they were receiving their stimulation from a distributor on a motor car, which stimulates all the spark plugs at different moments of each revolution of the engine.

The ship was doing only 10 knots at the time, to get to the next port at daylight and we ran through the area of patches in less than an hour; this confirms the radius of the area as about four or five miles. The patches appeared to be stationary and we even ran over a couple which were in our path.

When we were well into the area of patches we switched off the radar to see if the flashes would diminish at all. They did indeed get fainter until they were barely visible; then when the radar was switched on again they came back to life in a few flashes. Then they were observed to be fading out slowly and when the radar was switched off they went out altogether. Then we switched on again and the patches reappeared close to the ship, though not very bright and they faded continuously as we passed through the far edge of the area.

When we settled down to write out the report we had nearly recovered from our surprise that the bio-luminescence had flashed in time with the main engines. For the sound waves of compression travel better through the water than they do in the air and they would naturally be felt by the sensisitive microscopic plankton. What we had learned of importance was that the radar played a large part in the stimulation, as had been reported by two or three other ships, although not accepted by the scientists.

The larger forms of phosphorescent plankton, which show as individual points of light, are much more common. Some of them are often near the surface, stimulated by waves, including the bow wave of the ship, and others a few feet below and set off by the ship's lights. There are much more complicated patterns and beams of light which move over the sea, but I have not seen them, and I suspect that they have some connection with magnetic fields of fluctuating, pulsating or rotating designs, either due to the magnetic field of the earth, the ship, or a combination of these. There is still a lot to be found out about the subject.

There is also a great similarity between phosphorescence at sea and the illuminations in the sky known as the Aurora Borealis and Aurora Australis. The subject is too deep for me and will require co-operation between biologists, meteorologists, oceanographers and radio-physicists. It may even have to await future discoveries in general science, but in the meantime we have to take advantage of the rare manifestations to record their behaviour as accurately as possible, in order to give the scientists the basic evidence to work on.

Over a year has now passed since our last experience of phosphorescence at sea, but we are keeping a watch for any further signs of the mysterious phenomenon. I was now in a new ship, the m.v. *Tulagi*, built in 1955 to take over the run of the *Malaita* which has been transferred to the New Guinea run. The *Tulagi* has been called after a ship of ours which was built in 1939 and was sunk by a German raider in the Indian Ocean in 1942. There were only five survivors, three Europeans and two Malays, all of whom survived on a raft for the incredible time of 56 days, until they made land and were eventually brought back to Australia. The new *Tulagi* has her funnel aft and only carries 12 passengers, which gives me more time for my various occupations at sea and in the island ports. The ship is 2,700 tons, is registered in London, and carries a crew from Singapore of Malays and Chinese in addition to 15 white officers. She has the advantage of an extra knot of speed over the *Malaita*, and is a very successful ship for working the island ports.

On our last trip we ran into some trouble with our anchors and I've never seen anchors get into such a mess. We had used both our anchors to moor the ship off the loading site at Loavie, which until recently had a pontoon wharf of wartime steel cubes. When these rusted through, the pontoon began to sink and was towed away into deep water, apparently just about where we now have to anchor. As well as two anchors we secure the ship with two sternlines, as there is not sufficient swinging room between the reefs which line the foreshores. When we were ready to leave we cast off the sternlines and commenced to heave up the starboard anchor. This came up so far but no further and it was seen to be foul of the port cable with a very great strain on it. So we dropped the starboard anchor back on the bottom and started to heave up the port anchor, which was veered to 80 fathoms. A certain amount of this came up and then no more. At this stage the windlass would not pick up either anchor, despite its great power. There was nothing for it but to use the main engines. We went full astern to start with, then full ahead, hoping to clear one of the anchors at least. Even this was of no avail, so I decided to steam out into deep water to try to shake off the obstruction.

We were in 20 fathoms at the time, and by using full speed on the engines we found that we could proceed down the sound at about four knots, taking the anchors, etc., with us. What the " etcetera " was we could only guess at, but I believe that it was the sunken pontoon. It seemed to offer no great resistance to being towed into deep water, where we would have more room to manoeuvre.

We stopped the ship in an open area between the islands, where we were in 100 fathoms, and then tried to heave up the starboard anchor. This was achieved by helping the windlass, by running the wires from the two forward cargo winches, and the anchor slowly came to the surface, still bearing over one arm the bight of the port cable. We hove it up clear of the water, put our launch to work and after an hour were able to free the anchor and heave it right up to the hawsepipe. At this stage the port cable was held by the bight, which was heavily lashed by ropes. These ropes were then cut through and the bight fell down to its full length. I could feel the obstruction slipping down the cable a bit, as it now hung down freely in deep water, but it didn't slip right off as I had hoped it might. Now we helped the windlass to lift the port cable, which came up slowly with such heavy groans and shudders that we were afraid that the windlass would be wrecked if we carried on. So we stopped off the cable and proceeded at full speed towards shallow water, in the hope of tearing the " etcetera " off the cable against the coral reefs. By the time we stopped with the bow a few yards from a visible reef, the ship was in 17 fathoms and there was still a length of 50 fathoms of cable out. We picked up the slack, but

Plan of m.v. Tulugi *moored at Loavie*

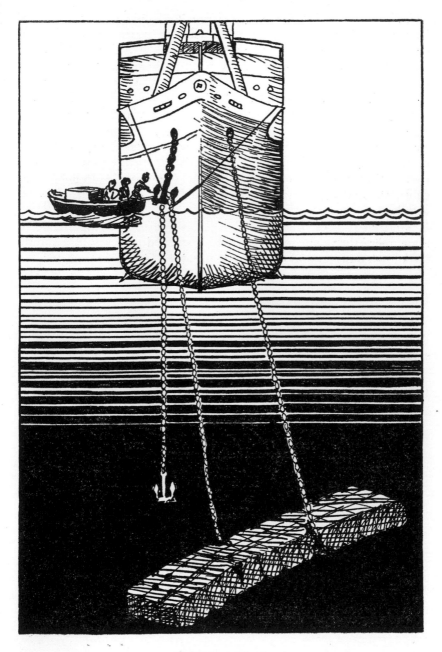

Foul anchors at Loavie

when we only had 35 fathoms left out, we could get up no more. The sun had set and our situation was not a safe one at all, so I decided to cut the cable and write it off as a bad debt. While the oxy-acetylene cutting gear was being brought up from the engine-room we took off at full speed for open water. When the cable was cut it fell, anchor, cable and " etcetera," into a depth of 160 fathoms, where it will worry us no more. That night we made our next port after dark, entering and anchoring by the aid of radar, for we had lost a total of five hours with our anchor exercises. Next morning we shackled our spare bower anchor to the remains of our port cable. Although we had lost about £400 worth of anchor and cable, we had cut it away before it did any damage to our vital windlass.

And so it goes, one trip with an adventure or experience to remember, then one or two trips to settle down, while avoiding the known dangers and trying to be prepared for the unexpected.

Chapter Twenty-One

History in the making

EVEN THOSE OF US WHO LEAD HUMDRUM LIVES ARE WEAVING the backcloth of the history of our times. The dramatic events of each period, when judged in retrospect, form the illuminating highlights of the long human story, like scenes in the Bayeux Tapestry. Some of the highlights remain after the background has been lost, while other highlights of our progress have passed unnoticed at the time and were not recorded. For example, who invented the magnetic compass, and where, and when?

Most discoverers, explorers and conquerors have a keen sense of history, like Julius Caesar, who valued the journals of his campaigns above all other personal possessions. But even his name would now be only one in the long list of Roman generals if it had not marked the beginning of recorded history for so many barbaric tribes of Western Europe, our ancestors.

Similarly in the South Seas, the history of each island is small compared with the details reported in the journals of the great discoverers. By the modern method of dating archaeological relics by Carbon-14 it appears that the Polynesian race has only been in the Pacific for about 2,000 years: in some island groups like Hawaii, there has only been habitation for half that time. This means that the migration and dispersal of this people, with a common culture and language, was about the time that Caesar landed in England and so well within the period of recorded history. Yet no record appears to even hint at the existence of this race. We do not know why or how these people spread right over the wide Pacific. They have been traced back to varying homelands by different experts. Their language is largely Malayan, which also extends to the island of Madagascar, showing that navigation was an extensive art in that period of unknown date.

Since Cook first cross-examined the Polynesians about their
navigation, many of us have studied that aspect of the Polynesian
mystery, but Cook is still the best authority on the subject. When I
went to the Gilbert Islands in m.v. *Tulagi* in 1956, I was told of some
coral stones on the island of Arorae which had been used for early
canoe voyages. The natives called them " Te Atibu-ni-Borau "
(the stones for voyages), but had no legends about their origin or
use. They turned out to be flat slabs of coral erected on edge and
paved around the base. They looked like grave stones, but had no
inscriptions on them except recent initials in Roman letters. The
stones pointed in almost all directions and were said to point the
path to the various neighbouring islands of the southern Gilberts.

Arorae is about five miles long and barely a mile wide, pointing
about south-east, into the trade wind. At the other end is a long
spit of sand, which has been extending through the centuries
because it is the lee end of the island. This is the site of the " stones
for voyages," which number eight or nine in all. There are a lot of
other flat stones standing on the island, but they are boundary
markers for plots of land and lines of coconuts.

The only safe landing place is about three miles from the site
of the stones, so I borrowed a bicycle, slung a boat's compass across
the handlebars and followed an elderly native guide along the track
of loose sand. I found it very hard work. As we neared the end of
the island we met the first stone, the largest of all, but it appeared
to mark only the entrance to the " navigation school." The other
eight stones pointed in five directions. Some of them were in pairs,
side by side, while others were alone. There was not much time to
spare, so I measured the direction of each as carefully as I could by
compass, made a rough plan of the layout and then tried to question
the guide.

I could speak only about ten words of Gilbertese and he spoke
about the same amount of English. He knew the islands to which
about three of the stones pointed, but nothing about their use. The
site was about 100 yards from the beach on each side and about
200 yards from the tip of the island. Owing to the presence of
various native huts and the vegetation of coconut palms and some
bushes, it was impossible to see the sea from the stones. I couldn't
see how they could be used for navigating canoes across the open
sea to other islands, so I returned to the ship to puzzle over the
problem.

The first job was to correct the magnetic bearings to true directions, by allowing the local variation as calculated from the ship's

observations. Then I plotted out the bearings on the chart and found that four of the directions pointed to the three nearest islands with a constant error of five degrees. Two of these courses were to windward of their island-goals, the other two were on either side of the nearest island, 52 miles distant.

Instead of taking a few days to solve the problem of how the stones could possibly have been used for navigation, it took me several months of research and deduction. We know that the native navigators used the stars by night to maintain a set course and two or three references turned up about the use of landmarks to set a canoe on its course in the late afternoon. We know of no other stones in the Pacific like those of Arorae, but they could easily have been unnoticed by Europeans and forgotten by the natives. The puzzle was therefore more difficult, but all the more important to solve.

I finally came to the conclusion that the stones were used in the following way: when the directions to the nearby islands had been related to certain stars at each hour of the night at a given time of the year, by trial and error over many years, some ingenious teacher hit upon the idea of setting up the stones as permanent sailing directions. They could have been used to check on the stars' positions and movement before the voyage was undertaken. On the afternoon chosen for the departure, the canoe would be launched at the landing place, sailed around to the tip of the island, and hove-to approximately in line with the correct stone or pair of stones. As these could hardly have been visible from a safe distance beyond the breakers, some temporary beacons must have been set up from the stone so they could be got in line, and placed right astern as the canoe made its departure. By the time the island was lost to sight the stars would appear, and be used throughout the night. Most of the voyages from Arorae were little more than 12 hours' sailing, so at dawn a masthead lookout would start scanning the horizon all round for the target-island.

The five degrees error on each course may have been an intentional allowance for the set of the equatorial current, while the navigator would have to allow something also for the leeway due to the trade wind. This would vary with the course, the strength of the wind, and the trim of the canoe.

One of the stones pointed exactly north-east, in which direction there was no island for 1,000 miles. I finally assumed that this course was given, with the usual ceremonies, either to unwanted visitors or to people being exiled for crimes against the community.

The mythical island to which they were sent off probably had a name like Limbo.

The stones, being so far from the sea, may have originally been on the tip of the island, but the extension of the island during the centuries has now left them out of sight of the sea. There are several good reasons for this assumption, but these conclusions still left several parts of the puzzle unsolved. How did these canoe navigators get back home again? The course they steered away from home included the five degrees allowance for the current and, if they steered the opposite course, it would put them five degrees to leeward and they would be lost. These islands are really only coral reefs with low banks of sand on them, up to about 12 feet above sea level. The palms reach a height of about 75 feet, so the islands are only visible from a canoe masthead at distances up to ten miles. The method of navigation I have described would not be successful over 100 miles, unless their island-goal was a high volcanic one, or a long chain of low islets. For in navigation it is not sufficient to steer a set course to reach a distant destination, as the set and strength of ocean currents is very variable. So the position of the ship has to be fixed at intervals, or the latitude fixed at least, in order to re-set the course as necessary to reach the destination. There is no evidence that the Polynesians could check their latitude and therefore we must assume that all their long voyages, up to 2,000 and 3,000 miles, were accidental or experimental, as Captain Cook was forced to conclude.

My next visit to the Gilbert Islands was in 1958. We made some charts in our spare time of two uncharted islands, Arorae and Tamana, and several plans of anchorages to make a little safety and precision available in this precarious trade. As in most of the island groups, navigational aids are crude and rude.

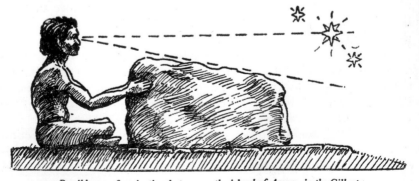

Possible use of navigational stones on the island of Arorae, in the Gilberts

Apart from the home-spun hydrography, we actually met up with two events of historical importance on this voyage. The more important of these, in the present day, consisted of a visit to Christmas Island while the H-bomb tests were being carried out. The other case of history in the making, which may be of much greater importance in future history, was the job we got to remove the entire population from Sydney Island in the Phoenix Group to a new home in the Western Solomons. The people numbered 215, the distance was 2,000 miles and the time taken was ten days in all.

The Phoenix Islands are a scattered group of tiny islands in the mid-Pacific, which were uninhabited when they were discovered, one at a time, in the years around 1850. Some were annexed by Americans, who stayed a while and then departed. Later the group was claimed by Britain, but no permanent settlement was made. Parties of copra-cutters visited the islands, six of which became the property of my employers, Burns Philp & Company. In 1937 Britain and the U.S.A. started selecting islands for air-bases across the Pacific and this led to several disputes. Britain decided to move some of the surplus population from the Gilberts to support her claims to the Phoenix Islands. This scheme was officially called the Phoenix Islands Settlement Scheme and it was too late when they found that the initials made up an Anglo-Saxon word !

Britain bought our six islands for £7,500 and settled about 500 Gilbertese on them, planting thousands of new coconuts on them at

The use of double navigational stones

the same time. Some of the islands prospered, but Sydney Island did not have enough rainfall or fishing facilities. The population went from 200 to 400 in the 20 years, by which time they were suffering badly from malnutrition. The island is only a mile or so in diameter, with a lake of salty mud in the middle, and a constant thunder of surf around it, making boat work usually impossible. It was therefore decided to move them to a fertile island in the Solomons. Small parties were moved by small government vessels over a period of two years, until only 200 remained for us to move. In one day of miraculous weather we embarked them all, with about 80 tons of personal effects and no less than 36 sea-going canoes. Ten days later we landed them at their new settlement at Gizo.

On this voyage a child died the first night, but a baby was born a week later, which balanced the tally. We had to feed them on atebrin each day to prepare them for the onslaught of malarial mosquitoes in their new home, as the Gilberts and all islands eastwards are free of this disease. Their new home has copious water, a very fertile soil, plenty of good timber trees, a sandy beach and a nice stretch of coral reefs to make them feel more at home. The Gilbert Islands could well afford to send thousands of their spare population to the many stretches of uninhabited land in the Solomons and other parts of Melanesia. Such an influx of new blood could be of great value in the future, when we may have some sort of general Confederation of Melanesian islands. This might extend from New Guinea to Fiji and include some three million natives with interests in common.

At present New Guinea, like ancient Gaul, is divided into three sections: Netherlands New Guinea (claimed by Indonesia), the territory of Papua (former British New Guinea) which is now owned by Australia, and former German New Guinea, now governed by Australia under trust for the United Nations. We can only hope that when self-government comes to this large island it will not be as premature as in the Congo, but more like the Indian example.

On our next voyage to the Solomons we picked up a party of five unusual looking natives at Gizo. They were the survivors of a drift in a canoe from the Laughlan Islands, at the eastern end of Papua, and we had to take them to New Guinea on their way home, at the expense of the Government.

This canoe voyage took three weeks and they only covered about 200 miles, so it was quite a minor affair by Pacific standards. Although there was practically no information to be extracted from the simple survivors, I was more interested in their case than in the various other cases which had come to my notice. They had left Woodlark Island, which is fairly large, after a trading visit by six of their canoes from the Laughlan Islands, which form an open coral atoll. The distance they had to cover was only 30 miles and they had sighted the first of their group when they were becalmed. According to the occupants of the five canoes which finally got home, the sixth was separated from them in a tide-rip and was missing next morning with seven natives aboard. We don't know how long the missing ones spent trying to regain their home islands, before resigning themselves to drifting aimlessly over the open ocean. After two weeks at sea, two of them died, a small boy aged about four, and the oldest man in the party. This left five, three men, a boy of about seven and a girl of 12. At the end of three weeks they were sighted by native villagers on the north point of Simbo Island, who set out to investigate the apparently lifeless canoe.

The meeting must have been poignant. The Laughlan Islanders are small at any time, with pale khaki skins and in an emaciated and dehydrated state they must have been pathetic. The muscular men of Simbo, with shiny blue-black skins, looked very like a band of well fed cannibals. In this predicament, the survivors' last hope was sanctuary at a mission station. The Simbos assured them that they were good mission boys themselves and took them in tow to the village where they got plenty of good food to eat.

From the Laughlans to the Solomons is a north-easterly course. Most of the other known drifts in the Pacific have been in an easterly direction, despite the fact that the south east trade is blowing most of the year. During the nor'west monsoon, which is also the hurricane season in the southern hemisphere, from Christmas-time to Easter, the wind is not steady like the trade; it generally blows fitfully, in fits and starts with calms between. Starting with a fierce westerly squall with torrents of rain, it peters out after a few days, and there might be light nor'east winds until the next westerly arrives. The south-east trade is so regular that it can be taken for granted, or allowed for in small craft navigation, but the westerly squalls throw them into confusion as well as reducing the visibility. It is therefore the westerlies which have caused most of the accidental drifts and may account for the spread of the Polynesians from the East Indies across the Pacific during many centuries.

These considerations, and other more obvious ones, led me to oppose the Kon-Tiki theory, put forth by Thor Heyerdahl so readably, in which he maintained that the Polynesians originated in South America. He claims that they were defeated in battle at Lake Titicaca and thereupon took to the sea and sailed into the setting sun to discover the South Sea Islands. In the first place all the races of the Americas are known to have come from Asia by the land route. They crossed the Behring Strait when it was either dry land or hard ice, the last of the races to arrive being the Eskimoes, who are definitely Mongols. In the second place Lake Titicaca is over 13,000 feet above sea level, like Tibet, and one might as well expect the Tibetans to hurry down to the coast near Calcutta, invent and build ships, and sail off into the Indean Ocean to discover unknown groups of islands by unknown processes of seamanship and oceanic navigation. These mysterious Polynesians all speak of their original homeland in the west and their language is in the same family as Malay, with many identical words. The only way in which Heyerdahl could be partly right in his theory is to accept, as most of us do, that some lost Polynesians must have reached both South and North America by accident. Then we have the possibility of some of them returning, under a leader called Kon-Tiki, towards the islands which they already knew about.

Last year I thought that I had stumbled on some material proof of this amendment to his theory. A friend of mine in the Solomons, named Ernie Palmer, often visited the more remote and outlying islands as a recruiter of native labour. He came back from Sikiana atoll one trip and presented me with a native piece of stiff cloth which had been woven on a primitive loom. This is a loose outfit hung from the wall of a house with the lower end secured around the waist of the weaver. It is called a " back-strap " loom, and is only known on a few islets in the Western Pacific. I found, quite by accident, that it appeared to be identical with those used in the Central and South American civilisations known as Aztec and Inca. But I learned on inquiry that they did not occur anywhere in the Pacific between Sikiana and South America, but there were some in parts of Indonesia and Micronesia. Then I found that there is an essential difference between the Pacific ones and the American so that they had certainly not come from that direction.

These may sound like theoretical considerations, but I am only interested in them from practical experience and observation. I am a firm believer in the infinite slowness of evolution and of the fundamental basis of heredity. My ancestors were Vikings who settled in England before the Conquest, becoming a staid line of yeoman farmers in Sussex. My hands are more suited, as you must agree, to the handle of a spade, or the loom of a steer-oar, than to the pen or the typewriter. Most of my writing, after the shining examples of Dampier and Cook, is designed to bring the " ivory-tower " philosophers down to earth, or down to sea level, on behalf of my fellow mariners, whether they be in ocean liners or in dug-out canoes.

To come to the point, I have a confession to make. My only real excuse is that if there is one thing I can't stand, or withstand, it is temptation. In spite of many months of resistance I have accumulated a new vice, which we will call a hobby. God save us from our friends. One of mine forced into my reluctant hands a hunk of insidious soapstone and suggested that I try carving it. I smuggled it aboard, hid it in my cabin, and took it out in secret to feel what it had to say to me. It turned out to be the usual sort of vice, a jumble of frustrations, sensuous delights and occasional satisfactions. It is carved with a strong knife and other implements and finally polished with beeswax and turpentine. So now I am a sculptor, in soapstone.

Because of the scarcity of soapstone, another friend gave me

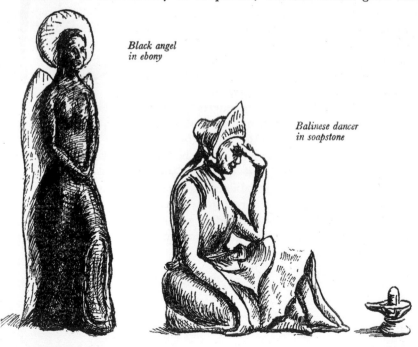

*Black angel
in ebony*

*Balinese dancer
in soapstone*

a choice piece of timber which had all the
properties of cast iron and it broke many a
chisel until I settled for a sharp fireman's axe.

My cabin has been alternately filled with
clouds of sawdust, flying chips of hardwood
and clouds of fine white powder from the
creations in soapstone. This type of rock is
ground up and sold in tins, with a little
scent added, as the best talcum powder. My
last burst of carving, from which my shipmates haven't yet recovered, was a whole
log of ebony from eastern Papua. It was as
heavy as lead, as hard as steel and as black as
sin. But the outer layer of " sapwood," much
to our surprise, was a light honey colour and
as tight and tough as anyone would desire.
The big problem was first to cut the log
into about ten pieces, each just too heavy
for a man to lift. Then I had to conceive
some plan by which I could make use of the
two different colours in the wood.

My first effort was a small wedge of
wood, from which I carved a rather down-
hearted black angel; the light wood formed
her halo and her wings, and she stood about
a foot high. Then I tackled a baulk about
three feet long, which turned into a figurehead for a ship, a honey coloured girl with
jet black hair right down her back. The
face was modelled from a young lady

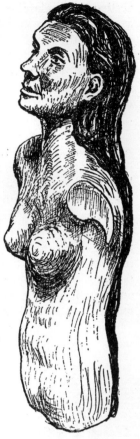

*Ship's figurehead
in ebony*

passenger, while the body had to be done from memory, as her
husband was aboard, and getting a bit restive. After the final
polishing my raven-haired beauty looked rather naked, and had to
be veiled, as she lay on my bunk by day, in a black lace shawl.
We'll eventually have to build a yacht to make use of her as a
figurehead, and that is going to cost someone a lot of money.

Chapter Twenty-Two

Royal rendezvous

NORFOLK ISLAND LIES ABOUT 800 MILES FROM THE COAST of New South Wales. It was discovered by Cook in 1774, and first settled in 1788, a few weeks after Sydney. It was a penal colony until 1856, when the descendants of the mutineers of the *Bounty* were transferred there. During these years it was often visited by British and American whaling brigs, who caught a fair number of whales in the vicinity. In 1880 the Government encouraged the islanders to start whaling from the shore. They built their own boats, which they sailed and pulled by oars to catch the whales. Having harpooned one, they were towed at high speed all over the ocean until the whale was tired and could be lanced to death.

The whale then had to be towed back to the island and dragged on to the beach at high water. At the next low water the whale was attacked with flensing knives by the whalemen, above the water level, and by sharks in the water. The blubber was cut into small pieces and boiled down in coppers on the beach, using wood fuel. It was not a very profitable business and slowly faded out after 1920.

In 1957 a new whaling industry was started on the island by an Australian company who spent a third of a million pounds on a modern whaling station and a chaser of 235 tons. They were allotted a quota of 150 humpback whales, which they filled without much trouble. We were very interested in the establishment of the station and watched its progress on each of our visits. We got photographs of the whales being towed to the station, hauled up the beach with a winch and then up a ramp to the flensing deck. Each whale weighs about 40 tons and is 40 feet long at least. About ten tons of oil are obtained from each and the whole whale is cut, ground up and boiled, not just the blubber. Even the bones are ground up, and the solid residue is sold as whale-meat for feeding

pigs or for fertilising the soil. The only parts wasted are the lines
of baleen from the mouth, which used to be used for " whalebone "
corsets, and the blood, gallons of which run off while the huge carcase
is being dismembered with great speed and high efficiency.

The whaling station was built at our usual anchorage, where we
land cargo in surf-boats, so we had a grandstand view of all the
proceedings. The season only takes two months of each year to fill
the quota, so we generally only see them in action once a year.

One afternoon in March 1958 we arrived at dusk, too late to
start work, and the master-gunner and his officers paid us an official
visit. It turned into quite a wild party; these whalers are tough, but
as I had arranged to go whaling with them next morning I went to
bed at 4 a.m. The Chief Officer called me at five and I climbed over
the side into our launch and went aboard the chaser. Most of the
crew were just returning from nocturnal adventures ashore and we
all ate a hearty breakfast of fried eggs and hot buttered toast,
washed down with draughts of strong tea.

When we left the shelter of the anchorage we found the sea
very rough, with a full gale blowing and driving rain squalls. The
chaser was put through her paces like a wild horse being broken in
and we all had to keep hold of our stomachs while hanging on to
stanchions to avoid being thrown overboard. It was really too rough
to do any serious whaling, but we chased after a few at high speed,
with the master-gunner on the bow with the harpoon gun at the
ready. We lost every whale in the high seas and rain squalls. Each
time the sun came out I took some photos, including some from
the crow's nest or lookout at the masthead. Then we sorrowfully
returned to port and spliced the main-brace.

Whales are very interesting animals, for they are mammals,

Whaling at Norfolk Island

as are we humans and their ancestors were once living on the land. There are many species of whales, some with teeth like the sperm, to which species the famous Moby Dick belonged. Their ancestors on land must have been equally varied, but I suppose they were similar to the present-day hippopotamus. The humpback whale, like many others, is based on the icy waters of the Antarctic, where its food, the plankton, is prolific. Once a year they set out and swim to the tropics for the mating season and then swim home again. During this long trek they don't appear to feed at all, as their stomachs are always found empty. When the whales are first hauled ashore it is impossible to tell the males from the females. After half an hour or so the males begin to show their maleness, until it extends to a good six feet. This is a sad sight, seeing that they are quite dead, and about to be cut up and reduced to a fine pulp. The whole business of killing these harmless, warm-blooded animals is sad, but they can never be exterminated. For after a few more years at the present rate of whaling, they will be too scarce and hard to find to make whaling profitable.

In March 1959 we left Norfolk Island bound for the New Hebrides and the Solomons. This was our usual run, but this trip we had a very special date by which we had to arrive in the Solomons, to meet the Duke of Edinburgh who was visiting the islands in *Britannia*. Se we had to reach Honiara by March 19, or be in dire disgrace.

As we steamed north we received weather reports of a cyclone passing down the other side of New Caledonia and therefore 500 miles clear of our track. It was not an intense cyclone, so we took no notice. The next day, Friday March 13, was really the Devil's Own and so was the cyclone.

I still don't know whether hurricanes love me or hate me. They get all wound up about it, and make straight for me when ever possible. On this devilish day I passed a quiet morning and, like a condemned man, ate a hearty breakfast. During the afternoon we received reports from both Fiji and Noumea to say that the cyclone had intensified and had altered course to intercept us. The force of the wind was now reported as up to 50 knots, with gusts up to 80, which qualified it as a hurricane. We therefore commenced to lash our boats, hatches, gangways and deck cargo with extra ropes.

Having been in six hurricanes before, including many worse ones than this, we pressed on at full speed to try to get across the predicted track before the storm reached the same intersection. My

previous experiences and studies had made me rather an expert
on hurricanes and, when I had to deliver a Presidential Address
to the Australian Institute of Navigation, my paper was entitled
" On the Avoidance of Hurricanes." This paper and its arguments
so aroused the ire of the Meteorological Office that they invited me
to be a delegate to the International Symposium on Hurricanes,
held in Brisbane in December 1956. I learnt a lot from the scientific
papers and discussions, but they were all at a high level in the
clouds, and of no practical use to a master mariner.

At 6 p.m. the wind was still only fresh, and from the north,
which was a head wind, so our speed was down to 10 knots. The
ship was well loaded and in good trim, so she could be expected
to handle very well if the storm got bad. The glass had fallen right
down to 29 inches, which was lower than that reported at the
centre of the storm, so the weather should not have got any worse.
There appeared to be so little to worry about that I had a drink or
two with the Chief Engineer and we both went down to the saloon
for dinner.

At 7.30 p.m. the glass was still falling and the crew were now
putting still more lashings on the boats, until they almost ran out of
rope. As the wind was now almost a gale, we headed straight
into it and reduced speed: we were therefore " hove-to." At

H.M.Y. Britannia

8 p.m. I decided that the wind had reached gale force and started to write out a weather report in plain language. The glass was now down to 28.66 inches, lower than I had ever seen it in my life and by the time I got to the end of the message I had to write " wind hurricane force." By this time it was starting to rain solidly, though it was difficult to tell which was rain and which was salt spray.

During the next hour things got worse and worse. Although the seas were not high for a hurricane, they were a bit confused, and made the ship roll violently. The glass fell and fell, very evenly but remorselessly. The wind force went from hurricane force to twice hurricane force and didn't pause for breath. It roared at us like the exhaust of a jet engine and then blew the bow away from the wind. I immediately rang for full speed and ordered the wheel " Hard a starboard ! " but to no avail.

As the bow fell away and the wind increased, the rolling went from devilish to fantastic. We were being thrown about and bruised, the boats were all working out of their chocks and gripes and odd waves were landing on the bridge from unseen directions. By this time we were broadside-on to the wind and seas, and things started to go wrong very quickly. The gangways were being smashed, the deck cargo had broken adrift and steel cylinders of acetylene were playing torpedoes in the well deck, ramming drums of high octane and other inflammables. At this moment the siren began to blow. It was normally worked by electric buttons on the bridge, but it also had a wire lanyard down the side of the funnel to the deck, and this was now catching the full force of the wind. It was an ominous note and I felt relieved when we had the air cut off it from the engine-room.

While I racked my brain for the means of getting out of the predicament, the ship was being wracked most dangerously. The bridge and wheelhouse were being swept by waves and the officers were thrown from one side to the other in a tangled mass of limbs. To add to our distress, the radar set broke away from the deck, and had to be disconnected before it electrocuted us all. It was then held up by superhuman efforts until it was shored up with timber. By this time the radio aerial had carried away and had wrapped itself, along with some signal halyards around the radar mast. The crew's and passengers' accommodation were flooded and about this time one single wave landed down the funnel. I could still find no means of getting the bow back into the wind and the situation became quite desperate. So I took a desperate chance, ordered the wheel hard a port, and turned down wind.

This put the stern into the wind, and we shipped some heavy seas aboard from astern. Speed was reduced and the ship steadied down a lot. My next worry was that we were driving towards the Loyalty islands, about 50 miles away, at what felt like a very dangerous speed. The time was 9.30 p.m. and, with most of the night still before us, we may have run into them without warning, now we had no radar and no visibility.

Twenty minutes after our desperate and precipitous retreat the wind suddenly stopped. So did the rain and we spied a few stars overhead. We had reached the centre, the eye or core of the hurricane. The glass stopped at 27.96 inches and the temperature was still 77° F. I was very relieved that we hadn't had to run all night on this course and we now had a quiet spell for about 20 minutes. We could expect to meet an opposite wind when the far side of the centre reached us and one of equal force. We soon saw the first cat's paws of wind coming at us from about west-sou'west. So we turned hard a starboard and around to a course of 080 true with the wind dead astern.

By 10.25 the glass was up to 28 inches again; by midnight it was 28.77, and by 2 a.m. it was up to 29 inches. It was therefore rising at exactly the same rate as it had fallen in eight hours. We were now heading for the southernmost islands of the New Hebrides, with perhaps 60 miles to go. By 3 a.m. we had cleared the wires and ropes from the radar mast and got the set going, just in time to pick up an island at 34 miles, on the port bow. We altered course to keep the wind and swell right astern, and passed the island at 8 a.m. By noon we were able to shape a course for Vila and resume full speed as we slowly relaxed.

I suppose all the damage could be called superficial. The hull was still in one piece, the funnel and masts and superstructure all intact, though a lot of paint had been stripped off. The bridge, the decks, the cabins, the storerooms and cargo holds, were in a fantastic shambles. During the next few days we cleaned up the mess, called at Vila and Santo and made for the Solomons at full speed. I was still puzzled at not being able to keep the ship's head into the hurricane, as I had always been able to do before, in much smaller and less powerful vessels. Then I sat down to do some sums relating to the pressure and movement of the storm. This eventually gave me the pressure gradient, which was ten times greater than that required to produce a theoretical " gradient wind " of 100 knots. The gradient wind was therefore exactly 1,000 knots. This is reduced by friction and by the tight curvature of the isobars, and

I feel sure that the actual wind was about 200 knots, or over three times hurricane force. Which is more than enough for anyone and far too much for the sanity of shipmasters. It was truly the Devil's Own hurricane.

We reached Honiara at 4 a.m. on the 19th, in time to welcome the Duke. That evening I was invited to Government House to a reception to meet H.R.H. I found him smaller than I expected, but far younger-looking, far more human, friendly and humorous. Later that evening we dined at the District Commissioner's home, where I met some of the Royal staff, including two very attractive secretaries. I also met Lord Frazer, of North Cape, a real sailor indeed, who was a passenger on the royal yacht. We were all in plain clothes that night, and without coats by the Duke's orders, owing to the hot and humid weather. This mufti attire led to some difficulty in identification and, when Lord Frazer and I were introduced to the newly-arrived British Judge for the Solomons, he assumed that I was the Admiral of the Fleet, and took the beardless Frazer to be the master of the *Tulagi*. His error may have passed unnoticed if he hadn't demanded of Frazer what had happened to the luggage which the judge had shipped in the *Tulagi* from Sydney !

Since then I have been transferred back to my best love, the m.v. *Malaita*, and have been working hard on these pages of my adventures. The month of March 1961 marked my 50th birthday and, after recording my harrowing experiences, I am surprised to find myself still alive. That last hurricane put a crop of grey hairs in my beard, so I may yet live to look like the Ancient Mariner, to harass the passer-by, yet unborn, with unpublished tales of the steamy South Seas.

THE END

INDEX